Trailblazer

Trailblazer

A Biography of Jerry Brown

Chuck McFadden

UNIVERSITY OF CALIFORNIA PRESS

Berkeley Los Angeles London

University of California Press, one of the most
distinguished university presses in the United States,
enriches lives around the world by advancing
scholarship in the humanities, social sciences, and
natural sciences. Its activities are supported by the
UC Press Foundation and by philanthropic contributions
from individuals and institutions. For more information,
visit www.ucpress.edu.

University of California Press
Berkeley and Los Angeles, California

University of California Press, Ltd.
London, England

Library of Congress Cataloging-in-Publication Data

McFadden, Chuck, 1937–.
  Trailblazer : A biography of Jerry Brown / Chuck
McFadden.
    p. cm.
  Includes bibliographical references and index.
  ISBN 978-0-520-27563-8 (cloth : alk. paper)
  1. Brown, Jerry, 1938– 2. California—Politics and
government—1951– 3. Governors—California—
Biography. I. Title.
  F866.2.B732M44 2013
  979.4'05092—dc23
  [B]   2012033542

Manufactured in the United States of America

22 21 20 19 18 17 16 15 14 13
10 9 8 7 6 5 4 3 2 1

In keeping with a commitment to support
environmentally responsible and sustainable printing
practices, UC Press has printed this book on Natures
Natural, a fiber that contains 30% post-consumer waste
and meets the minimum requirements of ANSI/NISO
Z39.48–1992 (R 1997) (*Permanence of Paper*).

for Barbara

It was a splendid population—for all the slow, sleepy, sluggish-brained sloths stayed at home—you never find that sort of people among pioneers—you cannot build pioneers out of that sort of material. It was that population that gave to California a name for getting up astounding enterprises and rushing them through with a magnificent dash and daring and a recklessness of cost or consequences, which she bears unto this day—and when she projects a new surprise the grave world smiles as usual and says, "Well, that is California all over."

Mark Twain, *Roughing It*

CONTENTS

ACKNOWLEDGMENTS

There is a truism about authorship: No book is the work of a single person. This biography is no exception. Without the help of many people, *Trailblazer* would not have come into being. They have my everlasting gratitude.

My remarkable wife, Barbara, gave invaluable encouragement and research help, and her editing abilities made the task easier and faster. She has a sharp eye for the occasionally clunky phrase and misplaced paragraph. Above all, she managed to put up with months of grumbling and muttering from the author.

Naomi Schneider, my editor at the University of California Press, set a high bar and made sure that I measured up. She guided an unknowing author through a series of hurdles with patience and good humor. She is responsible for the overall concept of the book—quirky state, quirky governor—and how the two have coexisted over the years. Her colleague Stacy Eisenstark handled the illustrations and vastly helped ease the way through the requirements of an academic press. Chris Lura, Lorraine Weston, and Rachel Berchten of the University of California Press have my gratitude as well, and so does copy editor Robin Whitaker.

There were so many others: Doug Willis, my comrade-in-arms for years at The Associated Press, provided so much insight and stories that he should probably be listed as a coauthor. Ron Miller, another old friend, was the source of much good cheer and encouragement over the months.

Dan Walters, who has observed Sacramento politics for more than forty years, shared his enthusiasm for California and generously provided a perspective on its problems, potential solutions, and Jerry Brown's approach to it all. He even provided the rare early photograph of Jerry Brown, his father, Pat, and Earl Warren posing with the Colusa rancher who hosted them on their duck-hunting expedition.

Steve Glazer, who managed Brown's historic 2010 win over Meg Whitman, provided insight into Brown's remarkable victory and how he might go about meeting the challenges of his new/old role as California's governor. Whitman's people have mystified political observers by refusing to speak of the election to reporters, pundits, political scientists, me, or, apparently, anyone else.

Oakland city councilman Ignacio de la Fuente, who ran against Brown for mayor and later became a Brown friend and colleague, provided a lively account of Brown's years as mayor, including previously unrevealed stories of their walks together through the city's toughest neighborhoods and a rollover accident on a Mexican highway that almost ended their careers and lives. Chip Johnson, the longtime East Bay columnist for the *San Francisco Chronicle*, shed light on Brown's unique personality and his years as mayor of Oakland, especially the last two years of the Brown administration, when the mayor began to look again at a possible run for statewide office.

Barbara O'Connor, professor emerita at California State University, Sacramento, was equally generous with her thoughts on the governor's approach to his new challenges, and brought to my attention the potential that Silicon Valley has for state leadership and for political/cultural leadership in addition to technology.

Doug Faigin, who served as Brown's press secretary during his early years in Sacramento, was extremely helpful in describing how his friend and former boss has changed over the years from the onetime enfant terrible of California politics to elder statesman.

Kevin Starr, Jerry Roberts, Sherry Bebitch Jeffe, Jim Brulte, Dan Schnur, Mark Hedlund, Larry Venus, George Skelton, and Peter Schrag, terrific and knowledgeable people all, contributed their time and vast expertise to the story of Jerry Brown over the years. Darrell Steinberg, the busy president pro tem of the California Senate, took time from his schedule to talk about Brown's relationship with the state Legislature and his ability to engage instantly in deep study of an issue. I am also grateful to Robert Dutton, the Republican minority leader in the state Senate, for his thoughts on the tax increase negotiations with Governor Brown. David McCuan, a thoughtful political scientist at Sonoma State University, provided invaluable help with the history of political techniques in California, especially in the rise of Whitaker & Baxter, the firm that brought stainless steel politicking to the Golden State long before it arrived nationwide. Jerry Meral, one of California's leading water experts, contributed to my understanding of the state's water challenges and possible solutions.

Thanks go also to Bill Boyarsky, author, editor, and astute political reporter, and Dale Maharidge, Pulitzer Prize–winning author, each of whom reviewed the manuscript and provided a number of suggestions that resulted in its great improvement. A third reviewer, who rescued me from what otherwise would have been two embarrassing mistakes, chose to remain anonymous. He or she has my gratitude.

I have been fortunate enough to know five photographers—Walt Zeboski, Eric Risberg, Sal Veder, and Rich Pedroncelli of The Associated Press and Dick Schmidt of the *Sacramento Bee*—who were not only leaders of the pack in covering breaking news but were also poets with cameras. Sal is a Pulitzer Prize winner; all of them should be. Dick made a series of terrific pictures from his private archive available. The wonderful Mary Lou Mangold engineered the connection that made the use of Dick's photos possible.

Dace Taube, assistant head of special collections at the University of Southern California's Doheny Memorial Library, rounded up sixteen boxes of material from the library's Jerry Brown archives and was an immense help in paving the way for access to them, as was Gareth Lacy of the governor's office. I am also grateful to the staff of the Bancroft Library at UC Berkeley for their help in researching additional material.

Despite my numerous attempts in person with staff members, e-mails, and telephone calls over a six-month period, Brown's staff failed to make him available to provide his perspective on this biography. Brown himself, in a five-word exchange with me, indicated a willingness to sit down and be interviewed, but his staff was unresponsive, and I regret that.

With that exception, all of those mentioned above made *Trailblazer* a richer and more complete book. I am deeply indebted to them. Any errors or misinterpretations are of course my own.

The Comeback Codger

I've been in office and I've been out of office. And if I were to choose, I'd rather be in office.

> Jerry Brown to George Skelton in "Capitol Journal," *Los Angeles Times,* January 19, 2004

Three thousand people crowded into Sacramento's cavernous old Memorial Auditorium on the sunny morning of January 3, 2011, all eager to witness a century-and-a-half-old ceremony. Most of the state's political establishment was there. The VIP list included Gray Davis, the cautious former governor who was recalled in 2003;[1] seated next to him was Arnold Schwarzenegger, smiling broadly as he enjoyed his last few minutes as governor of California, although within six months he would face horrific personal scandal. Next to him was his glamorous wife, Maria Shriver. Nearby was Gavin Newsom, the handsome mayor of San Francisco who had been elected lieutenant governor. He had defeated Republican Abel Maldonado, the son of immigrant Mexican American farmworkers. In keeping with the bonhomie of the occasion, the two men hugged each other while waiting for the festivities to begin. House speaker Nancy Pelosi, soon to become House minority leader, was seated close to Dianne Feinstein, the U.S. senator and former San Francisco mayor who some polls showed was the most popular politician in the state. In row after row of seats were most of the 120 state legislators. The crowd was boisterous and happy. Everyone was in a good mood, including those with famous names.

But the spotlight was not on them. Instead, all eyes were on a bald, slim, seventy-two-year-old in a severe dark suit who raised his right hand shortly after eleven o'clock and was sworn in as the thirty-ninth governor of California. Nearly four decades after his first inauguration, in one of the strangest journeys in American politics, Jerry Brown had once again stepped into the spotlight of America's most idiosyncratic, troubled, and glamorous state—a state that in many ways seemed ideally suited to a politician of Brown's talents and personality.[2]

He stumbled slightly while reciting the oath of office. It called for him to say that he took on the office of governor "without any mental reservation." Brown seemed to hesitate over the word *mental*, then smiled, turned to the audience, and said, "Really—no mental reservation." The crowd roared with delight. It was vintage Jerry Brown—informal, quotable, doing the unexpected.

He might have thought about the mental reservation. When he recited the oath of office, California had the worst credit rating among the fifty states, a bitterly divided Legislature, and an unemployment rate of 12.4 percent. It was one of the five states with the highest foreclosure rates in the nation. Pundits and political elites had taken to asking, without irony, if California had become ungovernable. It was too big, too diverse, too ideologically divided. It was saddled with a patchwork of governance hopelessly out-of-date and unable to deal with the complexities of what its boosters liked to describe as a twenty-first-century nation-state. A widening sense of malaise had overtaken the state's traditional buoyant optimism.

The pointed questions were put aside for the day, but they were on the minds of many in the 1927-vintage auditorium as well as those of California's thirty-seven million residents. Would Jerry Brown be able to ease a series of state government fiscal crises? What about the drooping economy? The environment? And water? Most of all, would he be able to restore the fabled California spirit? The new/old governor had become the man of the hour in a state that had lost its way.

Jerry Brown, in his eighth decade a man of seemingly inexhaustible energy, was now charged with solving the twenty-first-century problems of the most populous and complex state of the union. Even with his gymnastic abilities in navigating the shoals of American politics, this was an intimidating mandate. Whether he could prevail was an open question. But Jerry Brown's journey to this point had provided some clues that he would not be a victim of the formidable mix of economic travails and political gyrations that have permeated the twenty-first-century nation-state of California. One gleans, from his life story, both a flexibility and a resilience that have been central to his political survival for more than four decades.

Some additional light on Jerry Brown may come from a whimsical piece the decidedly unwhimsical Brown released during the 2010 gubernatorial campaign:

25 Random Things about Me
I've seen lists of "25 Random Things about Me" that people are sending around Facebook. I thought I would share my own list with you.

1. I got my first dog 13 years ago, a black Lab named Dharma.
2. At Yale, I took "Psychiatry and the Law" from Anna Freud, Sigmund's daughter. I also studied Roman law.
3. In 1958, I took vows of poverty, chastity, and obedience. Later, Pope John XXIII dispensed me from these obligations.
4. I took marriage vows for the first time 3 years ago.
5. I practiced Zen meditation under Yamada Roshi and Father Enomiya-Lassalle in Japan.
6. My official portrait as Governor was quite controversial and the legislature refused to hang it. My Father said if I didn't get a new one, I could never run again. It is now hanging and I am still running.

7. I am not fond of Mediterranean fruit flies, or of Malathion. Both are bad.

8. I dislike shopping.

9. I started 2 charter schools in Oakland, the Oakland School for the Arts and the Oakland Military Institute.

10. When governor, I decided not to have an Inaugural ball and my inaugural speech was 7 ½ minutes. For the inaugural dinner, we went to Man Fook Lo, a Chinese restaurant in the produce district of Los Angeles. It was once a favorite of Mae West.

11. I am a part owner of a ranch in Colusa County. It belonged to my Great-grandfather.

12. I worked with Mother Teresa in India at the Home for the Dying.

13. I've been duck hunting with Chief Justice Warren, but not with Vice President Cheney.

14. I sued Richard Nixon's lawyer for helping the President cheat on his income tax.

15. I like arugula and broccoli.

16. On my honeymoon, my wife and I canoed down the Russian River.

17. I was a cheerleader at St. Ignatius High School.

18. I knocked my opponent to the canvas in a 3 round boxing match at Senior Fight Night.

19. My favorite cereal is Flax Plus Multibran.

20. My first car was a 1941 green Plymouth. My most famous car was a 1974 blue Plymouth.

21. I own a colt 38, given to me by my father.

22. I went to Bangladesh as a CARE ambassador.

23. I hiked to the top of half dome. My first trip to Yosemite was when I was 4.

24. The first time I became Governor, I followed an Actor (Ronald Reagan).
25. My maternal grandfather was a San Francisco Police Captain. My paternal grandfather ran a poker club in the Tenderloin.

In this biography of one of the most idiosyncratic politicians in California history, I will explore the unique persona that is Edmund Gerald Brown Jr., son of California political royalty who forged his own unique political style against the tumultuous backdrop of a huge, balkanized state that goes its own, sometimes errant, way, shoved to and fro by complex currents. Plumbing his visionary impulses as well as his grandiose ambitions, my aim is to portray Jerry Brown through the lens of paradox: the intellectual who has thrown himself into a mean public arena, an idealist who has been willing to negotiate with all comers, a spiritual soul who has triumphed as a backroom politician.

Only in California could someone of such unusual traits emerge. This state on the edge of the continent has been a haven for outcasts for more than 150 years. The gold-seeking forty-niners, as adventurous and peculiar a bunch as one could imagine, were unhampered by the traditions and strictures of their old homes. Class and family background would no longer confine ambition. What a man—men were the only ones who counted—could accomplish in the here and now was what was important. The state was populated by family black sheep, adventurers, and hustlers from its beginning, but later waves of immigrants brought their skills, muscles, and hopes, increasing diversity in an already diverse population. By the twenty-first century, Californians had established the most diverse society on the planet, at one time or another home to Marilyn Monroe and Herbert Hoover, Steve Jobs and John Muir. The University of California claims fifty-six Nobel Prize winners; the state was also headquarters of the Flat Earth Society. Just south of Yreka, in the shadow of Mount Shasta, a sign promoting the State of Jefferson is painted on the roof of a large barn, one of the few remnants of a 1941 movement to create a new state from twelve of the northernmost California counties and seven southern Oregon counties. At the same time, several hundred miles to the south, a motorist in central Los Angeles can drive for block after block and see pink, turquoise, and red neon signs advertising various businesses—all in Korean.

At home and on the campaign trail with his father at a very young age, Jerry Brown absorbed California in all its grandeur and excitement. And while Pat Brown was an honest and effective public servant, his son quickly learned that politicians and the public live in two parallel universes: the things politicians talk about among themselves are a far cry from their utterances to the public. If a candidate or cause is to be successful, matters have to be presented in a particular way to voters, who are more worried about whether the refrigerator will hold up for another year than they are about whether state law should permit podiatrists to treat ankles.

"Except for brief interludes, the political history of the state has not been politically inspiring," historian Henry Cleland once observed.[3] Cleland's observation is debatable. It is lamentably true that California's political history has been marred by repeated outbursts of hysterical anti-immigrant agitation—particularly against Asians and later against Hispanics and "Okies"—but it is also true that while Californians were mining gold, developing the movies, and farming the Central Valley, they were concurrently creating a system of government that was intended to emphasize openness, honesty, and responsiveness to the electorate, virtues that Brown has touted consistently throughout his political career. Reform-minded progressives in the early years of the twentieth century gave California the initiative, the recall, cross-filing, and the referendum. These were designed to give the people a direct voice in how their state is governed, taking power away from what had become a corrupt, unresponsive, and lobbyist-riddled state Legislature. Historians point out, accurately, that the idealism only came in reaction to the power of the railroads and other big interests that had a stranglehold on the Legislature, but the outburst of idealism nonetheless did occur. No one at the time knew that the initiative process would become a fearsome tool of special interests that a hundred years later would reduce the Legislature to increasing irrelevance.

Jerry Brown's California is an abstraction, of course. His life has been shaped by an enormous and diverse place of 156,803 square miles and thirty area codes created by imaginary lines that emerged from war and were then embedded in law and treaty. But the state is more than that. It is a place that for more than 150 years has held forth a promise of life with a difference—warmer, sunnier, easier, a state where, if dreams don't always come true, they can come closer to realization than they can anywhere else. California promoters from Mark Twain to Southern California real estate hustlers have painted the state as a burgeoning, swaggering, wide-open place for anyone with talent who wants to break the mold, whether in business, science, show business— or politics. Because that fantastical picture grew from the real nature of California, Jerry Brown's ambition and idealism had great freedom and were even encouraged to develop. Brown has always been his own man, of course, but he could envision a political career for a person such as himself more easily in California, because in that freewheeling state it has been more acceptable for a political hopeful to be a little bit of an odd duck, wandering across the landscape of ideas and finding new intellectual playthings. In no other state would Jerry Brown have been as likely to achieve great success as a politician while talking openly of Zen, Mother Teresa, Catholicism, and the virtues of austerity. The tolerant, free-and-easy ethos of his home state has allowed Brown to blaze a trail of innovation in his appointments, his priorities, and his lifestyle. In California, he was a radio talk-show host long before this role became fashionable for politicians or even before talk radio became a national phenomenon. Jerry Brown lived in an ad hoc commune in Oakland, California, worked with Mother Teresa among the dying in Calcutta, studied Zen in Japan—and then, back in California, ran successfully for a third term as governor. Surfers and scientists, entrepreneurs and farmworkers, originators of social trends and the butt of mockery by some for "have a nice day" and alfalfa-sprout entrées, Californians developed as a separate breed, eager to move forward into whatever lay ahead. And so did their governor.

But paradoxically Jerry Brown has met political success in his freewheeling native state by consistently telling Californians what most state politicians would never tell them—that there are limitations on government's ability to make things better. Austerity had worked politically for him thirty-seven years earlier, when he proclaimed that Californians were in an "era of limits." Considering the difficulties the state faced in January 2011, limits would probably be front and center again as he began his third administration.

Jerry Brown's father, Edmund G. "Pat" Brown, who was also an idealist, didn't much believe in limitations. He was the perfect man to govern the rapidly growing California of the 1950s and '60s—eager to build more educational institutions, more freeways, and more water projects. Pat's philosophy meshed perfectly with his exuberant California. Jerry Brown has shared Pat's ambition but in many respects has been his exact opposite. Jerry has preached frugality, limits, and realistic views of what can be accomplished, yet at the same time has practiced his own brand of push-the-envelope idealism, appointing unprecedented numbers of women and ethnic minorities to high positions. In the post-Pat '70s, Jerry's particular alchemy created a political persona that sold well among Californians, who were recovering from a twenty-year building binge and beginning to worry about higher and higher taxes.

Jerry Brown's idealism has been shaped and enhanced by a powerful California institution—the Catholic Church, whose ranks include roughly one in four Californians.[4] From the fourth grade through his twenty-first year, the serious-minded and idealistic Brown was educated in Jesuit institutions. The cumulative effect of those many years was that he took the teachings of the Jesuits to heart more than did most of his peers. He took them seriously enough so that by the time he was seventeen, Jerry had determined that he wanted to become a Jesuit priest. He devoted three and a half years of his life to an austere, demanding, but limited seminary education. Although he eventually left the seminary, he has never entirely turned from his idealism or intellectual bent. The two characteristics have merely been expressed in different ways. Brown is one of the few politicians who examines an idea for its intellectual charm as well as its political value. Few politicians sprinkle the occasional Latin phrase into public conversations. Jerry has, declaring at the end of his 1991 announcement for president *"Annuit Coeptis"*—"may God bless this undertaking." Fewer still allow it to be known that they are interested in the devotional pronouncements of St. Ignatius as well as the party registration numbers in Fresno.

A second paradox in Jerry Brown is that, along with the intellectualism and idealism, he has a great understanding of California's unique, stainless-steel political system coupled with an unmatched ability to recognize and seize opportunities. When no one else did, ambitious Jerry realized the political possibilities in an obscure state office and made full use of them to catapult himself into the governor's office. When aspiring Jerry ran for governor in 1974, he realized more than any of his contemporaries and rivals did that California voters were suspicious of Sacramento after eight years of antigovernment rhetoric from Ronald Reagan. Californians feared their heritage was being eroded by secretive deals in Sacramento. Brown campaigned, therefore, on a platform of bringing honesty and transparency to the Capitol. Four years later, again sensing the public mood better than anyone, he campaigned on a platform of limiting the malevolent influence of lobbyists. In 2010, Brown divined that even during a national tide of revulsion against incumbents, Californians wanted an experienced hand in the governor's office, not another "run government like a business" type. Voters rewarded him with the governorship each time.

Whether from conviction, or his keen political antennae, or both, Brown as governor cannily manipulated symbols designed to show voters that he was not going to live luxuriously on the taxpayers' dime. He loudly refused to live in the new governor's mansion; he eschewed the gubernatorial limousine. Early on he realized that the Golden

State, its romance frustrated by what many regarded as Sacramento's insider politics, was made to order for his own designer-brand mix of populism and idealism. In a media-soaked state of more than thirty-seven million people, a few limited, large brushstrokes work best, and Brown has made use of them better than anyone.

To my knowledge, it has been nearly thirty years since a biography of Jerry Brown has been published, and millions of Californians know relatively little about the man who has become their thirty-ninth governor. His story is alternately heartening and discouraging, but it is always a California story. *Trailblazer* will discuss the changes that have occurred within Brown himself over his forty-plus years in the political arena, from a thirty-six-year-old governor to the seventy-two-year-old Comeback Curmudgeon. The following chapters chronicle the biography of this larger-than-life politician against the template of this larger-than-life nation-state.

The son of a governor, Jerry Brown grew up in an intensely political household and began absorbing politics with all its splendor and heart-break while still in his high chair. While growing up, this offspring of Protestant and Catholic immigrants from Germany and Ireland became more and more interested and involved in religion, specifically the teachings of the Jesuits. In addition to tracing his background and youthful development, chapter 1 will describe the election of Jerry's father, Pat Brown, as a result of William Knowland's bullheaded ambition, the idealist Jerry's conflict with his father over the Caryl Chessman case, and the Pat Brown–Ronald Reagan gubernatorial election of 1966, with its continuing ramifications for California politics and its effect on Jerry Brown.

Some might describe him as altruistic, while others might call him flaky, but Jerry Brown is one of the most ambitious, canny, and opportunistic politicians around. He made a very well-calculated entry into elective politics, using his famous name to win a spot in 1969 on the Los Angeles Community College Board of Trustees, and quickly established a reputation as a social liberal and fiscal conservative. Jerry's decision to go statewide by insightfully running for secretary of state, his hunt for headlines on the fringes of Watergate, and his preparations for a gubernatorial campaign are the themes of chapter 2.

The campaign that followed came amid a crowded and rancorous field of seventeen candidates, but Brown easily won the Democratic nomination for governor in 1974. He went on to be elected to the governorship over the Republican Houston Flournoy in the general election. Jerry's deft use of voter-pleasing symbolism and his political idealism in the governor's office make up the themes covered in chapter 3, along with his romance with Linda Ronstadt, his first run for president, and his paradoxical liberal/conservative "canoe politics."

Four years later, despite being distracted temporarily by his presidential ambitions, California's popular young governor won a landslide victory and a second term over the Republican attorney general Evelle Younger. The campaign's high point—of a sort—included the advice of the Republican gubernatorial hopeful Ed Davis on handling airplane hijackers: "Hang 'em at the airport!" Also making up chapter 4 are descriptions of the governmental malpractice that resulted in Proposition 13, the "Governor Moonbeam" nickname, Brown's 1980 bid for the presidency, his unsuccessful bid for the U.S. Senate, the nosedive in his popularity, and his Proposition 13 and Medfly flip-flops.

Out of statewide office after twelve years, Brown turned to spiritual matters—temporarily. He spent years studying Zen in Japan, working with Mother Teresa in Calcutta, and hosting the *We the People* talk show from his Oakland loft residence on the left-leaning radio station KPFA. I examine the concurrent and contradictory spiritual/political course of his years in Oakland and his friendship with Catholic philosopher-priest Ivan Illich in chapter 5, as well as the beginnings of his political comeback, serving as chairman of the California Democratic Party.

The former governor evolved from California's philosopher-prince to a pothole-filling mayor interested in downtown development and education during his eight years as mayor of gritty Oakland. He also got married at age sixty-seven to his longtime companion Anne Gust, a high-powered woman who was to influence him greatly both personally and politically. Brown reentered the statewide political scene by becoming California attorney general in a bitter election that ended in an overwhelming win for him. All that is described in chapter 6, along with his actions as attorney general, including the high-stakes Countrywide financial settlement and his controversial refusal to defend Proposition 8.

Continuing his lifelong tactic of using one office as a springboard to another, higher, one, Brown sought to return to the governor's office in what became one of the more remarkable political campaigns in recent American political history—how, with a small paid staff and relatively meager budget, Attorney General Brown defeated the Republican candidate Meg Whitman, who brought a mostly self-funded $180-million war chest to bear. Some strategists argue that the bitter Republican primary, and even the oceans of cash available to the Whitman campaign, may have ultimately been fatal to her hopes. Chapter 7 puts that campaign in its historical context, describing the invention of modern campaign techniques in California, a defense of the Whitman campaign from none other than Brown's campaign manager, and what it all augers for the future of California politics.

California's morale at the time of Brown's third inaugural was at a low point, with polls showing a large majority of citizens saying the state was headed in the wrong direction and, as we've seen, some pundits pronouncing the state as ungovernable. What might a man of Brown's background and temperament bring to bear on California's multiple and daunting challenges in governance, education, and infrastructure, along with a host of others? Can Jerry Brown make the planet's most diverse society work in an era of severe budget restrictions at all levels of government and in the face of a pallid economy? Can the onetime apostle of frugality and lowered expectations be an effective state cheerleader, restoring to an enormously changed state the robust "can do" spirit that motivated California fifty years ago? Has he even wanted to be an effective cheerleader? With comments from allies and adversaries, chapter 8 addresses those vital questions.

Barring the unexpected, Brown will continue to write additional chapters in California's history. The wide assortment of problems he faced in the first year of his third term would in all likelihood require a wholesale reworking of California's political culture to solve with any degree of permanence, and they may not be solved at all. What I hope the reader will gain from *Trailblazer* is a better understanding of what has gone into the makeup of this quirky and idealistic man and the state that has nurtured him. It is a story unparalleled in American political history.

CHAPTER ONE

Early Years

Politics and Religion

It is not just my family but every Californian is heir to some form of powerful tradition, some history of overcoming challenges much more daunting than those we face today.

  Jerry Brown, third inaugural address,
  January 3, 2011

Californians in 1938 were busy. In Hollywood, producer David Selznick was masterminding a nationwide search for the young woman who would play Scarlett O'Hara in the forthcoming supercolossal epic *Gone with the Wind*. (There were salacious rumors that he was conducting part of his talent hunt on the casting couch.) In the hills above Berkeley, Ernest Orlando Lawrence was working on his atom-smashing cyclotron, a scientific advance that would win him the Nobel Prize in Physics in 1939 and contribute to the development of the atomic bomb. The *San Francisco Chronicle* and the *Examiner* carried headlines about distant war in Asia and potential war in Europe, but they had little immediate significance to most people, who were still getting used to driving on the Golden Gate Bridge, just eleven months old, and the Bay Bridge, a mere seventeen months old. The Golden State's burgeoning population was soaring from 5.6 million in 1930 on its way to 6.9 million in 1940, even while families were feeling the effects of the Great Depression.

An ambitious young San Francisco attorney named Edmund G. "Pat" Brown became the father of a baby boy on April 7, 1938, the third of what would be Pat and his wife Bernice's four children. They named the new arrival for his father, Edmund Gerald Brown, but most people called him Jerry. He had no brothers. His three sisters were Barbara and Cynthia, both older than Jerry, and Kathleen, the youngest, who came along in 1945, seven years after Jerry.

Jerry Brown is a fourth-generation Californian, born into what passes in that state for a family with ancient roots there. One side of the family came from Germany, the other from Ireland, and both arrived in 1852. Augustus Fiedler Schuckman, from Westphalia, settled in the Colusa County town of Williams, amid wheat and barley country. He was one of the thousands of settlers who flooded into California four years after gold had been discovered in the tailrace of a lumber mill in the Sierra foothills owned by an enterprising Swiss immigrant named John Sutter. But Augustus sought his fortune in settled, peaceful farming in California's Central Valley, not panning for gold in a rough miner settlement.

He came to a place isolated from the rest of the nation and, indeed, the world. A popular song of the era declared of those who would come to California:

They swam the wide rivers and crossed the tall peaks
And camped on the prairie for weeks upon weeks.
Starvation and cholera and hard work and slaughter,
They reached California in spite of hell and high water.[1]

Augustus kept his own more personal record of his six-month trip to California. It was a classic pioneer saga. Here are excerpts from the diary he kept during the trek:

On the 26th of June, we came to the first sand desert—it was 41 miles. We went there at night and rode 19 hours in it. . . .

On the 26th of July, we came to the second large plain—also 40 miles long. Here we lost seven oxen which died of thirst. . . . Thousands of cows, horses and mules were lying about dead. . . .

The discarded wagons by the hundreds were driven together and burned. We saw wagons standing that would never be taken out again and more than 1,000 guns that had been broken up. Here on this 40 miles are treasures that can never be taken out again.[2]

Schuckman did well enough in his new surroundings to build Mountain House eventually, a stage stop in Sonoma County that included a bar, a post office, lodging, and a small store. He and his wife, Augusta, had eight children. One of them, Ida, found herself drawn in 1896 to the glamour and wealth of San Francisco, the commercial center of the West Coast with a growing population of three hundred thousand.

Amid the towering ten- and fifteen-story buildings, plush hotel lobbies, and breathtaking views of sparkling San Francisco Bay, Ida met and married Edmund Joseph Brown, the son of an Irish Golden Gate Park gardener named Joseph Brown. Joseph and his wife, Bridgette, had come from Tipperary, in County Cork. They sought their fortune in a two-year-old state where, it was well known, one could pick gold nuggets right up off the ground, the climate was always miraculously sunny, and the scenery was astonishing. The settlers found that at least the last part was true.

Joseph managed to stay married to Bridgette and employed by the city and was apparently a satisfactory gardener, even though he did occasionally go off on three- or four-day benders. It happened only two or three times a year, however, and Joseph took vows of sobriety after each frolic.

Joseph was content to remain in his humble job, tending the flowers in Golden Gate Park, but that was an unusual characteristic among Jerry Brown's ancestors. Joseph's son Edmund, Ida's new husband, aimed higher. Edmund was a merry, free-spirited Irish Catholic who wanted to make his fortune in business. And why not? San Francisco was full of opportunity. Edmund started by opening a cigar store on Market Street and in 1905 branched out, opening a nickelodeon. As the years went by, the family's fortunes gyrated with the prudence of free-wheeling Edmund's various financial ventures, which in addition to the cigar store and the nickelodeon included at one time or another a laundry, a penny arcade, and a full-scale vaudeville theater that tanked. The great 1906 San Francisco earthquake and fire forced the Browns to move briefly across the bay to almost-untouched Oakland, the city that would elect Jerry Brown as its mayor ninety-three years later.

Along with the nickelodeon acquisition, the year 1905 saw the arrival of a son, named Edmund Gerald Brown. When he was twelve years old, the future governor would acquire his nickname, "Pat," for Patrick Henry, after giving a sales pitch for World War I Liberty Bonds and ending it with "Give me liberty or give me death!"

Young Pat was an intelligent and convivial child who grew up to be an outgoing, likable man and a natural politician. He was not fond of the up-and-down entrepreneurial life led by his father and sought something that would give him respectability and a more secure income—like the law. There was the added advantage that it would provide an appropriate springboard for the political career Pat was already thinking about. Pat attended the San Francisco College of Law, won his law degree in 1927, passed the bar that same year, and went into practice, working for Milton Schmitt, a blind attorney who became his mentor.

By the time Jerry came along, Pat was prospering as an up-and-coming young attorney who could now afford some of the better things in life. Even though their circumstances were comfortable, Pat Brown disputed the idea that his son was born with a silver spoon in his mouth.

"We never had any money to speak of," he told interviewer Orville Schell. "When I ran for DA of San Francisco, I was only making $8,000 a year. I had won some lawsuits, but I never had any money. We never took any trips."[3]

Jerry was born at St. Mary's Hospital, the first in a series of institutions that had "St." or "Sacred" or "Santa" as part of their names and would largely influence his first two decades. He grew up in a white, five-bedroom Mediterranean-style house on Magellan Avenue in the desirable Forest Hills section of San Francisco.

Magellan Avenue today seems little changed from the time young Jerry Brown was there. Despite the nearby busy streets, it is a quiet, pleasant, tree-lined upper-middle-class neighborhood, with a mixture of large Italianate, Tudor, and Spanish-style houses. Home prices today range from $1.5 million and up, with most fetching far more than that.

His parents had a lifelong love affair. Bernice Layne Brown was the stunningly good-looking and enormously intelligent daughter of a San Francisco police captain. She graduated from high school at age fourteen and from the University of California's Berkeley campus at eighteen; she was teaching school at nineteen. If the career straitjackets imposed on women at the time had not been present, there is no telling what Bernice Layne Brown might have attained in a professional life had she been inclined to pursue one.

Bernice had first attracted Pat's eye when she was only thirteen, when they were in the same history class at Lowell High School. Lowell was and is an elite public school that numbers among its graduates actors Bill Bixby and Benjamin Bratt, U.S. Supreme Court associate justice Stephen Breyer, Alexander Calder, the artist who invented the mobile, and actress-singer Carol Channing. Pat had almost immediately tried to get a date with pretty Bernice, but her parents ruled that she was too young to go out with boys. But Pat persisted, and after years of courtship, he and Bernice eloped to Reno, Nevada, on October 30, 1930. They had to elope and marry on the sly because women teachers in 1930 were not allowed to marry. Pat was twenty-five.

In contrast to her ebullient, politicking husband and her non-ebullient, intellectual, politician son, Bernice was ambivalent about politics. In a 1960 news release, the governor's office said, "Mrs. Brown frankly admits that she never would have chosen a political career for her husband if the choice had been hers to make." But she "gracefully assumed the role of First Lady. As First Lady, she was a popular speaker, often offering intimate stories of family life in the governor's mansion."[4]

Pat made friends easily, an asset that fueled his political ambitions. Just one year into his law career, in 1928, he ran for the state Assembly as a Republican but lost. At the urging of a friend, labor lawyer and fellow Lowell High alumnus Matthew Tobriner, he switched to the Democratic Party in 1932, and in 1939 he ran for San Francisco district attorney against incumbent Matthew Brady. He lost again. But in 1943, when Jerry was five, indomitable Pat ran again, and this time he won. He would be in public office for the next twenty-three years.

As the district attorney of San Francisco with an eye for higher office, Pat eventually performed what was almost a rite of passage for law enforcement officials of that era, even in wink-at-sin San Francisco. He launched a headline-seeking campaign against vice. He cracked down on bookies and led a raid on San Francisco's most elegant bordello, run by Sally Stanford. Most political observers at the time credited the antivice campaign, especially the 1949 raid on Ms. Stanford's popular establishment, as a major factor in Pat's successful campaign for California attorney general a year later.[5]

In 1946, as the well-regarded Democratic district attorney of a major California city, the ever-ambitious Pat had thought himself well poised to run for state attorney general. He took on Frederick Howser, a former member of the Assembly who was the district attorney for Los Angeles County. Howser beat him. But four years later, with the Sally Stanford raid under his belt, Pat tried again and beat Republican opponent Ed Shattuck by 225,000 votes. In what would be regarded as freakish today, parts of California were plastered with billboards urging voters to cast ballots for Democrat Brown and the ever-popular Republican governor Earl Warren. The governor had not liked Howser, but he did like the affable Brown and looked favorably on Brown's use of his name. Brown was the only Democrat to win statewide election in California that year, which saw Earl Warren win a third term as governor. Brown's son Jerry, in a somewhat parallel triumph, was to be a Democratic victor in a mostly Republican year when he was elected secretary of state twenty years later, in 1970.

Although he was a politician to his core with an eye for the next chance to move up, Pat had a strong sense of right and wrong—most of the time. He opposed the forced relocation of some ninety-three thousand California residents of Japanese descent, including those who were U.S. citizens, during the early days of World War II. It was a courageous stand, especially for a politically ambitious young man. The relocation had been endorsed by Franklin D. Roosevelt and most other army and civilian authorities, and Brown's opposition stood in marked contrast to the position of his friend Earl Warren, who as governor endorsed the policy. (Warren later said he regretted his role in the relocation.)

Pat Brown was a visionary and an idealist who sought to make California a better place by being a civic booster on a grand scale, building freeways, opening new university campuses—three University of California branches in one year, 1965—and creating an enormous water project. Jerry absorbed his father's sense of vision but manifested it differently. More reserved, intellectually inclined, and with a strong commitment to personal austerity, he grew up questioning his father's backslapping ebulliency and unswerving devotion to pouring concrete. Despite his more self-reflective nature, however, Jerry also internalized his father's ferocious ambition.

Both Pat and Jerry were entranced by the rough-and-tumble game of moving masses of people in a desired direction, and both were prepared to do what was necessary to accomplish political goals. Pat could pull an occasional dirty trick; if Jerry ever did, it escaped public notice.

Jerry's political heritage was therefore formed as he grew up in a serious, but certainly not gloomy, household where law, politics, religion, and ambition dominated the adult conversation that Jerry eagerly absorbed and would adumbrate his lifelong interests in politics and various intellectual or spiritual pursuits. He was an inquisitive, intelligent child who listened closely to adult dinner-table discussion and asked endless questions. Despite his idealism, he learned early the value of playing on voters' fears and ignorance, campaign tools used even by candidates such as his father, who told fearful voters he would stand up against eastern hoodlums and communist subversives.

There is little evidence that humor played much of a role in Jerry's upbringing. While it is true that Pat Brown was an outgoing man who was extremely likable, he was not known as a great teller of jokes, nor was Bernice. Young Brown grew up in an atmosphere emphasizing achievement, substance, and serious concerns. Humor was not a mainstay of life on Magellan Avenue. Politics was.[6] "I was attracted and repelled by what I saw of politics in my father's house. The adventure. The opportunity. The grasping, the artificiality, the obvious manipulation and role-playing, the repetition of emotion without feeling— particularly that—the repetition of emotion. . . . I've always felt I could see the limitations because I was brought up in it," Jerry said years later.[7] Jerry also got a close-up look at California politics on the campaign trail, accompanying Pat as a twelve-year-old in 1950 when his father endeavored to show voters up and down the state that a good family man was running for attorney general.

But it wasn't all politics in the serious Brown home. Spiritual concerns have always been an important part of Jerry's life. In his first twenty years, they manifested themselves in his intense devotion to the Catholic Church. He attended St. Brendan's, a Catholic grammar school near his home, then San Francisco's St. Ignatius High School—now known as St. Ignatius College Preparatory—founded by the Jesuits in 1855. He graduated in the school's centennial year, 1955.[8] He was devoted enough to the Catholic Church to attend services on his seventeenth birthday, causing him to miss a surprise birthday party his friends threw for him.

As he matured and learned more about the world and its inhabitants, however, Brown became less attached to the formal teachings of the church. By the time he was twenty-one, he had left his seminary in a rebellion against the strictures of Jesuit teaching. Brown then began to express his moral convictions in more secular and independent ways, opposing the death penalty, working on behalf of farmworkers, and bringing those who were previously excluded into the mainstream of state government. He discovered that his idealism could be expressed through, of all things, nitty-gritty politics.

Jerry Brown therefore grew to maturity with two concurrent streams of thought running through his young psyche: his love-hate relationship with the facts of life involved in big-city politics, and the pursuit of Catholicism's lessons. Catholicism and political ambition are a combination that many Irish politicians grew up with, in Boston, New York, and other big cities, but few of them pursued the theological side of the combination with the dogged persistence, moral conviction, and intelligence of Jerry Brown.

Every biography of Jerry Brown that covers his youthful years paints a picture of an essentially serious, highly introspective young person who nonetheless played football with his friends in the neighborhood and indulged in the usual adolescent adventures, even while being occupied with thoughts of the important matters of politics and religion. But unlike most of his friends, Jerry found argument with adults enjoyable for its own sake. He asked questions persistently at the Brown dinner table and loved conversations about abstractions. He constantly sought answers to the Big Questions.

At St. Ignatius, Jerry was a debater and a cheerleader, but "the only reason you would be aware of Jerry at that time is he was the son of the attorney general," said Frank Damrell, a debate opponent from Modesto who later became a college roommate.[9] But biographer Roger Rapoport, in his dual biography of Jerry and Pat Brown, *California Dreaming: The Political Odyssey of Pat and Jerry Brown,* has a differing version of Jerry Brown's days at St. Ignatius, saying that Brown "distinguished himself in the oral arts. No one at St. Ignatius could match his verbal abilities." Rapoport reports that Brown was a star on the debate team and won freshman elocution and sophomore oratorical contests.[10] He developed a technique of picking apart an opponent's case with a series of strategic questions.

When he graduated from St. Ignatius at age seventeen, Jerry wanted to enter a seminary and train for the priesthood. But he had to be eighteen to do that without parental consent, and Pat refused to give it. He advised his son to attend college for a year, and then, if Jerry still wanted to become a priest, he would consent.

Brown may very well have had spiritual reasons for wanting to enter the seminary, but it's a good bet that he also wanted to out of rebellion, said George Skelton, the longtime political columnist for the *Los Angeles Times* who has covered Brown for more than four decades. "He was rebelling against society, I guess—against the way things work," Skelton said.[11]

Acceding to his father's wishes, Jerry, with a few of his St. Ignatius friends, entered Santa Clara College, a pleasant and quiet males-only Jesuit institution thirty miles south of San Francisco, in the heart of what was then known as the Valley of the Heart's Delight and would later become Silicon Valley. Santa Clara College appeared to be an ideal place to begin higher education for a thoughtful young man with a strong religious bent and some thoughts about politics. Now a university, Santa Clara declares its goal to be "the preparation of students to assume leadership roles in society" through liberal, professional, and preprofessional education.

During his year at Santa Clara College, Brown had a reputation as a night owl, fond of staying up late, not to carouse, but to discuss philosophical questions with roommate Damrell, the former debate opponent. To continue their discussions past lights-out, the roommates tucked towels under the doors to block the light. Jerry continued to be a debater at Santa Clara, once participating in a debate in which one of the judges was Marshall F. McComb, a justice on the state Supreme Court.[12]

Despite the intellectual attractions and pleasant student life at Santa Clara, the desire to be a priest still burned in Jerry Brown. After a year at Santa Clara, on August 15, 1956, the now-eighteen-year-old Jerry entered a seminary to begin training as a Jesuit. The institution he chose was Sacred Heart Novitiate, founded in 1887 in the Santa Cruz Mountains near Los Gatos, a town some sixty miles south of San Francisco. Jerry was one of forty incoming novitiates, including two close friends—Peter Finnegan and Damrell[13]—who drove down to Los Gatos together to enter the seminary. They entered on the day of the

Feast of the Assumption, the traditional day that aspiring priests enter the seminary.

Young men studying to become Jesuit priests face a long process, as much as fifteen years. It requires consistent, long-term dedication. The novitiates' studies included the classics, theology, languages, and literature (within limits). Some parts of Brown's new life were familiar. He had already been steeped in Jesuit education by the time he arrived at Sacred Heart, including his enrollment at the Jesuit Santa Clara College and his high school attendance at St. Ignatius, which was named after the Jesuits' founder, St. Ignatius of Loyola. Ignatius was a charismatic and devout Basque Spaniard of noble birth who experienced a religious epiphany after being wounded in battle. He founded the Jesuits—the Society of Jesus—in 1534. The order emphasizes rigorous religious education, intellectualism, obedience, poverty, and chastity, all of which were visited upon the young men at Sacred Heart. The Jesuits were also then interested in proselytizing, attempting to stop the spread of Protestantism. Of formidable intellect and deeply dedicated, they have been referred to as "the Pope's Marines." They have also been accused of intellectual arrogance and having an unfeeling attitude toward fellow human beings, even while engaged in education and charitable works. Because the educational institutions they founded were at that time far superior to those otherwise available, Jesuits trained lawyers and public officials; their educational institutions have spread around the world. Jesuits came to California in 1849, when two Jesuit priests originally from Italy, Michael Accolti and John Nobili, arrived in San Francisco from Oregon.

Life as a seminarian was tough, especially for a young man raised in relatively affluent circumstances. Shortly after their arrival, novitiates at Sacred Heart began a thirty-day retreat designed to cleanse their minds of secular biases and ponder the meaning of Jesus. They were housed six to a room, and the room was austere, with no running water. The day began at 5 A.M. and was spent in meditation, learning Latin, attending Mass, doing kitchen chores and other housekeeping, and learning the rules of life laid down by the order. Other physical labor was also required at times. Sacred Heart's stately main structure is located in the midst of a vineyard, and the novitiates spent each October being hot, sweaty, and juice-stained, picking the grapes for the esteemed dessert wines of the Sacred Heart winery.

Novitiates spent their long days mostly in silence. No casual conversation was permitted. Parents or close relatives were allowed one two-hour Sunday visit per month and one letter per week. Except for what they learned through the visits and letters, novitiates knew little of what was occurring "outside," because newspapers, television, and radio were forbidden. There was no smoking. Dates with women were out of the question. The Jesuits wanted no distractions or interference with the business of instilling their ideas in young heads. It was total immersion.[14] Occasionally, Brown and his fellow novitiates engaged in a practice called "taking the discipline," which involved wrapping wire around a leg to produce discomfort that was thought to increase spiritual awareness and penitence. Brown on occasion wrapped the wire so tightly that he limped, according to fellow novitiates. Self-denial was daily preached and practiced.

Although a novitiate was severely constricted in reading material and outside influences, the inward life of the mind suited Jerry at that point in his life. He felt it gave him inner discipline, and he enjoyed the pure intellectual exercises involved in meditating on life's most important issues through the lens of the Jesuits. It instilled in him a certain amount of intellectual arrogance, a sternness, a liking for austerity, and a sense of righteousness (critics would say self-righteousness) that has manifested itself throughout his political career. Years later, as a member of the Los Angeles Community College Board of Trustees, as secretary of state, as governor, and as a mayor, he lectured fellow politicians, voters, and reporters on what was important. He has continued the practice in his third gubernatorial term, telling voters that they have to face up to "tough choices" and be realistic about what government can do.

Although he had taken his initial vows and been elevated to the "juniorate" level on the pathway to priesthood, by 1960 Jerry had become frustrated and grown tired of the limited life of a seminarian. He was restless, and his intellectual curiosity had begun to burst the boundaries of the Jesuits' rigorous, but constricted, educational outlook. Jerry had begun to question some of the Jesuits' teachings, including chastity and obedience to a set of unshakable rules on how one should live one's life. He was unhappy with the Jesuit Province's decision to forbid Sacred Heart juniors from reading the works of Pierre Teilhard de Chardin, a Jesuit intellectual Jerry admired who became internationally famous as a paleontologist but whose writings on science, especially cosmic history and evolution, disturbed the Vatican.

Along with his scientific studies, Teilhard de Chardin was an explorer of the spiritual. He told his admirers that they were not human beings in search of a spiritual experience; they were spiritual beings immersed in a human experience. And he instructed that our duty, as men and women, is to proceed as if limits to our ability do not exist, adding that we are collaborators in creation. But the authorities in Rome distrusted Teilhard de Chardin and did not want young would-be priests exposed to what they thought could lead to an undermining of Catholic doctrine.

On one of the monthly visits of his parents, Jerry unburdened himself, declaring, "I sit here in poverty, but it isn't real poverty. I don't buy anything. I don't own anything, but I don't have to worry about it either. The mystical Three Degrees of Humility elude me, too.[15] And chastity seems like just another form of detachment and separation. What's the point of being here?"[16]

Jerry decided to leave Sacred Heart. He went through the necessary paperwork, giving up his Jesuit connection and its pathway to priesthood, and was placed in El Retiro, a sort of Jesuit halfway house where young men who wished to leave the seminary stayed briefly. He then hitched a ride home to Magellan Avenue with Mark McGuiness, a friend from Jerry's boyhood in San Francisco. At the end of his three

and a half years at Sacred Heart, Jerry Brown emerged with two concurrent drivers in his life: first, the Jesuit-influenced approach to
political and personal challenge, emphasizing intellectual rigor and
personal austerity, and second, his previously developed idealism and
desire to make the world a better place, even if that eventually involved
doing the unconventional, as well as the assiduous study of what political ploy works best to influence voters.

James Straukamp, a former priest who was a teacher at St. Ignatius
when Jerry was a student there, told Brown biographer Robert Pack
that among Jesuits "there is a process, an attitude, an underlying
approach to problem solving and people relationships that remains.
Your will and mind are in control all the time, and therefore there is a
danger of being too heady and not having enough heart. Oh, you're
going to feel emotion, but I think that there is a mechanism that
controls the external expression."[17]

During his time of isolation, introspection, self-denial, and inward-
looking intellectual exercise at Sacred Heart, Jerry had become the son of
the governor, although it had made little difference in his daily life. Pat's
campaign for governor came as he was nearing the conclusion of his
second term as a popular attorney general, well poised to become the
Democratic gubernatorial nominee. Then, on top of that, he was handed
an opportunity politicians can only dream about. It came as a result of one
of the most infamous instances of political bullying in California history.

The incumbent governor was Goodwin Knight, an affable, outgoing
Republican who enjoyed his job. He had been lieutenant governor
under Earl Warren and found himself in the governor's office in 1953,
when Dwight Eisenhower rewarded Warren's support by appointing
him chief justice of the U.S. Supreme Court. Knight was elected governor on his own in 1954.

Knight's happy life as governor came to an end in 1958 because of the
ambitions of U.S. senator William Knowland, who was also an assistant
publisher of the newspaper the *Oakland Tribune*, owned by his father. Knowland was the Republican leader in the U.S. Senate and one of the most

powerful, best-known, and bullheaded politicians in the country. He harbored presidential ambitions and thought his chances would improve if he were the sitting governor of a large state such as California rather than one of many in the Senate.[18] Knight stood in Knowland's way. Knight enjoyed his job and wanted to keep on being governor. But Knowland, aided by Richard Nixon and even President Eisenhower, convinced (some would say muscled) Knight to run for Knowland's Senate seat instead of another term as governor.

Pat took advantage of this gift from the political gods in the 1958 campaign, hammering at Knowland's stance on right-to-work, the big switch, and the disarray in Republican ranks caused by Knowland's ambition. And he won the governorship easily, beating tone-deaf Knowland by more than a million votes. The jovial Knight lost his senatorial campaign by 10 percentage points to Clair Engle, a Democratic congressman from Red Bluff, a small agricultural community in the northern Sacramento Valley. Knowland committed suicide in 1974.

Immediately after Jerry Brown left Sacred Heart, he enrolled at the University of California's Berkeley campus as a second-semester junior majoring in the classics. He stayed at International House, on the campus, which was open to both American and foreign students. Two fellow lodgers were Rose Bird, whom Jerry would appoint as chief justice of the California Supreme Court, and Ken Reich, who later covered Brown as an able political reporter for the *Los Angeles Times*. Frank Damrell, who had left the seminary as well, also enrolled at Berkeley.

The big, bustling, sophisticated Berkeley campus, with students discovering 1960s folk music that spoke to social injustice, was a different universe from the quiet, austere Sacred Heart, but Brown retained his idealism. In coffeehouses near the campus, students talked about racial integration in the South, capital punishment, conditions for farmworkers, the merits of the Kingston Trio, and the morality of the atomic bomb. It was, again, a place where Jerry found satisfying intellectual discourse, but this time it was free and far-ranging, in contrast to that at Sacred Heart.

He became interested in the plight of California farm laborers and sought to improve conditions in California's fields, working with members of the Berkeley campus's Agricultural Organizing Committee and the Catholic Worker Movement. Jerry and a friend, Carl Werthman, volunteered to help take students to work in the fields on weekends to help pick strawberries near Stockton so that they would form an up-close idea of what farm labor was like. He spent additional time researching farm labor law. That interest was made concrete in 1975, when Brown, as governor, created the Agricultural Labor Relations Board.

However, what may have been Jerry's most direct demonstration of continued idealism, an issue that brought him into direct and heartfelt conflict with his father, was the case of Caryl Chessman. Chessman was a career criminal with a long record who was on parole when he was arrested near Los Angeles on suspicion that he was the notorious "Red Light Bandit" who used a red light on a car spotlight to deceive young couples into believing that a policeman was behind them. When they got out of their car, the bandit would rob them and rape the women. Chessman was convicted of seventeen assorted counts of robbery, kidnapping, and rape in July 1948 and sentenced to death. He repeatedly appealed his sentence over the twelve years he spent on San Quentin's death row and won worldwide fame from his cell as an author. Chessman sold the rights to his autobiography, *Cell 2455, Death Row*, to Columbia Pictures.

By early 1960, however, Chessman was reaching the end of his appeals. Pat Brown, an opponent of the death penalty, was his last chance. Chessman had not been accused of murdering anyone, but under California's "Little Lindberg" law, kidnapping with intent to inflict harm was a capital case. Forcing victims to move even a few feet constituted kidnapping under the law. Since Chessman was a man who hadn't killed anyone but still faced the death penalty, his case became a worldwide cause célèbre. Brown was deluged with appeals for clemency from, among many others, Billy Graham, Marlon Brando, William Buckley, Aldous Huxley, Ray Bradbury, Norman Mailer, Robert Frost, and Eleanor Roosevelt.

For Berkeley undergraduate Jerry Brown, Chessman's was a clear-cut moral case. He hadn't committed murder. The death penalty was a leftover from the Dark Ages. California was better than that. Jerry repeatedly appealed to his father to follow his conscience and grant clemency. Pat, pulled between his personal beliefs, the impassioned appeals of his son, and the demands of the law, listened, argued, and wavered. In the forlorn hope that the California Legislature would somehow act on his plea to abolish the death penalty or at least place a moratorium on it and erase his agonizing dilemma, he granted a sixty-day stay of execution in February 1960, hours before Chessman was due to enter the gas chamber. The stay ran out in April, the death penalty remained in effect, Pat Brown refused executive clemency, and after a few unsuccessful last-ditch appeals, Chessman was executed on May 2, 1960.

Jerry's opposition to the death penalty did not waver. In April 1967, seven years after Chessman's execution, Jerry was among those outside the gates of San Quentin Prison when Aaron Mitchell, screaming, "I am Jesus Christ!" was executed for killing a Sacramento policeman during a 1963 robbery. A year earlier, toward the end of his term, Pat Brown again had refused to grant executive clemency. In 2011, as governor, Jerry Brown halted construction of a new, state-of-the-art, multimillion-dollar gas chamber at San Quentin. He cited budgetary concerns.

Although the Chessman case had harmed Pat Brown politically, causing him to be labeled a "tower of Jell-O" because of his perceived indecisiveness, the damage did not prevent him from being a giant-killer two years later, when he defeated former vice president Richard Nixon by three hundred thousand votes to win a second term. Idealist Jerry flew home from Yale, where he was studying law, to engage in street-level politics, campaigning energetically for his father in the heavily black Hunter's Point area of San Francisco. Nixon was handicapped by an accurate perception that he would use the governorship as a stepping-stone for another bid to become president.

The morning after the returns were in, an unshaven, pale Nixon held his famous "You won't have Nixon to kick around anymore" news conference in the ballroom of the Beverly Hilton Hotel, in Beverly Hills. Nixon's pout and the fact that a former vice president had been defeated for a mere governorship, even if it was in a state the size of California, took some of the national media limelight off Pat. But he had won, and won convincingly.

Jerry Brown graduated from Berkeley with a bachelor of arts degree in classics in 1961. District Court of Appeals judge Matthew Tobriner, who had convinced Pat Brown to switch from being a Republican to a Democrat nearly thirty years earlier, convinced Pat's son that he should attend Yale Law. Jerry set off for New Haven.

At the suggestion of his father, Jerry performed legal research in the Yale Law Library for Stephen Reinhardt, a Los Angeles attorney who had recently brought a legal action against Pierre Salinger, formerly President John Kennedy's and then Lyndon Johnson's press secretary. Salinger, a former reporter for the *San Francisco Chronicle* before he went to Washington, had been appointed to the U.S. Senate to fill the unexpired term of Democrat Engle, who had died of brain cancer. He then filed to run for a full six-year term. Even though Pat Brown had appointed Salinger to the Senate, Brown and Reinhardt opposed Salinger's candidacy and sought to derail it on the grounds that Salinger was not a legal resident of California. Salinger won the case, even with Jerry doing opposition legal research, defeated Alan Cranston in the Democratic primary, and went on to be defeated in 1964's general election by former MGM song-and-dance man George Murphy.

During his time at Yale, Jerry formed two other friendships—with former Louisiana seminarian Don Burns, a brilliant student who later became a member of his cabinet, and with also-brilliant Tony Kline, who became Jerry's legal adviser and a state appeals court judge.

Jerry did not go to Fort Lauderdale to frolic with girls in bikinis during Yale's spring break. Instead, he went to Mississippi to observe the struggles of those attempting to win civil rights for African Americans. He arrived in Jackson, talked with civil rights organizers, and dropped in unannounced to chat with Ross Barnett, the segregationist governor. Barnett, an unlikely friend of the senior Brown from governors' conferences, phoned Pat to tell him that Jerry was running around with the wrong sort of people. A few days later, Jerry returned to New Haven. "It got really heavy," Jerry told his father. "I was really nervous so I got out of there."[19]

Jerry graduated from Yale in 1964, returned to California, and clerked for Matthew Tobriner, then a justice of the state Supreme Court who had been appointed to that court in 1962 by Pat. (Jerry breezed into the clerkship after getting his law degree but before passing the bar examination; he was, after all, the son of the governor.) Jerry confidently took the California bar exam, and flunked it. In Jerry's defense, the three-day California bar examination is generally regarded as one of the most difficult in the nation. Determined to pass the next time around, Brown hunkered down in the 1877-vintage, three-story, white Victorian governor's mansion in downtown Sacramento and studied. He passed on his second try, after taking a three-month refresher course at McGeorge School of Law in Sacramento.

Whether he was influenced by Yale, his rebellion against the severity of Sacred Heart, a resurgence of interest in secular intellectual pursuits, or, as is most likely, a combination of those factors, Jerry Brown after graduating from law school pointed his life in a direction that was new in locale but familiar in background—politics. The idealism remained, but gone was any desire for an official attachment to the Catholic Church. He decided to strike out afresh in a new political arena. He went to work at $640 a month for Tuttle & Taylor, one of the more prestigious law firms in Los Angeles, located in the former 20th Century-Fox studio lot remade into the sleek Century City office area.

Tuttle & Taylor was a firm that emphasized collegiality, relatively low billable hours, schedule flexibility, and high academic achievement among the attorneys it very selectively hired. The combination was ideal for a young man ready to explore options.[20] But before taking the Tuttle & Taylor job, the ever-restless, ever-inquiring Jerry Brown embarked on a six-month study tour of Latin America, which saw him stopping in Mexico City, Honduras, Costa Rica, Guatemala, Venezuela, Colombia, Brazil, and Uruguay.

In 1969, not long after beginning the private practice of law at Tuttle & Taylor in vote-rich Los Angeles, former Jesuit seminarian Jerry Brown entered what was to be his lifelong occupation—elective politics.

CHAPTER TWO

Going Statewide

Learning the Ropes and Hunting Headlines

Nothing in life is so rigid that there aren't developments.
That's true in politics. That's true in theology. That's true in
personal relations.

Jerry Brown, speech to high school students, 1979

Just as Jerry had begun to settle into life in Los Angeles, his father found himself in the political fight of his life, scrambling to retain his governorship against a Hollywood actor named Ronald Reagan. The election that followed had repercussions that echoed down the years for Jerry Brown and all California politicians.

From the conventional political standpoint of the mid-1960s, even with its revolution against societal norms, Reagan was regarded by Pat Brown and his inner circle as an impossible candidate; *movie stars* did not run for office, even in celebrity-struck California. The famous, but probably apocryphal, story has movie mogul Jack Warner reacting when informed that Reagan was running for governor: *"No—Jimmy Stewart for governor—Ronald Reagan as 'best friend.'"*

For the most part, elected officials in the state's highest offices prior to Reagan had been people—almost all of them men—who had devoted their lives to politics. Earl Warren, Goodwin Knight, William Knowland, and Pat Brown were experienced, professional, and used to making deals. They sought to win voters by talking about how their policies were good for people and their opponents' policies were not. They did not rely primarily on personal charm, although it was regarded as an asset. They sought to project themselves as competent and reliable. Warren and Knight worked at having a cordial relationship with the state's civil servants. Being charming on television was terra incognito.

Reagan upended that world forever, a lesson not lost on Jerry Brown. Reagan proved that a political outsider, one who had never before faced a general electorate and who had a background professional politicians would laugh at, could steamroll an experienced, competent incumbent through his appeal to the media. Dramatically exploiting themes that resonate with voters had long been a standard part of the political armamentarium and still is, but Reagan's twinkly-eyed ability to connect with voters, especially on television, took the tactic much further. The trick is finding the themes. In California in 1966, the right themes were the perception of misbehaving students at Berkeley and the rioting blacks in Watts.

The late Mario Savio and other young firebrands of the 1964 Free Speech movement at the University of California's Berkeley campus could not have known it at the time and would probably deny it today, but they and a group of conservative California businessmen formed an unknowing and odd combination that helped open the door for Ronald Reagan to eventually occupy the White House. They unwittingly helped elect him governor, and a California governor is automatically a potential president. Reagan would indeed be elected president in 1980.

The chain of circumstances stretched across many years. For nearly a century, the university had been a beloved California institution, enabling millions of young people from modest circumstances to receive an excellent education and move up the economic and social ladder. UC was, and still is, a major driver of California's and the nation's economies. But beginning in 1964, millions of voters discovered to their horror that the university had some students who engaged in unruly conduct, became active politically, defied police, and generally behaved in ways that, in the minds of many voters, university students were not supposed to behave.

The Free Speech movement was not the first demonstration for idealistic causes at the University of California's Berkeley campus. Demonstrations for one cause or another dated at least back to the 1930s, and the campus was roiled by a 1960 demonstration against the ROTC. In 1949–51, the entire university system was embroiled in controversy over the Board of Regents' decision to require a loyalty oath. In addition, students in 1960 went across the bay to be part of the San Francisco city hall demonstration against the House Un-American Activities Committee, which was holding hearings in the same building. But the Free Speech movement was the seminal student activism event, leading to at least some consequences the demonstrators and their leaders never had in mind.

Reagan and his campaign strategists realized the impact the Free Speech movement was having on a large portion of the California electorate and moved effectively to seize the opportunity presented by offended voters.[1] Among those offended was Jerry Brown. When the Free Speech movement erupted at Berkeley, Jerry Brown, by then a Yale Law graduate clerking for state Supreme Court justice Matthew Tobriner, went over to the campus to take a look. He was not impressed by the students' righteousness, reportedly saying that he didn't see the point of breaking a law in support of some other grievance.

The campus unrest, combined with the Watts riots of 1965, was fatal for Pat Brown's reelection hopes. The six days of race riots across eleven square miles of Los Angeles left thirty-four people dead, more than a thousand injured, and a feeling on the part of voters that Brown had not moved effectively to stop the violence. Brown had been on vacation in Greece when Watts began burning, and although he called out the National Guard and flew back to California once he realized the seriousness of the situation, millions of voters thought he was not on the job.

Handsome, stern, and reassuring Ronald Reagan promised to whip the university and its ungrateful students into shape. "Obey the rules or get out," he declared. Voters eagerly gave him a chance to fulfill his promise. Reagan defeated Brown by nearly one million votes—3,742,913 to Brown's 2,749,174. Reagan carried fifty-five of California's fifty-eight counties, with more than 57 percent of the popular vote. Pat carried only 42.3 percent of the popular vote and won in only three counties.

Some political observers have argued that Jerry felt his father lost the election because he wasn't agile and flexible enough—that he allowed Reagan to paint him as ineffectual in dealing with problems instead of nimbly leaping to the forefront of the attack against unruly students and rioting blacks. In subsequent years, Jerry Brown—the supreme opportunist—has proven himself able to take quick advantage of the tide of public opinion. The most blatant example, discussed in chapter 4, is Jerry's overnight about-face on Prop 13. He had campaigned against it as governor, but hours after it won overwhelming voter approval, Jerry pronounced himself a "born-again tax cutter."

With his new job at Tuttle & Taylor, lifelong Northern Californian Jerry Brown immediately wove himself into the fabric of Los Angeles. With the help of his parents, Jerry bought a house in Laurel Canyon with a swimming pool. He started forming acquaintanceships. If he was to launch a political career, Jerry knew he needed a foothold in Los Angeles—some sort of public office that could serve as a launching pad. Pat Brown, ever helpful, called a friend, Los Angeles County supervisor Kenneth Hahn, who promptly arranged to have the newly arrived Jerry appointed to the Los Angeles County Delinquency and Crime Commission. It was a start.

Those expecting a soft approach to crime from the son of the notably liberal governor Brown were in for a surprise. He reportedly told his fellow commission members that his philosophy was that it is better to catch people at the beginning, give them a sentence of a substantial time in prison but not a draconian period, then let them out, and if they fail again, bring them back and keep them longer.

At the same time that the newly arrived Southern Californian was delivering hard-line lectures on juvenile delinquency and feeling bored with routine legal work at Tuttle & Taylor, he took an interest in presidential politics and the Vietnam War. He wrangled an invitation to speak at a California Democratic Council (CDC) meeting in Long Beach and spoke in favor of an immediate cessation of the bombing of North Vietnam, advocating a prompt start of truce talks. That was not what many CDC members wanted to hear. They wanted a call for immediate withdrawal.

But Jerry, while seen as a moderate, was also dovish enough to be selected as the Southern California finance chairman of a CDC "peace slate" favoring the rebellious presidential candidacy of Minnesota senator Eugene McCarthy. Pat Brown favored Lyndon Johnson and thought his son's advocacy of McCarthy was helping to destroy the Democrats' chances of retaining the White House in 1968. The situation grew more complicated when Robert Kennedy, the senator from New York and brother of the late president, entered the race and Lyndon Johnson declared he would not seek reelection.

The president's decision to bow out placed McCarthy and Kennedy in head-to-head competition in the California Democratic primary. Jerry worked hard for McCarthy, finding him an agreeable intellectual companion, familiar with Latin and able to discourse on theology, poetry, and politics.

Robert Kennedy was assassinated in the kitchen of the Ambassador Hotel in Los Angeles minutes after learning that he had defeated McCarthy in the primary and telling his cheering supporters "On to Chicago!" After Kennedy's assassination, Jerry and others briefly considered the possibility of resurrecting the McCarthy campaign, but it ultimately failed to gain traction. Hubert Humphrey, Johnson's vice president who had been endorsed by Pat Brown, won the Democratic nomination at a tumultuous convention chiefly remembered afterward for television footage of Chicago police beating antiwar street demonstrators.

Early in 1969, after Humphrey had been defeated by Richard Nixon, Jerry decided to run for the new Los Angeles Community College

Board of Trustees. It was the next step up. Community colleges—originally "junior colleges" until educators decided "community colleges" sounded more grown-up—had been educating students for forty years when the state Legislature separated the nine-campus system from the Los Angeles Unified School District in 1969. The colleges would now be governed by their own seven-member Board of Trustees. Jerry Brown, working in corporate law at Tuttle & Taylor, saw election to the board as an obvious move in his nascent political career. Service on a school board has long been a traditional way for ambitious Californians to begin careers in elective office, and many Los Angelenos have realized that. There were 133 candidates for the seven trustee positions in the 1969 election.

Many would argue, justifiably, that Jerry breezed into his first elective office because his last name was Brown. His father's friend Matthew Tobriner was not alone in observing that had Jerry's last name been Green, he would not have achieved his immediate success. But it is equally true that Jerry worked hard and intelligently. His name and ambition alone would not have been enough to sustain a political career—certainly not one that has carried him to three terms in the governor's office. They had to be combined with a high intellect, a canny political instinct, and a finely tuned sense of what gains favorable recognition in the media.

But because he was the son of a governor, the unproven Jerry Brown in his first elective venture had the widest name recognition and cruised to victory. He became one of the fourteen finalists selected in a preliminary round of voting and was the top candidate in the runoff, beating second-place Mike Antonovich by sixty-one thousand votes.

There was never any doubt in anyone's mind that Brown viewed his trusteeship as nothing more than a temporary, entry-level position and that even before his election, he had his sights aimed higher, undoubtedly at statewide elected office. Antonovich, not surprisingly, believes that Brown's entire service on the board was aimed at creating an effective springboard for higher office. "I don't think his heart was in serving on a college board," he told Brown biographer Robert Pack. "I think that was all contrived to project his name in the paper and then to be elected secretary of state."[2]

Brown was one of at least three newly elected board members who had their sights set on higher office. Brown, Antonovich himself, and Robert Cline were three intelligent and ambitious young men who all viewed membership on the Board of Trustees as a first step in their political careers. But ambition was about the only thing they had in common. Cline and Antonovich were Republicans. Brown was not only a Democrat; he was the son of a man who until recently had been the most visible Democrat in the state.

Antonovich, a conservative Republican and former public school teacher, later served three terms in the California Assembly before winning election to the Los Angeles County Board of Supervisors.[3] Robert Cline, another conservative Republican, was also elected to the Assembly.

During his eighteen months on the board, Brown quickly established a paradoxical reputation that has remained with him throughout his political life: He is a dead-serious fiscal conservative and a social liberal. He voted against an appropriation to provide private offices for the seven trustees; comfortable in his own ability to generate media attention, he opposed hiring media relations people for the district as an unnecessary expense; he was a "no" vote on a sixty-dollar appropriation to allow Antonovich to attend a conference at Stanford University. He was mostly on the losing side in these issues, with Antonovich and Cline voting against Brown and with the majority. But, according to his conviction and his view of political necessity, he carved out a reputation for himself as someone distinctly different from his free-spending father.

On social issues, idealist Brown was a consistent liberal "yes" vote. He favored, for instance, recognizing Martin Luther King's birthday as a holiday and opposed a requirement that district employees be fingerprinted.

Brown also came up with some off-the-wall ideas designed to show voters that he was not completely a squishy liberal. Keenly aware of the continuing public antagonism toward angry students, he advocated prohibiting students from transferring into the district if they had been convicted of a campus disruption sometime during the previous three years. In a notion that today sounds silly, he suggested formation of "an airborne campus strike force to curb student violence" that would employ "no-nonsense tactics" against the hated student disrupters. It would have a fleet of jets, and members of the strike force would equipped with crowd-control devices such as tranquilizer guns, wood pellet guns, and water cannons. He also suggested that the state's nationally admired Master Plan for Higher Education be scrapped in favor of turning two-year junior colleges into four-year institutions. Although helicopters were used by Reagan to quell student disorders at Berkeley, the airborne strike force never flew, and the Master Plan for Higher Education has remained in effect. All of Brown's suggestions were styled to receive maximum media attention, a practice Jerry was to follow through the coming decades.

The major liberal/conservative dispute during Brown's time on the board revolved around Deena Metzger, an English teacher. A majority of the board voted to fire her after she read a poem titled "Jehovah's Child" aloud in class. Cline and Antonovich were among the board majority who regarded the poem as advocating abnormal sex, among other things. Brown voted to retain Metzger but lost. The case became a Los Angeles cause célèbre, winning headlines for Brown as an advocate of freedom of expression.[4]

Almost simultaneously with his election to the college board, Jerry met Tom Quinn and began a friendship that was to benefit both of them immensely over the coming years. Brown needed favorable notice in the media if he was to advance his political career beyond the board. Few could equal Quinn as a master at creating headlines and using the news media to the advantage of a candidate or cause.

Quinn came by his abilities naturally. He is the son of Joe Quinn, a former executive at United Press International who, with former Los Angeles mayor Fletcher Bowren, founded City News Service. CNS is a local wire service that for eight decades has provided local news on a fast-breaking basis to media outlets, first in Los Angeles and later to much of Southern California. It features a daily morning "budget" listing of scheduled events such as news conferences, and it is avidly read by city editors and television assignment editors as an important resource in determining how to deploy reporters and camera crews.

Tom Quinn in 1966 had formed Radio News West, an audio version of CNS that feeds audio reports to radio stations. Such a background meant that Tom Quinn, more than most news executives, was from an early age acquainted with the news business—its customs, techniques, problems, people—and what makes a news story.

Brown and Quinn talked about what path might prove most beneficial in advancing Brown's political ambitions and quickly settled on a target—California secretary of state. To say that the office of California secretary of state was obscure in 1970 is to elevate its profile. Few Californians, even those who worked in state government in Sacramento, had much of an understanding of, or cared to learn, what the secretary of state does. The joke around Sacramento was that the chief duty of the secretary of state is to polish the state seal.

In fact, the secretary of state is a sort of county clerk, except that he or she serves a state rather than a county. The office is responsible for a number of functions, nearly all of them boring. It oversees the state archives; it keeps an official record of all laws passed by the Legislature; it records the sales of farm equipment and the registration of farm names; it registers the names and insignias of fraternal organizations; it registers aircraft brokers and notary publics.

Not only was the office of secretary of state an obscure paper-shuffling backwater in 1970; it was also an oddity. Since 1911, with the exception of two years, 1940–42,[5] it had been filled by Frank C. Jordan and then his son, Frank M. Jordan. Both died in office.

It was an office that most aspiring politicians thought little about. Who would want to wind up in such a dead-end job? But as Jerry Brown would many times in the future, he proved himself more intelligent than his fellow politicians and potential rivals. Unlike the hordes of ambitious individuals in Sacramento and elsewhere across California, Tom and Jerry took the trouble to study the duties of the office in some detail. They realized that the secretary of state was, after all, a state-wide office, but because it was so lightly regarded by the ambitious, there would be little or no topflight competition. There was no incumbent. And while most of the office's duties were dull, it had potential: *the office interprets and enforces the state's election laws.* What could be a better platform for a clean-government crusader?

Jerry declared his candidacy on March 2, 1970, and zeroed in on the office's hitherto-unrealized potential for creating headlines. Brown told reporters in a news release that he would "vigorously enforce campaign disclosure laws now on the books. These laws require candidates to report the precise source of all contributions. Yet most reports are so vague they're actually more funny than informative." He added, "I will refuse to certify the election of any candidate who fails to fully and honestly report every campaign contribution."[6] Brown and Quinn had seized upon a previously neglected potential headline grabber within the labyrinthine functions of the office of secretary of state. It was a masterly display of finding a political golden needle in a haystack.

The combination of Brown's name identification, the headlines promising a crackdown on rule-evading politicians, and Californians' distrust of Sacramento, encouraged by Reagan, combined to give Jerry 70 percent of the vote over two opponents in the Democratic primary. His chief intraparty rival was Hugh Burns, a Fresno Democrat who had been a major power in the California Senate for more than thirty years and, ironically, had been one of Pat Brown's chief lieutenants in getting Pat's huge water plan through the Legislature. He had achieved some notoriety through his chairmanship of the state's Un-American Activities Committee, but by the time he ran against Jerry Brown, Burns, no longer in a Senate leadership position, was very nearly a spent force. His longtime financial backers absented themselves, and Brown spent two dozen campaign dollars for every dollar spent by Burns. Pat also helped, sending his longtime supporters a letter asking them to contribute a hundred dollars toward his son's campaign. There was also money originally pledged to a 1970 Pat Brown comeback campaign for governor that never happened. Jerry Brown and Pat Brown biographer Roger Rapoport wrote that Pat was dissuaded from making the rematch race against Reagan by Bernice, who told him that two Edmund G. Browns on the ballot was not a good idea.[7] Burns afterward found a sinecure through appointment to the Alcoholic Beverage Control Appeals Board.

Brown's Republican opponent in the general election was James Flournoy, an African American attorney in Los Angeles.[8] With the backing of the Reagan forces, James Flournoy campaigned against Brown on a theme of toughening laws that governed corporations, declaring that there was some evidence of an underworld influence. He also said he wanted to bridge the "polarization gap" between the races, although it was uncertain how he could do that as secretary of state.

Sensing the growing voter distrust of politicians and all that went on in Sacramento, Jerry Brown said he would reduce the "hidden influence of lobbyists" in political campaigns by requiring candidates to file more complete reports on their campaign expenditures. He said election laws should be liberalized to allow voters to register as late as two weeks before election day and suggested that television stations be required to donate time to political candidates as a remedy for the vast amounts of campaign money that had to be sought on behalf of political candidates. Brown himself benefited from help given by Pat's former financial backers, including San Francisco hotel magnate Ben Swig. Swig occasionally locked up potential donors in a hotel ballroom until they unlimbered their checkbooks.

Brown went on to a victory in the general election with a margin of three hundred thousand votes. He had 50.4 percent of the vote, Flournoy won 45.6 percent, Peace and Freedom candidate Israel Feuer won 1.7 percent, and American independent Thomas M. Goodloe had 2.3 percent.[9]

Jerry had achieved a Democratic victory amid a mostly Republican year. Ronald Reagan, whom Jerry regarded as an intellectual lightweight, was reelected governor by a 501,000-vote margin over Jesse Unruh, the longtime speaker of the Assembly nicknamed the "Big Daddy" of California politics.[10] Houston Flournoy was elected state controller, Ed Reinecke was elected lieutenant governor, and Ivy Baker Priest was elected treasurer. All were Republicans. It was not, however, a complete Republican sweep. Wilson Riles became California's first statewide elected African American official, winning the nonpartisan state superintendent of public education post. Riles was a Democrat; Max Rafferty, the incumbent that Superintendent Riles defeated, was a conservative Republican.[11] And Democrat John Tunney was elected to the U.S. Senate, defeating Republican incumbent George Murphy.

Reagan, justifiably confident of his own victory, campaigned hard for his old movie-days friend Murphy and was disappointed when Murphy lost. Murphy's forlorn reelection campaign was handicapped by his undistinguished six years in the Senate plus throat cancer, which forced him to make platform speeches in a throaty whisper.

On January 4, 1971, Jerry was sworn into office by Earl Warren, with his parents, siblings, staff, and grandmother, Ida Schuckman Brown, looking on proudly. Standing before the 150 people assembled to witness his inauguration, the new secretary of state turned to his mother and thanked her for naming him after his father.

Early in his tenure as secretary of state, Jerry met Jacques Barzaghi at a party in Los Angeles and shortly afterward appointed him to his staff as a file clerk. That was the title, although Barzaghi was really a staff utility man, friend, political and spiritual adviser, futurist, confidant, decorator, and personal stylist. Barzaghi was an enigma to Brown's other staffers. However, he was to remain at Brown's side during the next thirty-plus years, far outlasting other members of the Brown team who eventually went their separate ways.

Despite being the son of a governor, Jerry Brown had spent little time in the state capital. He was a creature of San Francisco and then Los Angeles, where he had quickly become part of the city. The Sacramento that Jerry Brown confronted upon taking up his new position was, like Jerry, full of contradictions. It had a reputation of being dull. A long-standing quip had one of its residents saying, "Sacramento used to be a little cow town. Now it's a big cow town." Nancy Reagan was famously quoted as saying of Sacramento, "Nobody does hair there."

Dull or not, Sacramento was the capital city of the nation's most populous and complex state. And it was sophisticated. But the sophistication was political, much too specialized to be appreciated in the wider world. Lieutenant Governor Ed Reinecke once told me that, counting the 120 legislators, lobbyists, staff members, and reporters, only about 2,000 Californians were daily concerned and knowledgeable about what went on in the Capitol, while the rest of the state knew little about internecine Sacramento political happenings and didn't much care. Back in the districts, constituents didn't know much about the realities faced by lawmakers, who sometimes had to make ugly compromises to get desired legislation passed. Lobbyists got it; constituents didn't.

The political players—legislators, their staffs, and lobbyists—had their own jargon, their own watering holes, and, in cow town Sacramento, a certain amount of well-hidden contempt for civilians unfamiliar with their tribal rites. In a quote that has been repeated for more than fifty years, Unruh once declared, "If you can't eat their food, drink their booze, screw their women, take their money, and vote against them, you have no business being here."

Unruh's legendary quote has been accurately interpreted as a commentary on being independent and tough-minded in the face of blandishments by lobbyists, but it also gives insight into the prevailing atmosphere in Sacramento. Republican and Democratic legislators got to know one another at private parties that lobbyists hosted in the Senator Hotel, across the street from the Capitol. In his book *A Disorderly House,* James Mills, a scholarly legislator who was one of Unruh's top lieutenants in the Assembly and later became the president pro tempore (leader) of the California Senate, tells of magnificent feasts with distinguished wines topped off by brandy and cigars.[12] State senators formed the Derby Club, where lobbyists paid for jolly lunches every Wednesday at Posey's, a nearby restaurant that posted a black derby hat atop its sign. The California Assembly and Senate were gathering places for 120 extroverts, and because their wives and children were most often at home in the districts, they were on their own.

While they were guilty of occasional idealism, the eighty members of the Assembly and forty members of the state Senate, along with the constitutional officers who were elected statewide, had for the previous 120 years spent most of their waking hours scheming and posturing to move out of the Triple-A League politics of California's capital to the Major Leagues, either by getting elected governor—and therefore becoming automatically mentioned as a potential president—or by getting elected or appointed to a suitably prominent position in Washington. There was nonstop plotting, maneuvering, and backstabbing.[13] Everyone also wanted to do good, of course—whatever that might be—but most of all, everyone wanted to do well.

In 1966, four years before Jerry's arrival in Sacramento, voters approved a measure authored by Mills to create a full-time legislature with an annual salary that went from six thousand dollars to sixteen thousand. The idea was that a more professional, better-paid legislature was appropriate for a complex state that in 1962 had surpassed New York to become the most populous in the nation. For many lawmakers, the higher salary allowed them to live in Sacramento year round, some with their families, and become even more wrapped up in the world of the Capitol.

Into this long-established cauldron of ambition, warfare, idealism, and sin came thirty-one-year-old Jerry Brown, a former Jesuit novitiate, austere idealist, and opportunistic antipolitician politician. "I would say it was a culture shock," recalls Doug Faigin, Brown's press secretary in the secretary of state's office and later his press secretary as governor. "Reagan and his people would go to the Firehouse, which was about the only really fine restaurant in Sacramento at the time, but we would go to the Virgin Sturgeon. Sometimes Jerry would be there."[14]

It took a year of simmering resentment before the Sacramento political establishment moved to put the brash, self-righteous newcomer with the famous name in his place. In June 1972, legislators did what they usually do when an agency head or elected official displeases them—they cut his or her budget. When he took office, Jerry had established his main base of operation in sleek Century City, not far from his previous perch at Tuttle & Taylor.[15] Not only were the offices handsome and modern, but Jerry was driven to them every day in a Cadillac—a far cry from the famous blue Plymouth he later used during his years as governor as an emblem of his frugality. Then the Assembly's budget committee took away the rent money for the Century City office and cut two positions from his staff, including an "editorial assistant"—a public relations position. The cuts were included in the budget that was sent to Reagan for his signature.

Brown was furious. He told Doug Willis of The Associated Press that the move was nothing less than revenge for his attempting to expose big campaign contributors. "For the first time, the secretary of state has made politicians report where they get their campaign money, and they don't like it," he said.[16]

But Willie Brown, the San Francisco assemblyman who headed the budget committee—and who was later to become mayor of San Francisco while Jerry was mayor of Oakland, across San Francisco Bay—said the secretary of state's office was merely being made to comply with the restrictions placed on other offices. And anyway, there were vacant offices in state buildings. The state did not need to shell out fourteen hundred dollars a month for Brown's Century City offices, Willie Brown pointed out. The irony of protesting the cutting of a public relations position from his office only a few years after he had voted against hiring media relations people for the college district was lost on Jerry, at least publicly.

"Some of the leadership in the legislature doesn't want the public to know where their campaign money comes from," Brown said. Asked by Willis which legislators were attempting to cloud campaign cash reporting, Brown replied, "I would single out the speaker and his lieutenants. They don't want this done."[17]

More was involved than mere displeasure or a simple budget cut. Willie Brown was a top lieutenant to Bob Moretti, the speaker of the Assembly who was eyeing a 1974 run for governor, as was Jerry Brown. Even as early as 1972, it appeared they would probably be opponents in the 1974 Democratic primary. The budget cut was a shot across the bow, letting Jerry know that he would not always have clear sailing if he persisted in crusading against lawmakers to gain traction for a run at the governorship. Brown himself said the Democratic primary was too far away to be "a main issue" in the dispute.

Willis's story drew headlines across California—the then-named *Long Beach Independent, Press-Telegram* proclaimed, "Brown Says Top Solons Trying to Cripple Him." It was just the kind of idealist-against-the-entrenched-establishment headline that Jerry sought.

Jerry's indignation was part of a consistent program. No one in the ranks of Capitol reporters, legislators, staff members, or lobbyists doubted that ambitious Jerry Brown was determined to follow in his father's footsteps and become governor. His challenge was to find a way to turn a moribund office into a dynamic center of political reform and let California voters know about the good work that was being done.

To do that, Jerry and Tom Quinn had to raise Jerry's visibility as an active, corruption-fighting political comer whom voters would be well advised to promote to a higher position in the next statewide election. To do that, they had to create headlines. And to do that, they had to find ways of entrancing the California news media, most particularly the approximately seventy men and women who made up what was

usually called the Capitol Press Corps. The Sacramento Capitol reporters were not the only media people Jerry dealt with—he spent much of
his time in Los Angeles, running the office with a telephone from
poolside—but they were the single most important cluster of reporters
in California on political subjects.

In 1970, every large- and medium-sized daily in California had at
least one reporter in Sacramento. The Capitol bureau was considered a
plum assignment. There were full-time television crews from Los
Angeles, San Francisco, and Sacramento as well as radio reporters from
all-news radio stations. The four largest bureaus were those of the *Los
Angeles Times*, the *Sacramento Bee*, United Press International, and The
Associated Press. Competition was intense, especially between the two
major wire services, UPI and The AP.

For the seven reporters in the AP bureau, the height of success in
daily reporting (along with beating UPI on a breaking story) was to get
a story on the "A" wire—the national wire that was put together by the
general desk in New York and carried the top stories of the day around
the world. Even better was to get a story on the A wire "budget"—the
listing of the dozen or so top stories of that day's news cycle. A story
that went national on the A wire was a career booster. Because there
were then both afternoon and morning dailies, there were two A wire
budgets in each twenty-four-hour news cycle. There were also two
California-only budgets a day for the top state stories selected by The
AP's hub bureau in Los Angeles.[18]

Jerry and his staff were well aware of the people and pressures that
made up the Capitol Press Corps. They correctly surmised that the
best angle of attack for them was the "clean up politics" theme, which
would work particularly well against the backdrop of a famous and
popular governor who spent much of his time attacking state government and the politicians in the Legislature. Adopting this theme was an
ideal melding of Brown's inherent idealism and his calculating political
instinct. But there was an attendant challenge: Reagan's antipolitician
attitude was helpful as a sort of reinforcing backdrop, but would the

"clean up politics" message that had carried Brown to victory in the election continue to win headlines when Reagan, embarking on his second term and with great ambition of his own, was still sucking all the oxygen out of the room in terms of major state and national coverage? What would be the follow-through?

Brown and Quinn felt they had to jump at every opportunity. They were not always certain when real opportunity presented itself, so they just kept jumping. Brown's office thus began issuing what became a torrent of news releases. Many of them had only a tenuous connection to the work of the secretary of state's office, but most of them managed to be of interest to reporters, even while they chuckled at their typewriters. Through his numerous news releases, Brown in effect became a commentator on the passing scene. He praised César Chávez for his work on behalf of farm laborers; he called for a "massive national debate" that would end with the impeachment of President Nixon and Vice President Spiro Agnew;[19] he announced support for a bill that would allow women to use "Ms." before their names when registering to vote. ("Miss," "Mrs.," and nothing were also acceptable.)

Jerry also took on Attorney General Evelle Younger, who would become his Republican opponent in the 1974 gubernatorial race. Younger had issued an opinion declaring that college students should not be entitled to vote at their college addresses but instead should have to vote at their parents' addresses. While not having the force of law, the attorney general's opinions are generally given great weight. Younger's opinion was generally regarded as a move to safeguard Republican candidates running in college towns, where perceived left-leaning students were more likely to vote for a Democrat. In a rare and audacious move, Democrat Brown challenged the ruling and embarrassed Younger by winning in a case that ultimately went to the California Supreme Court. Brown, in a news release, also declared that the 1971 calm on California college campuses was the result of allowing eighteen-year-olds to vote, adding that those young voters would create a revolution at the ballot box.

Three weeks after taking office, Brown announced he was filing a $250,000 lawsuit against foes of a ballot measure that would have allowed gasoline taxes to help finance rapid transit. He charged that they had illegally kept their donations secret. Within a few days, oil companies, chief backers of the "anti" forces, were forced to disclose their contributions. The lawsuit won headlines and sharpened Jerry's emerging image as a crusader against corruption, exactly the portrait Brown and Quinn wanted to cultivate. "Laws aimed at guaranteeing open and honest elections must be enforced because the public has a right to know all the facts," Jerry declared in a statement.[20]

In September 1971, Brown announced that he would enforce the law requiring political candidates to fully disclose their campaign contributions, giving the 134 named individuals a deadline of October 15. "We looked at the books that were supposed to contain the records of campaign contributions, and we found that anything of interest was redacted—blacked out," Faigin said.[21] Brown and his staff called a news conference in the Capitol and displayed poster-sized copies of the blacked-out pages.

If found guilty, Brown said, those failing to produce complete reports faced jail time of up to five years in state prison. Almost all complied, including Norton Simon, a longtime friend of Pat Brown who had run in the Republican U.S. Senate primary against George Murphy. No one went to jail. Brown biographer Robert Pack pointed out, "Brown got good mileage from the original admonitions to the 134 candidates, only 33 shopping months before the Democrats had to choose their 1974 gubernatorial nominee."[22]

Then, in August 1972, Brown's staff discovered that both the pro and con arguments intended to be distributed to voters by the secretary of state prior to an upcoming state ballot measure had been typed on the same typewriter. The ballot measure was Proposition 8, intended to give property tax relief to businesses that cut down on pollution. Brown's news release accused two executives of a major oil company and a staff member of the state Senate's Revenue and Taxation Committee of getting together in a Capitol committee room and writing both arguments.

It all amounted to a fraud on the public, Brown declared in a news release, indicating that the arguments against the measure were actually written by people who wanted the measure adopted.[23] In one of the stupidest public relations decisions of the twentieth century, the oil company loudly protested, saying the secretary of state had no business meddling in ballot arguments. That jaw-dropping move raised the visibility of the matter even more and further enhanced Brown's knight-on-a-white-charger image.[24] Jerry had two Democratic Assembly members rewrite the con argument.

While Jerry Brown and Tom Quinn pursued headlines, the nonpartisan legislative analyst's office, headed by the respected A. Alan Post, issued a series of reports critical of Brown's administration of the secretary of state's office, saying that the office charged fees that were too high, didn't have enough employees to handle requests efficiently, creating a backlog, and had a turnover rate of more than 3 percent a month.[25] One report in the series declared that such a high turnover rate is generally considered by those in state government to be indicative of undesirable conditions.

Jerry's high-minded pursuit of headlines was not slowed by commentary on his administrative style. In April 1973, representatives of Common Cause, the People's Lobby, and Brown announced plans to gather initiative signatures for the Fair Political Practices Act on the June 1974 primary ballot. Edwin and Joyce Koupal had founded the People's Lobby in the late '60s with the aim of giving ordinary citizens more power through direct democracy, using the mechanism of the initiative. For Jerry Brown, the campaign on behalf of the Fair Political Practices Act was ideal for his patented merger of opportunism and idealism. In addition, it was a tailor-made vehicle for a gubernatorial campaign that would emphasize clean and transparent government.

Brown and his allies were successful in gathering signatures, and the measure was given a ballot designation as Proposition 9. Brown declared, "This measure will be the most fundamental and far-reaching reform of our California governmental system in more than 60 years."[26] It required that candidates' and ballot measure committees' spending reports be audited, that lobbyist gifts to lawmakers be limited, and that public officials disclose their assets, and it forbade them from acting on any measure in which they had a financial interest. In addition, it established the California Fair Political Practices Commission to enforce its provisions. Daniel Lowenstein, a member of Brown's staff, drafted the bulk of the measure.

Many members of the state Legislature, while occasionally acknowledging the malevolent influence of lavish lobbying, nonetheless argued that ideologically opposed legislators could get to know one another better during dinners paid for by lobbyists in their Senator Hotel suites across the street from the Capitol or at Frank Fat's, the legendary Chinese restaurant a few blocks from the Capitol. They maintained the result was intelligent compromise that was in the public interest, no matter the circumstances under which the give-and-take occurred. But their almost wistful argument was mostly made privately. No one was going to publicly defend the idea of legislators receiving sumptuous dinners from lobbyists.

Voters certainly would have none of it. They overwhelmingly approved Proposition 9 in the June primary, at the same time that Democrats chose Jerry Brown as their gubernatorial nominee. Brown said Proposition 9's ten-dollar-a-month limit on what lobbyists could spend on a single legislator meant they could buy the lawmaker only "two hamburgers and a Coke."[27]

Proposition 9 was challenged in the courts and modified, but the Fair Political Practices Commission survives. Its Web site, echoing the rhetoric of Jerry Brown, declares that before its creation, "laws governing the conduct of public officials and campaign committees were few, weak and largely ignored." Then, in March 1974, just three months before the June gubernatorial primary, came a big break.

Frank DeMarco, a law partner of President Nixon's personal attorney, Herbert Kalmbach, had notarized the document by which Nixon had donated his vice-presidential papers to the National Archives in return for an income tax deduction of five hundred thousand dollars. A comparison once again of typewriters showed that DeMarco had backdated the document in order to take advantage of a law that had been repealed prior to the donation. Some of those involved went to jail. But all that Brown could do, as a secretary of state, was revoke DeMarco's notary public license, which he proposed to do—at the top of his lungs.

How could such a picayune matter as revocation of a notary public license create headlines across California? The nation was at a fever pitch over Watergate. Anything having to do with alleged chicanery by Nixon or his associates, even something as minor as revocation of a Nixon-connected notary public license that was not directly related to Watergate, was grounds for extensive media coverage and reportorial career advancement.

Brown's case against DeMarco was furthered because political reporters in Sacramento, three thousand miles from Washington, had read and heard, day after day, sensational stories about dirty tricks, the Watergate break-in, and the congressional investigation headed by Senator Sam Ervin. This was the political scandal of the century, and the frustrated Sacramentans thirsted for a piece of the action. Jerry Brown gave it to them, even if it was on the fringe, and they seized upon it. Although the notary public license was minor, it was connected to what appeared to be a major case of underhanded dealings by a president, or at least by those representing him.

Reporters in the state Capitol knew very well that Jerry was reaching for headlines by using a trifle to take advantage of a national obsession with Nixon's misdeeds. But it was a symbiotic relationship. Jerry got his favorable publicity; reporters got their big headlines and top-of-the-newscast placement. As one of the reporters in The Associated Press Capitol bureau at the time, I knew we were being had, and so did my fellow reporters. But we wanted a bite of the Nixon-Watergate apple somehow, so we gleefully went along with it. Everyone was happy, except, perhaps, Kalmbach, DeMarco, and Nixon.

With the achievement of statewide recognition as a crusader for open and honest government, Jerry Brown was now ready for bigger things.

CHAPTER THREE

The Big Show

California is the most influential state in the nation. What we do here will not only help our own citizens; it will provide a model for the entire country.

Jerry Brown, first inaugural speech, January 3, 1975

Carrying with him a strong, Catholic-inspired sense of moral rectitude and a rapidly developing sense of how to practice statewide politics, Jerry Brown became California's secretary of state on January 4, 1971. He was thirty-two years old and fired with ambition. Even as he settled into his new job, he and a few confidants were assessing the tactics they would use to win the governorship in four years.

It was not an unrealistic goal. Jerry occupied a statewide office with hitherto unrealized potential for creating positive headlines, and he was most certainly prepared to take advantage of it. He had a famous name. He could tap into his father's network of supporters for campaign funds. And if he were to win the governorship, he would be able to put into practice the ideals that had motivated much of his life—concern for minorities, attention to the nonmaterialistic aspects of life, perhaps even an end to the death penalty.

The first hurdle was the 1974 Democratic primary. Jerry had several advantages. His name was Brown, giving him name recognition and conjuring up good feelings among California Democrats who had fond memories of his father. Moreover, Jerry had cannily moved to Southern

California to begin his political career. That meant that in addition to the familiarity his name already had with voters, his well-publicized service on the community college board had given him another layer of name recognition in a vote-rich area of the state.

Perhaps more important, however, Jerry had a keen sense of what would work in the California political world of the mid-'70s. The opportunity was there. From Chula Vista to Arcata, voters in 1974 were ready for someone who touted honesty and frugality in state government, even after eight years of the self-styled citizen-politician Ronald Reagan. They had listened to and liked Reagan's oft-expressed counsel that politicians were ready to swallow freedom and raid pocketbooks unless taxpayers kept close watch and demanded frugality.

It is not much remembered today, but Reagan's fiscal conservatism was more symbolic than real. Upon assuming office, he was forced to ask for what became the biggest tax increase in California history, partly to erase a budget deficit bequeathed to him by Pat Brown and partly to ensure a cushion so that he would never have to ask for a tax increase again. Reagan accused the Brown administration, not inaccurately, of having "looted and drained" the state's fiscal resources and is said to have stated more than once that his administration would have to "cut, squeeze, and trim." The increased state revenue eventually produced a budget surplus, which Reagan attributed to his administration's managerial skill. Nonetheless, Reagan rode his reputation as a fiscal conservative all the way into the White House and beyond.

As the 1974 race for governor began, five of Brown's sixteen rivals for the Democratic nomination race were potentially formidable foes. They all had more money or political experience than Brown, more loyal followers or admirers, stronger political networks, and more personal warmth and charm. But they all lacked one important asset for the primary 1974 race: they didn't have the Brown name. And they didn't have the political media skill that enabled Jerry, the son of a two-term governor, to style himself somehow as a fresh new face. Houston Flournoy, Brown's Republican rival in the general election, echoed

Matthew Tobriner when needling Brown in one of their joint appearances in the fall campaign: "If your name was Jerry Green you wouldn't be here today."

Brown had five formidable opponents in the Democratic primary: George Moscone, Jerome Waldie, Bob Moretti, William Matson Roth, and Joseph Alioto.

The handsome, sunny, and popular majority leader in the state Senate, George Moscone, of San Francisco, was almost unknown in Southern California, where most of the votes were. To remedy that, he had started a strenuous routine of flying to Los Angeles once or twice a week to give speeches before Rotary clubs and other organizations. But campaign money was in short supply, and Moscone dropped out, deciding instead to run in 1975 for mayor of San Francisco.

Jerome Waldie, also known as Jerry, was a congressman from Antioch, a small town in the San Joaquin–Sacramento Delta. He had earlier served as the majority leader of the Assembly in 1961. He vowed to walk the entire length of the state to meet voters but had to interrupt his campaign for the Watergate hearings, an interruption that was fatal to his hopes.[1]

To the extent he was known at all, Bob Moretti, the intense, hard-driving speaker of the Assembly, was regarded as a member of the Sacramento establishment. Moretti was an able legislative negotiator, but when he voiced his own radio commercials he sounded as if he were trying to make a deal with voters. He tended to say "made a judgment" instead of "decided."

The San Francisco multimillionaire William Matson Roth was the aristocratic but likable heir to a shipping fortune. He was a member of the University of California Board of Regents.[2] Roth ran a credible campaign but finished with only 10 percent of the vote.

Like Jerry Brown, Joseph Alioto was a San Francisco native. He was the energetic, cosmopolitan, and articulate mayor of San Francisco who had strong support from labor unions. He had made a fortune as a top antitrust lawyer. And also like Jerry Brown, Alioto had begun his political career by serving on an education board—in his case, the San Francisco Board of Education.

The 1974 campaign for the Democratic gubernatorial nomination was long, raucous, and unenlightening. Moretti campaigned as someone experienced in getting things done in Sacramento; Alioto told voters that as a big-city mayor, he was well suited to administer the state; Waldie had Watergate; Roth styled himself as an experienced businessman, an international diplomat, and a fresh face.

Brown, aided by his last name, campaigned on a theme of austerity and honesty, telling voters that state government could not do everything for them. He said California was in need of political reform and that, given his record of forcing politicians to follow the law, he was best suited to make reform a reality.

The Brown campaign shied away from taking clear stands on controversial issues. Jerry was ahead in the polls and did not want the pot stirred too vigorously. Polls conducted by Brown aide Richard Maullin showed that after eight years of Reagan versus the Democrats, voters wanted peace and quiet from Sacramento, along with honesty and frugality. Barzaghi designed the television spots, emphasizing Maullin's data on integrity and reform. Jerry managed a campaign promising honesty and decency, styling himself as the young candidate on a white charger, ready to take on the dark doings in Sacramento.[3]

From the standpoint of reporters covering the 1974 primary campaigns, one of the highlights came on May 23, when Moretti and Brown had a sometimes insulting head-to-head confrontation in room 1190 of the state Capitol, where governors and other officials hold news conferences. Moretti had reserved the room for thirty minutes, with Brown scheduled to follow at the conclusion of Moretti's news conference. But Moretti, finishing his meeting, lay in wait for Brown. When Brown showed up, Moretti challenged him to a debate, right then and there. Brown angrily declared that it was his news conference, not Moretti's, and rejected the challenge. But then Brown conferred with aides, agreed to a debate, and stepped back to where Moretti was waiting. In the impolite, sometimes heated exchange that followed before two dozen delighted reporters, Moretti accused Brown of lying and said Brown had little knowledge of state government.

"Stop blowing smoke in your own face. What you know about what goes on in this building could be put on the head of a needle," Moretti said.[4]

Brown, countering, stuck to his transparency-in-government theme. "There is still secrecy in this building," he declared.

The two Democrats also each claimed to know more than the other about poverty and who had been forced to struggle most in the climb to success. Moretti said he had been forced to "live in the real world," and Brown, the son of a former governor, pointed out that, of the three major candidates (himself, Alioto, and Moretti), "my assets are the least in number," and that he had marched along dusty roads on behalf of farmworkers and cleaned toilets as a seminarian.

Both men claimed victory when the forty-five-minute exchange ended. The verdict from the reporters afterward was that Brown was calmer and smoother and that Moretti, behind in the polls by almost 20 percent, was the more aggressive. Alioto, seeking to rise above it all, said the encounter was "unseemly adolescent behavior."

On June 4, 1974, California Democrats made a judgment. Brown's still-important name identification and his four years as secretary of state, during which he cultivated an image as a young, vigorous man who would bring honesty and frugality to state government, demolished the opposition. Jerry took nearly 38 percent of the Democrats' votes, Alioto came in a distant second with slightly fewer than 19 percent, Moretti was third with 16.6 percent, Roth was fourth with slightly more than 10 percent, and Waldie was fifth with nearly 8 percent.[5]

Moretti theorized later that the presence of Proposition 9 on the primary ballot had benefited Brown by adding another layer of emphasis on political reform, one of the main themes of the Brown candidacy. The kidnapping of newspaper heiress Patty Hearst shortly after Brown had announced his candidacy also helped Brown, according to Moretti, because it commanded great media attention, lessening the coverage of the campaign, and helping Brown with his built-in advantage of name recognition.

With a comfortable primary win behind him, Jerry now faced the general election. His opponent was Houston (Hugh) Flournoy, the handsome and well-liked state controller. Flournoy was a moderate, academically inclined Republican with a PhD in politics from Princeton. He had been a faculty member since 1957 in the Pomona College Department of Political Science and in 1960 ran for the California Assembly, where he befriended Moretti. In 1966, he was elected state controller. He was reelected in 1970.

The race pitted two men with high intellectual credentials against one another—Flournoy with his Princeton PhD and tenured professorship, and Brown with his Yale JD—but, as in most campaigns, intellectualism did not peek through. Brown, consistently ahead in the polls, ran a campaign designed to avoid rocking the boat, while Flournoy circled for an opening.

Flournoy had won the 1974 Republican gubernatorial nomination over the more conservative Ed Reinecke, Reagan's handpicked lieutenant governor, after an earlier round of political musical chairs. Reinecke, who had had served in Congress since 1965, resigned on January 21, 1969, to become California's lieutenant governor. He replaced Robert H. Finch, who had resigned in order to become secretary of health, education, and welfare under his old friend Richard Nixon.

Reinecke had thought that being the popular Reagan's lieutenant governor would place him in an advantageous position for a run at the governorship in 1974, but it was not to be. The Reagan magic did not rub off on his affable lieutenant governor. A little less than two months after Flournoy defeated him, Reinecke was convicted of perjury by a federal district court jury in Washington. Reinecke was convicted of lying during testimony in connection with a pledge of four hundred thousand dollars from the International Telephone and Telegraph

Corporation to the Republican National Convention. Reinecke resigned as lieutenant governor on October 2, 1974. His conviction was eventually overturned but too late to revive his political fortunes.

There were six televised debates between Brown and Flournoy, and Flournoy left them frustrated. He told reporters that Brown had ducked specifics and had concentrated on "phony" issues, such as Brown's refusal, if elected, to live in the governor's mansion. Brown and his aides disagreed, saying he had been specific but that the media had been so locked into a storyline about a young reformer running against a traditional Republican that they had paid scant attention to what the candidates were actually saying. Brown advocated lessening penalties for marijuana possession and eliminating the death penalty while Flournoy wanted to keep the draconian marijuana penalties on the books and favored the death penalty. Their differing positions did not seem to make much difference to voters.

In one of the more bizarre events of his campaign, Flournoy flew some twenty reporters in five private twin-engine planes to the small Tehama County town of Flournoy for a picnic, just to prove, he said, that a town named Flournoy really exists. In blistering heat, Flournoy stood in his shirtsleeves and announced under a mulberry tree that he would not deliver a campaign speech. "It's too hot for that," he said. But some hundred Flournoy supporters and the twenty reporters had a good time at the picnic, and the event made headlines as far away as Long Beach.

While Flournoy was picnicking in the north, Jerry Brown was holding a joint news conference in his Hollywood campaign headquarters with his former foe Moretti. Although Moretti had accused Brown in the primary campaign of not knowing much about what went on in the Capitol, all was forgiven as he endorsed fellow Democrat Brown. "That was what I thought before we had a chance to really sit down and talk at length," Moretti told reporters. Moretti had given up his Assembly seat to run for governor, and there was some talk of a postelection appointment if Brown, as expected, were to win the governorship. Moretti was indeed appointed to the California Energy Commission, created under legislation signed into law by Reagan in 1974. Moretti served from 1975 to 1977 and died of a heart attack in 1984. He is memorialized by a bench in Capitol Park.

Jerry did not bring his father into the campaign, seeking to portray himself as a candidate who would bring fresh ideas and innovation to state government. He realized that the old-style "build California" ethos of Pat Brown's administration would not fly in 1974.

As election day drew near, Jerry found himself mysteriously slipping in the polls. No one could figure out why. One theory was that Jerry had somehow failed to distinguish himself from liberal Republican Flournoy; another was that Jerry had attempted to position himself more forcefully as the head of the Democratic ticket and that had diluted his white-charger campaign. Jerry probably added to his campaign's distress by foolishly canceling television advertising for a week in an effort to save money on the theory that his ideas had been sufficiently established in voters' minds. Flournoy, with his own last-minute television blitz, began making even more dramatic gains. The Brown campaign hastily allotted $250,000 for television at the last minute.

On November 5, Jerry Brown was elected, barely, as California's thirty-fourth governor. He won by a mere 2.9 percentage points, or 180,000 votes. It was the closest California gubernatorial election in fifty years, but Jerry had gone from being a member of a community college board to governor of the nation's largest state in a little more than four years.

Flournoy blamed the September 1974 pardon of Richard Nixon by President Gerald Ford for his loss and never ran for political office again. He died in 2008. Brown had a different interpretation from that of Flournoy, saying that the vote was more complex than that and no single factor could account for Flournoy's surge and near victory. He said that although he had started the race with an advantage of name recognition, Flournoy closed the gap as his candidacy emerged more clearly.

Some observers believed that Brown's victory came about because of what turned out to be an essentially dull campaign, resulting in low voter turnout that added to his name-recognition advantage. In his official summary of the results issued as secretary of state, Brown declared, "The biggest vote of all last November was a vote of no confidence. More than half of the people who could have voted refused, apparently believing that what takes place in government has so little impact on their lives that they need not pass judgement on it."[6] He had a point. The turnout was about 45 percent of those eligible to register and vote. The previous two gubernatorial elections had turnout rates of 54 percent in 1970 and 59 percent in 1966, when the charismatic Reagan was running for governor.

The statement reflected Brown's belief that a fresh wind needed to sweep into Sacramento and shake up a fossilized and opaque political establishment that had lost contact with the people. How Brown managed to paint himself successfully as a fresh new face while concurrently taking political advantage of the Brown name is one of the more remarkable feats of political legerdemain in campaign history. Jerry's narrow victory was part of a Democratic sweep. The only statewide office going to a Republican was attorney general, where Evelle Younger was reelected. Democrat Alan Cranston was reelected to the U.S. Senate by 1.5 million votes, a stark contrast to Jerry's squeaker. Mervyn Dymally, a state senator, was elected lieutenant governor, defeating Republican John Harmer, a fellow state senator.[7] Dymally was a former schoolteacher and had worked on behalf of Robert Kennedy's presidential campaign. Jerry and Dymally were not close, in fact barely knew each other. They did not campaign as a ticket.

On January 6, 1975, Brown took the oath of office. He was the youngest governor in the nation and the sixth-youngest governor of California. In his brief (1,059-word) inaugural address, Brown stressed regaining the trust of the people, eliminating unnecessary spending, and improving the state's job picture. He said he would cut his office budget by 7 percent and would push for unemployment benefits for farmworkers. Parts of his 1975 address, as evidenced here, sound as if they could have been delivered at his third inaugural, thirty-six years later: "Today, unemployment in this state is well above the national average. That is not just a statistic, it is a reality. Men and women whose futures are uncertain, whose families are anxious, look to us for answers. I know much of the solution lies at the federal level, but I also know that California is the most influential state in the nation. What we do here will not only help our own citizens, it will provide a model for the entire country."[8]

Brown was also specific about two goals, bringing collective bargaining to farmworkers and state employees:

> I also believe it is time to extend the rule of law to the agriculture sector and establish the right of secret ballot elections for farm workers. The law I support will impose rights and responsibilities on both farm worker and farmer alike. I expect that an appropriate bill that serves all the people will not fully satisfy any of the parties to the dispute, but that's no reason not to pass it.
>
> As we bring collective bargaining to the fields, we should also establish appropriate mechanisms for public employees to choose the bargaining representative of their choice. All workers, whoever they are, and wherever they are, should be strongly represented and have an effective voice in the decisions that affect their wages and working conditions.[9]

The new governor's administrative style was the polar opposite of his predecessor. There was a nonchalant, '60s-style free-spiritedness about the new Brown administration. Reagan insisted on crisp, one-page memos that outlined a problem and recommended a solution or options and maintained an orderly schedule for the day's events. Brown's style was New Age, loose, flexible, and adventurous. He liked to examine ideas and used the word *dialectic* in conversation with reporters. Writers such as Ken Kesey and Ray Bradbury, along with celebrity thinkers such as Carl Sagan, Buckminster Fuller, and Jacques Cousteau, trooped through the horseshoe-shaped suite of gubernatorial offices. Brown's daily schedule was a mystery that unfolded hour by hour.

While his conventional predecessors, including his father, Pat, wanted to have early warnings on potential difficulties ahead so that they could be dealt with before they became larger, Brown preferred to let a problem boil up into a crisis before acting. "When I try to slow government down, I see that as a very progressive idea," he said at a news conference early in his administration.[10]

Brown biographer Robert Pack has a blunt assessment of Brown's administrative style: "Jerry Brown would prefer to avoid mistakes by not acting at all," Pack declared in his 1978 biography, *Jerry Brown: The Philosopher Prince.* What Brown called his "creative inaction" meant that he was slow in making appointments, leaving many policy-making jobs unfilled for months. To Moretti, creative inaction meant "sitting on your ass."[11]

Wilson Riles, the state superintendent of public instruction, was frustrated by Brown's ad hoc last-minute style. When Reagan was governor, Riles and his staff would work with lawmakers and the governor's advisers on an issue or piece of legislation for months. Knowing what Reagan's position was on the matter, they and the sponsoring legislator could adjust language accordingly and be assured that, with the changes they had negotiated, the bill would be signed. That was the way lawmakers and constitutional officers worked with most governors.[12] But Riles frequently did not know how Brown stood on a proposal until a piece of legislation was on Brown's desk. There had been no prior communication, no opportunities to compromise. Brown would sometimes veto the bill, raising objections that had never been raised before and deeply frustrating Riles.

In his four years as secretary of state and before that on the community college board, social liberal Brown had promoted fiscal restraint. When he took office as governor, Brown wasted little time in reinforcing his image as a skinflint. Fewer than twenty-four hours after signing the 1975 state budget, he sent a memo to department heads declaring, "I intend to take every step possible to avoid a general tax increase in the next fiscal year. Accordingly, new programs which cost money require corresponding reductions in other programs."[13]

The new governor came through quickly on a major campaign promise. Only five months after his inaugural address, he signed into law the Agricultural Labor Relations Act, the first of its kind in the nation. The ALRA gave California's 250,000 farmworkers the right to decide, by secret balloting, whether they wanted to be represented by a union. It was a fulfillment of Brown's longtime belief that California farmworkers deserved better treatment. Although the board created by the ALRA did not fully live up to the hopes Brown and his allies held for it, its creation is regarded as one of the signature achievements of Brown's years as governor.

A number of people were involved in writing the bill and pushing it through the Legislature. Rose Bird, Brown's friend from their days at International House on the UC Berkeley campus, was one of the chief writers of the bill as Brown's secretary of agriculture and services. She worked with Los Angeles labor lawyer Stephen Reinhardt, for whom Jerry had done legal research while at Yale, aimed at derailing Pierre Salinger's U.S. Senate bid. Paul Halvonlik, Brown's assistant for legislative affairs, talked to the various interested parties, including growers, the United Farm Workers, and the Teamsters Union. The UFW and the Teamsters each wanted to represent the farmworkers. Brown himself shuttled between the interested parties in the Capitol, playing a large and unaccustomed role as diplomat-in-chief during the difficult negotiations that resulted in the final bill.

Democrat Howard Berman, himself a labor lawyer, sponsored the bill in the Assembly, a task made somewhat more difficult because the bill was presented as a fait accompli, with the governor's office decreeing that no changes could be made. But Berman also said securing legislative approval was not as difficult as the negotiations within the governor's office had been. Bird, Brown, and other members of the administration team felt the "no changes" stance was necessary because the bill was delicately balanced among the various interest groups, primarily the growers, the UFW, and the Teamsters, and any revisions by legislators would mean the unraveling of the whole package and probable defeat.

Willie Brown, who was then a bit of a Jerry Brown nemesis, thought the system had been circumvented (it had) and that the Legislature should have been allowed to work its will in representing the people instead of acceding to the product of closed-door negotiations.[14] State senator George Zenovich, from Fresno, was sympathetic to the growers and said Bird had told him that any changes imposed by lawmakers would kill the bill. Zenovich said that in his fifteen years in the Legislature, he had never before heard that.

The bill provided for the five-member Agricultural Labor Relations Board to oversee farm labor elections. Brown appointed LeRoy Chatfield, a former leader of the UFW who had participated in the writing of the bill; Joe C. Ortega, a lawyer active on behalf of farmworkers; Catholic bishop Roger Mahoney of Fresno; Joseph R. Grodin, a labor law professor; and Richard Johnson Jr., executive vice president of the California Agriculture Council. The growers felt betrayed. They believed the appointments of Chatfield, Ortega, and Mahoney meant a board weighted 3 to 2 in favor of the unions. Brown himself argued that he had envisioned the board as balanced, with Ortega and Chatfield representing the unions, Johnson and Grodin representing the growers, and Mahoney serving as a swing vote.

Three months after its formation, the board began to run into trouble. It had burned through its initial funding of $1.3 million, and the Department of Finance loaned it another $1.2 million. But the Legislature, still rankled by the manner in which the legislation was presented and sensitive to the complaints of the growers, refused further money. Brown attempted to secure an appropriation for additional funding and won a majority of votes, but the appropriation did not receive the required two-thirds majority.

Brown named three new board members to replace the three who had resigned while the board languished without funding. The Legislature eventually appropriated $6.8 million to renew funding. While that was happening, the UFW had received enough signatures to place a farm labor initiative on the ballot. In essence, it embedded the Agricultural Labor Relations Act, not subject to change by the Legislature. Change could come only as the result of statewide voter action.

The initiative went onto the November 1976 ballot as Proposition 14 and was overwhelmingly defeated despite Brown's campaign on its behalf. One of the major factors in its defeat was a provision that would have allowed union organizers to come onto private farmland to organize workers. Voters thought that was a violation of property rights, an issue that was vigorously highlighted by growers in their advertisements against Proposition 14.

Proposition 14's landslide defeat had repercussions. Democrat John Tunney, who had defeated George Murphy in the 1970 U.S. Senate race, lost his 1976 bid for reelection to S. I. Hayakawa, a San Francisco State University professor who had won fame for yanking the wires from a student public address apparatus during a campus demonstration. Tunney blamed his defeat on the wave of opposition to Democrats generated by Proposition 14.

Despite its shaky beginning, the board managed to continue in operation and in 2011, as a longtime established part of state government, had a full agenda of cases to consider and regional offices in El Centro, Salinas, and Visalia.

In a related effort, Brown was successful in September 1975 in pushing legislation that extended unemployment benefits to farmworkers, fulfilling the hope he had voiced in his inaugural address. Such legislation had passed the Legislature five times before only to be vetoed by Reagan.

Creation of the farm labor act was one of two achievements of which Rose Bird was most proud. She was also instrumental in the success of legislation that required state regulatory boards to have inexpert public representatives as members. Bird said it opened up the boards to the citizens. In a signing statement, her friend Jerry declared, "The legislature recognizes that ordinary citizens are as competent to make public policy in the regulated areas as the professionals themselves." He said that the inexpert public members would be "lobbyists for the people."[15]

Every new governor vows to bring in a new era. Jerry did so, in big blinking neon. The emphasis was on intellectual ability, not administrative or business experience. With few exceptions, his was to be a businessperson-free administration. Everything was going to get a fresh look. There was to be austerity and idealism, an unusual combination in Sacramento, although politicians paid separate lip service to each when they sensed that they needed to.

As his chief of staff, Brown passed over his top campaign aides in favor of young Gray Davis, an aide to Los Angeles mayor Tom Bradley. The two had met when both spoke at a labor luncheon in 1974. Davis had been running for the Democratic nomination for state treasurer but had been shouldered aside by the much-better-known Jesse Unruh, who went on to win the job in the 1974 general election.

Brown burned with a desire to bring more women and minorities into state government, which he felt had for too long been the exclusive bastion of white males such as himself. Through late August 1977, he had made 1,862 appointments, including members of the executive branch as well as judges. Of that total, 31 percent were women, 10 percent were Hispanic; 8 percent were African American; Asian Americans were 3 percent; Indian Americans, 2 percent; and Filipino Americans, 0.5 percent.[16]

When set against California's twentieth-century history of reserving top positions in government almost exclusively for white males, Brown's appointments to the executive branch and the judiciary were revolutionary. These were people who agitated for the rights of the poor and ethnic minorities, represented indigent criminal defendants, and fought for environmental and consumer protection. Many of them lacked experience in state government, something Jerry did not find disqualifying and even found refreshing, in light of his anti-Sacramento-establishment philosophy. The Capitol was full of self-satisfied people adhering to the outmoded, to the detriment of the common good. Why not shake things up? Since when was meeting a payroll a prerequisite for high office?

In addition to his unprecedented appointments of ethnic minorities, he appointed more young people. Davis, Brown's chief of staff, was only thirty-two; Rose Bird, his secretary of agriculture and services, was thirty-seven when appointed to that job and forty when Brown named her to the state Supreme Court.

Mario Obledo, of Mexican descent, was made head of the Health and Welfare Agency, the largest single state department. Obledo's life was a testimonial to the American dream, political version. He was born in San Antonio and in his early childhood slept on the floor of a hovel with twelve siblings. Somehow, he made it to the University of Texas's flagship campus in Austin and became a pharmacist. Obledo was a fiery advocate for Hispanics, declaring that they would no longer "take a back seat to anyone" in American society. And he became the first Hispanic in modern California history to mount a serious campaign for governor in 1982, as Jerry was completing his second term. Obledo spent the rest of his life advocating for Hispanics, sometimes vociferously. He was awarded the Presidential Medal of Freedom in 1998 by President Bill Clinton and died in 2010 at seventy-eight.

African American Leonard Grimes headed the Department of General Services and then became head of the Agriculture and Services Agency when Rose Bird departed. Grimes became the first African American in California history to serve in a governor's cabinet. His appointment, along with Brown's other minority appointments and the 1970 election of African American Wilson Riles as state school superintendent, shattered forever the white monopoly on high state office.

Brown's most controversial appointment, one that still set off an argument decades later in 2011, was of Rose Bird to the state Supreme Court as its chief justice in February 1977. Bird was born near Tucson, Arizona, in 1936. Her father, a chicken rancher, had deserted the family (some biographers say the parents separated), then died when Rose was five. She grew up in New York amid poverty but graduated magna cum laude from Long Island University. She also attended UC's Boalt Hall School of Law, graduating in 1965 with honors for oral advocacy and brief writing.

The new state Supreme Court nominee was another Brown appointee with a series of firsts in her biography. She was the first female law clerk in the Supreme Court of Nevada, she was the first female deputy public defender in Santa Clara County, and she was the first woman to hold a cabinet-level job in California as secretary of agriculture and services. Bird was part of a trifecta of trailblazing appointments: Wiley Manuel was appointed with Bird and became the first African American on the state high court, and Cruz Reynoso became its first Chicano.

The Bird appointment to the California Supreme Court would not have happened without an act of political courage from Brown's adversary Evelle Younger. Judicial appointments in California must be confirmed by the Commission on Judicial Appointments, made up of the attorney general (Younger), the chief justice or acting chief justice of the Supreme Court, and the senior presiding justice of a state court of appeal. The acting chief justice was Matthew Tobriner, mentor to Jerry Brown and longtime friend of Pat Brown. He voted for confirmation. Parker Wood, the presiding justice of the California Court of Appeals, Second Appellate District, Division One, voted against confirmation, citing Bird's complete lack of judicial experience. That left it up to Republican Younger to cast the deciding third vote. Republicans up and down the state were outspoken in their opposition to Bird, but Younger, in a gutsy move that reflected his integrity, reluctantly voted to confirm. In a statement, he declared, "During his campaign Brown described the kind of appointments he would make. Rose Bird fits the model. The decision as to the kind of chief justice California would have was, in effect, made by our voters in November, 1974."[17]

In a statement, Bird said she was "deeply honored" by the confirmation, adding, "I hope to dedicate my professional life to assuring fairness and that justice is done. I hope to dedicate all my energies to that end."[18]

When she was sworn in on March 26, 1977, Jerry Brown shattered another precedent by administering the oath himself. As acting chief justice, Tobriner would normally have done the honors. Jerry's insistence on administering the oath himself was another instance of his desire to demonstrate contempt for the way things had always been done in the capital. *Los Angeles Times* columnist George Skelton said the naming of Bird as chief justice, along with a host of other precedent-shattering appointments, was evidence that Brown's rebellious streak, demonstrated years earlier by his decision to enter the seminary, was still alive in the governor's office.

Bird promptly began shattering precedent herself. In actions that reflected those of her friend the governor, she sold the Cadillac that had been made available to the chief justice and returned the money to the state, and she stayed at inexpensive hotels when traveling. During her time on the court, it upheld stronger environmental regulations, abortion rights, tenant rights, and more gender diversity in California courts.

Like the governor, she was an ardent opponent of the death penalty at a time when 80 percent of the California public favored it. That proved to be her undoing after nine years on the court. California had reinstated the death penalty in 1977 over Brown's veto, sending numerous cases to the state Supreme Court for review. The justices reviewed and decided on sixty-one death penalty cases during Bird's time there, and with no exceptions, Bird voted to overturn lower-court death sentences. It was plain that Bird, a brilliant student of the law, had somehow found a legal reason to overturn in every one of the sixty-one cases, despite an earlier promise to uphold the death penalty if she found that the trial was fair and the law constitutional. Death penalty advocates, including district attorneys, Republican lawmakers, and California's post–Jerry Brown Republican governor, George Deukmejian, were outraged by Bird's consistent finding that the death penalty was unjustified. Growers were also unhappy with Bird because of her role in creating the Agricultural Labor Relations Board.

By 1986, nearly four years after Jerry had left office and Bird had been on the court for nine years, she came up for a retention vote in a state whose electorate favored the death penalty. Retention votes for judges were normally routine and little noticed, but not this time. Opposition was well organized and active, accusing Bird of ignoring the tragedy of the victims while being sympathetic to cold-blooded murderers. Republican governor George Deukmejian, who had campaigned as a strong law-and-order candidate, and three organizations led the anti-Bird fight: Crime Victims for Court Reform, Californians to Defeat Rose Bird (led by Howard Jarvis and Paul Gann, the authors of Proposition 13), and the Bird Watchers Society, led by hard-right Orange County Republican congressman William Dannemeyer. Bird was voted off the court, along with fellow justices Reynoso and Joseph Grodin. They became the first California Supreme Court justices in history to be removed by voters in a retention election.

Bird maintained a low profile after her removal. She taught briefly in Australia, did volunteer work at a food bank, and lectured. She died of breast cancer in 1999 at age sixty-three.

Although she was the most visible, Bird was not the only high-level Brown appointee to run into trouble. Obledo was criticized for being a poor administrator and for unfairly favoring Hispanic job applicants; Dr. Jerome Lackner, head of the Department of Health in Obledo's agency, was also criticized as a poor administrator; seven months into his administration, Brown fired James Lorenz as director of the Department of Economic Development. Lorenz and his staff had created a jobs plan that involved, among other things, collectives. A copy of the plan fell into the hands of reporters, headlines talked of a "secret plan," and some business leaders called it socialistic. Lorenz had proved to be too visionary for a visionary administration.[19]

As governor, Brown practiced the same paradoxical attitude he had displayed while on the Los Angeles Community College Board of Trustees: fiscal restraint and social liberalism. Although he firmly opposed the death penalty, he otherwise pleased conservatives with a tough law-and-order stance, signing legislation that imposed mandatory sentencing, with a long list of mandatory sentences, to replace the previous indeterminate sentencing policy. But at the same time, he appointed liberal judges to enforce the law.

The freewheeling Brown administration set a Sacramento trend toward three-piece suits, challenges to the status quo, and informality. The lights in the governor's offices burned late into the night, creating an image of young people putting in long hours. Detractors argued, however, that they were more probably indulging in late-night, college-style bull sessions over the nature of power.

Whatever their penchant for late hours, Brown and his staff paid assiduous attention to the news media, even late in his administration. Between January 2 and December 24, 1981, for instance, he and his staffers made 203 broadcast appearances, roughly four a week over the year-long period. A handful were made by chiefs of staff Davis and B. T. Collins, but the overwhelming number were by Brown himself.

One measure of the Brown phenomenon is the staggering number of letters the governor received during the first year of his administration. The correspondence office set the number at six hundred thousand.[20]

Former Jesuit priest-in-training Jerry Brown brought home his luxury-free ethos by selling Reagan's armored limousine in favor of a blue Plymouth Satellite sedan, one in Sacramento and a second in Los Angeles. He stopped the issuance of handsome tan leather briefcases to state bureaucrats, saying it was his experience that the amount of "paper expands to meet the available briefcases."[21] Using his own money, he rented a $250-a-month apartment across the street from Capitol Park, refusing to live in the new governor's mansion. That twenty-five-room, twelve-thousand-square-foot home was built by private donations after Nancy Reagan refused to live in the downtown Sacramento mansion, reportedly declaring it a firetrap. The replacement mansion in suburban Carmichael, fifteen miles from the Capitol, boasts a ballroom, a formal dining room, eight bathrooms, two kitchens, and lavish teak cabinetry. It was sold in 1975, after Brown's refusal to move in.

The ideas that Brown's apartment was spartan and that Brown slept on a mattress on the floor, however, were false. The apartment was in one of the more desirable downtown Sacramento apartment buildings, and Brown slept on a mattress atop a box spring set.

It all pleased the public. A 1975 poll showed that voters who approved Brown's performance as governor outnumbered those who disapproved by 7 to 1. In that year, Jerry Brown was the most popular politician in the history of California public-opinion polling.

CHAPTER FOUR

Romance, Flip-Flops, and Moonbeams

We have only so many cookies in the cookie jar, and if Proposition 13 passes, the jar will be empty.

Jerry Brown, campaign speech against
Proposition 13, 1978

I am a born-again tax cutter.

Jerry Brown, statement to reporters after passage
of Proposition 13 in June 1978

Early in March 1976, barely past the first year of his administration, Jerry was riding high in the polls. Californians liked the continuing shake-up he had brought to Sacramento. And then, amid all the presumably important things going on in his still-young administration, Jerry Brown announced he was running for president. In the annals of "I'm running for president" announcements, few could come close to Brown's offhand approach.

His announcement, such as it was, came late on a Friday afternoon in March 1976 during a chat with three reporters he had invited into his office for coffee. Doug Willis, former chief California political writer for The Associated Press, recalled the incident vividly:

The event was a Friday evening children's art show in the governor's conference room. There were three reporters there: Nancy Skelton of the

[Sacramento] *Bee*, Jerry Goldberg, who covered the Capitol for several weeklies, and me.

Nancy and I were there because the deadlines for many of the final presidential primaries were approaching, and we knew Brown was pondering it. We also both thought that when he decided he would probably tell the first person who asked him. Goldberg was hoping to question Brown about highway projects affecting his client newspapers.

Answering Goldberg, Brown cited experts who believed that more highways don't relieve congestion but instead attract more traffic.

"And that's the dialogue and dialectic that I intend to bring to this campaign," Brown said.

Still focused on highways, Goldberg continued asking about specific highways in his area. After a few moments, Nancy and I broke in and simultaneously asked, "What campaign is that? Are you running for president?"

"Yes. I'll be filing the papers on Monday," Brown replied in a matter-of-fact manner without any fanfare. But he stressed that he wasn't going to run as a favorite son, but as a serious candidate in all of the remaining primaries. [And it was a serious campaign, winning five primaries as the last Anybody-but-Carter contender in the race.]

Since no other reporters were present, Nancy and I didn't rush to the phone. Instead we conducted a thorough interview of 30 to 40 minutes. When Brown's press secretary, Dave Jensen, came in we insisted that he just sit and listen and not call any other reporters until we were through.

When Nancy and I had all that we needed, I borrowed Brown's phone from his desk to call AP's San Francisco bureau, explaining to a rewrite man that I had an exclusive which should be a state wire bulletin and an urgent to New York for AP's national wire.

With Brown watching over my shoulder and occasionally suggesting changes, which I ignored, I dictated about 800 words from my notes. At one point the reporter taking my dictation asked me what the background noise was. I explained that was Brown trying to convince me that a different quote was more important than the one I was dictating at the time.[1]

That was it. The governor of the most important state in the Union had just "announced" he was running for president not yet a year and a half into his administration. It was typically quirky Jerry Brown, ignoring customary political protocol, strategy, and even rhetoric. Few, if any, politicians have ever used the word *dialectic* in a candidacy announcement. But even reporters who had grown used to Brown's sometimes unusual way of doing things were caught off-guard. This was bizarre, even for Jerry Brown. He had intended to make a normal announcement at a press conference or a reception earlier in the day—but no one had asked him, Brown said later.

Anyone who manages to become governor of California is automatically a potential president. Earl Warren, Pat Brown, Pete Wilson, and Ronald Reagan had all harbored presidential ambitions during their time in the governor's office. But a California governor with thoughts of being president has to walk a cautious tightrope. California voters are jealous of their governors, and overt flirtation with the presidency causes resentment. Governors are expected to tend to state business in Sacramento, not go skylarking across the nation in pursuit of selfish ambition. But to flatly deny any presidential ambitions whatsoever before launching a presidential campaign is likely to inflict a sizable dent in one's credibility. The time-tested strategy for sitting governors, therefore, is to say something along the lines of "Being governor is a big job, and I am devoting all my time to it. I'm too busy to devote much time to thoughts of the presidency." Adhered to faithfully—and if reporters don't press too hard—the strategy presents a picture of a hardworking executive devoted to making life better for Californians while keeping the door open to a possible presidential campaign.

But Jerry did not follow the script. There had been speculation about a Brown presidential run, as there would be for any popular California governor, and reporters had begun to pay closer attention to Brown's movements, because it was, after all, a presidential election year. Nonetheless, his casual declaration before three reporters was a bombshell. Not even his press secretary at the time, Dave Jensen, had known in advance.

Late on a Friday is regarded as the worst possible time to make an important announcement. Saturday newspapers are thought to be slim and neglected over the weekend, and broadcast outlets do not get the attention they receive during the week. However, Jimmy Carter on that same Friday evening was appearing at a fund-raiser in Los Angeles, and some speculated that Brown had timed his move to make his entry the major political story of the day, not the California visit of putative front-runner Carter. But he would have accomplished the same thing and enabled television stations in those days of film to shoot footage and get it onto the eleven o'clock news had he made the announcement earlier in the day.

Whatever the nature of Jerry's entry, and illustrative of the gulf that exists between elected officials and the general public, he and his closest advisers had been secretly discussing a possible presidential bid as early as six months into the new administration, while Californians were still getting used to their new governor. Those against it felt the nomination was almost sure to go to a Democrat who was in a different stage of development. Leo McCarthy, the speaker of the Assembly, felt a failed attempt could hurt Brown fatally with California voters. But there were other factors weighing in: the incumbent president had not been elected, Republicans were badly wounded by the Watergate scandal, and Jerry could be put forth as an exciting young candidate who would bring honesty and innovation to the White House.

Acting on the advice of Nancy Pelosi, a rising political fund-raiser in San Francisco, Jerry entered the May 18 primary in Maryland. His opponents on a crowded ballot included George Wallace, the governor of Alabama who had campaigned against "pointy-headed intellectuals"; Senator Henry "Scoop" Jackson of Washington State; Carter; Morris Udall, a lanky, witty Arizona congressman; and Ellen McCormack, running as an antiabortion candidate.

There was enormous and instant national interest in Jerry's candidacy. The campaign issued 150 credentials to reporters who traveled in two press buses. As a candidate who was concurrently the fresh new face and son of a former governor, Brown captivated the East Coast public and press. Just as he depicted himself in his bid for the governorship of California, Brown had remounted his white charger, galloping in to clean up politics as usual. In Kennedyesque speeches, Brown declared that he had come to Maryland to test whether the state and this nation were ready for a new generation of leadership.

And again, it worked. The Brown formula proved to be portable outside California. Jerry took slightly more than 48 percent of the vote, soundly drubbing Carter, who placed second with just under 40 percent. Udall finished a distant third, with 5.3 percent. A few days later, Brown repeated his winning performance, easily winning the primary in Nevada with nearly 53 percent of the vote as against Carter's slightly more than 23 percent.

Jerry's momentum slowed in Oregon despite a near-miraculous political performance. The Oregon secretary of state ruled that late-entry Brown could not appear on the printed ballot, so he was forced to wage a write-in campaign. Brown fielded thousands of volunteers and campaigned furiously, telling voters in his stump speeches to bring their pencils to the polls. It almost worked. Brown received 25 percent of the vote, a remarkable achievement and the highest vote total ever achieved by a write-in candidate in Oregon. Idaho senator Frank Church came in first with 34.6 percent, Carter was second with 27.4, and Brown was in third place with 23.3 percent—96,486 write-in votes.

Jerry now faced Super Tuesday—primaries in California, Ohio, and New Jersey. He was not on the ballot in Ohio, so the hope was for an indecisive vote there, a big win in home state California, and a sizable vote in New Jersey. That would muddle things enough to throw the decision to the convention, where Jerry and his people hoped to pull it out on perhaps a third ballot.

Jerry won nearly 60 percent of the vote in California compared with Carter's 21 percent and Church's dismal 7 percent. In New Jersey, Jerry eked out what was considered a solid victory through an unusual agreement that saw an uncommitted slate billed as a joint Brown–Hubert

Humphrey delegation. It won 42 percent of the votes. But Ohio did him in. Carter had campaigned hard there and rolled up an impressive 52 percent of the vote. That meant that there would probably be no muddled situation that would force the choice onto the convention. The media highlighted the Carter win.

Jerry did not give up, although it was plain his presidential campaign was not going to be successful. He made a last-hurrah nationally televised speech, spoke before the National Press Club, and decided to have his name formally placed in nomination at the convention. He did not release his approximately three hundred delegates.

After some tense negotiations, Jerry was denied the right to appear at the podium to move that Carter's nomination be made unanimous, giving him one last shot in the national spotlight. Instead, he won the right to have California recognized first in the roll call, and he was able to make an announcement from the floor that California was switching its delegates to Carter. It was half a loaf, but Jerry was in the spotlight again briefly.

In all, Brown had won 2,449,374 total primary votes, or nearly 14 percent of the total and second place, compared with Carter's 6,971,770-vote total, or 40.16 percent. George Wallace was third with 2,236,186 votes, or 12.75 percent. Hubert Humphrey, who had been the Democrats' 1968 presidential nominee, was far down in fifteenth place with 61,992 votes, or 0.35 percent.

A little-remembered bit of historical speculation about the 1976 presidential contests is that while Jerry was campaigning among Democrats, Ronald Reagan was making his own determined bid for the Republican nomination, seeking to oust incumbent but unelected President Gerald Ford. Reagan didn't manage it, but if he had—and if Jerry had won the Democratic nomination—the nation would have witnessed a contest between two successive California governors for the presidency.

Jerry returned to his office in Sacramento a defeated candidate—but a still ambitious national political figure.

While Jerry Brown was serving his first term as governor and running for president, rumblings of discontent were gathering strength in California. Property taxes were rising so fast that some people feared they would lose their homes, and no one in Sacramento seemed to be listening.

Property tax bills in California, as elsewhere, are the result of two factors: the tax rate and the *assessed value* of the property. The rate can stay the same, but if the assessed value goes up, so does the tax bill. In California, property values and therefore assessments had been rising rapidly during the second half of the 1970s. The *Los Angeles Times* reported they had gone up by 120 percent in the Los Angeles area between 1974 and 1978. There was fear that lower-wage workers and seniors on fixed incomes would be forced out of their homes by high property taxes.

County assessors, dependent on voter approval for reelection, had managed to hold the line against rising tax bills to some extent by limiting assessed home values, resisting pressure from local officials desperate for dollars to build the schools, parks, and other infrastructure required in a rapidly expanding state. Assessors usually set assessments on businesses at a higher rate, in effect creating an informal "split role" between business and homeowners without lavishing undue attention on that role. Then, in 1965, Assessor Russ Wolden of San Francisco was convicted of giving lower assessments to businesses that paid him "consulting" fees.

The statewide scandal that erupted over assessors' discretion in setting assessed values resulted in legislative action. In 1966, with the best of intentions, the Legislature enacted, and Pat Brown signed, AB 80. The new law ended assessors' flexibility and set assessed value at 25 percent of market value. Since most home assessments across the state had been considerably lower than that, thanks to assessor discretion, home assessments shot up, and so did property tax bills.

Another factor contributing to homeowners' increased restiveness was the California Supreme Court's 1971 decision in *Serrano v. Priest,* which held that the amount of funding going to schools in wealthier areas was disproportionately favoring the wealthy. Under the equal protection clause of the U.S. Constitution, some way had to he found to equalize school spending, the court ruled. Prior to *Serrano,* local taxes went to local schools in both wealthy and poorer districts. Wealthier districts could amply fund their schools with a lower tax rate because of their higher real estate values and assessments.

The Legislature's answer was to limit the amount of money that a school district could receive. Leftover money in the wealthier districts would be sent to less affluent districts. While that caused rejoicing in the poorer districts, wealthier Californians resented an arrangement in which their tax dollars were not all being spent on their own children but were instead siphoned off and shipped across town to the less affluent.

The solution, such as it was, came from an unlikely source. Howard Jarvis, a lobbyist for the Los Angeles Apartment Owners Association, was a crusty, blunt-talking antitax activist and a failed Republican candidate for the U.S. Senate and mayoralty of Los Angeles. He teamed up with Paul Gann, a fellow antitax activist from Sacramento, to mount an initiative campaign aimed at halting the escalation of assessments. It would be called the People's Initiative to Limit Property Taxation, and its first paragraph declared, "The maximum amount of any ad valorem tax [tax based on the value of real property] on real property shall not exceed one percent (1%) of the full cash value of such property. The one percent (1%) tax to be collected by the counties and apportioned according to law to the districts within the counties."

The proposition set assessed property values at their 1975 value. It limited annual increases of assessed value of real property to no more than 2 percent per year. The base year of assessed value could not be changed unless the property changed ownership or it was new construction. The initiative also required a two-thirds majority in both legislative houses for future increases of any state tax rates or amounts of revenue collected, including income tax rates. In addition, it required a two-thirds vote majority to increase local special taxes. All of the provisions were to be made part of the state constitution, subject to change only by a vote of the people. It could not be modified by the Legislature.

Jarvis, his wife Estelle, and volunteers collected enough signatures to put their measure on the June 1978 primary ballot as Proposition 13. The Legislature finally awoke to the situation and started a frantic round of bill consideration. Lawmakers had clear ideas of what needed to be done. The problem was that twenty-two clear ideas were introduced. None of them won approval. Jerry Brown, apparently practicing creative inaction, was mostly silent.

After Jarvis had qualified Proposition 13, however, the Legislature did come to a consensus and rushed a rival measure onto the ballot as Proposition 8. It, too, aimed at lowering property tax bills. But while it would have cut homeowners' property taxes by 30 percent, the Legislature's version did not contain a cap on property assessments. Furthermore, it could be amended by the Legislature. Stung into action, Governor Brown also began to campaign vigorously against Proposition 13, calling it a fraud and a rip-off in speeches up and down California.

All to no avail. An aroused 70 percent of voters went to the polls, and Proposition 13 won in a landslide, with nearly 65 percent of the vote. Proposition 8, the Legislature's tax-cutting proposal, trailed badly with 47 percent. Instantly, Jerry Brown performed one of the most dazzling flip-flops in the history of American politics. Proclaiming himself a "born-again tax cutter," he embraced Proposition 13. He embraced it so convincingly that he earned the nickname "Jerry Jarvis," and polls several months later showed that a majority of Californians believed he had been for Proposition 13 all along. His outward enthusiasm for Proposition 13 was so intense that Howard Jarvis himself did a political commercial for Brown in the November general election.[2]

Idealist Brown's flip-flop on 13 illustrated an important, if contradictory, part of his philosophy—do what the political situation seems to demand, said *Los Angeles Times* columnist George Skelton. "I think he's more practical than idealistic," Skelton observed.[3]

It is hard to overstate Proposition 13's continuing effect on California governance. With nearly 57 percent of their tax revenue wiped out, local jurisdictions were in deep trouble. The Legislature rode to the rescue, sending the state's five-billion-dollar budget surplus to local jurisdictions. But the bailout in effect meant that fiscal control shifted to the state, the source of money that has kept local services afloat. Local school districts, cities, and counties from 1978 on have looked to the state, not to local taxpayers, for large amounts of their operating funds. Local jurisdictions have since then also resorted to an imaginative series of fees and special assessments, including fees imposed on developers, in an effort to replace lost revenue.

But there is more to the story than fiscal rearrangement, far-reaching and consequential though it was. The Proposition 13 saga was governmental malpractice on a grand scale. Leo McCarthy, the late Assembly speaker and later lieutenant governor, summed it up in an interview: "I think a lot of us in Sacramento... really didn't measure the distress of homeowners accurately enough.... We sort of said, 'Well, they've got this big asset, a home, that's being greatly inflated now, and that's going to be good for their kids, their families, whoever inherits it' and so on. We didn't understand, and should have, the fears of a lot of these homeowners."[4]

The governor, the Legislature, and local governments all failed to act in a timely and effective manner to deal with a major crisis. The California electorate as a result concluded, in this case accurately, that the state and local governments were unable to meet the voters' concerns. Layered on top of Ronald Reagan's mantra, "government is not the solution to the problem, government is the problem," was an enormous loss of governmental credibility that continued through the ensuing decades. Proposition 13's detractors call it a meat-ax approach to a complex problem; its defenders say if the voters had not taken the initiative (literally) nothing would have been done, and property taxes would have continued a cruel and inexorable climb. If Proposition 13 was not written with the sophistication and nuance that a legislative solution would have contained, Californians reasoned, that is a small price to pay for the needed relief. Proposition 13 continues to be popular with voters, with many political writers calling it the "third rail" of California politics. If it were to be put on a ballot in 2013, it would probably win by a larger margin than it did in 1978.

In the 1978 November general election, incumbent Brown had no major opposition in the Democratic primary and was therefore able to bring a considerable campaign war chest to bear. The Republican primary was much more interesting and hard-fought. The favorite was Evelle Younger, the state attorney general. Younger was a former FBI agent who had served as the Los Angeles County district attorney and a municipal and superior court judge. He had achieved a substantial career in public service but was limited by what many considered to be a wooden speaking style. Ed Davis, the former Los Angeles police chief who was a primary opponent, called Younger "as exciting as mashed potatoes" in numerous campaign speeches. Davis, a state senator, was probably the most colorful of the Republican primary candidates. He had a tough law-and-order reputation, enhanced, as previously mentioned, by his suggested treatment of airliner hijackers, which he often reiterated while campaigning: "Give 'em a fair trial, and then hang 'em at the airport!" State senator Ken Maddy, of Fresno, and San Diego mayor Pete Wilson were the remaining candidates, both regarded as moderates.

When the tallies were in, Younger had 40 percent of the vote, Davis had nearly 30 percent, Maddy had slightly more than 19 percent, and Wilson was in fourth place with slightly more than 9 percent.

Proposition 13 played a major role in the November general election, which saw Jerry winning a second term. Younger, who had favored Proposition 13 all along, attempted to grab its momentum and paint himself as the proposition's champion as opposed to Brown, who had campaigned against it. It didn't work. In Jerry's remarkable turnaround on Proposition 13, he told voters that the people had spoken and that as governor he would diligently enforce their will. The statement won the day. Younger was simply drowned out. Brown won by a huge margin, with more than 56 percent of the vote to Younger's 36.5 percent. His margin of victory was greater than that amassed by Ronald Reagan when he defeated Jerry's father. He had 3.87 million votes to Younger's 2.52 million, for a margin of slightly more than 1.3 million votes.

Lieutenant Governor Mervyn Dymally was not as lucky. He lost to composer and record company executive Mike Curb, who had been urged to enter politics by Reagan. Dymally's loss was merely a single chapter in a political career arc that is one of the more unusual in California history. He was first elected to the Assembly in 1963 and was elected to the state Senate in 1966. He was elected as lieutenant governor in 1974 and served until losing to Curb. After stepping off the political stage for two years, he won election to Congress from a Los Angeles–area district in 1981. He served until 1993, when he retired again. He came out of that ten-year retirement and was elected to the Assembly in 2002, where he had started out almost forty years earlier.[5] His attempt to return to the state Senate in 2008 after three terms in the Assembly, however, ended in defeat.

Curb composed music for movie soundtracks such as Clint Eastwood's *Kelly's Heroes* and had a hit recording of "It's a Small World." He composed songs successfully enough to make him a major player in the music business, creating his own record label, Curb Records. He formed his own musical group, the Mike Curb Congregation, and was an outspoken enemy of drug use among musicians and an advocate of gay rights. Republicans regarded the boyish Curb as a fresh face who could go far. He was a major thorn in the side of Brown. Jerry was frequently absent from the state while campaigning for the presidency in 1980, and as acting governor, Curb took full advantage of the situation. He vetoed legislation, issued executive orders, and even made appointments. Curb's actions eventually wound up before the California Supreme Court, which ruled that he had acted within his constitutional prerogative.

Curb ran for the Republican gubernatorial nomination in 1982 but lost to Attorney General George Deukmejian, who went on to win the governorship. Curb tried again to become lieutenant governor in 1986 but lost to Leo McCarthy in a bitter campaign that prompted a seven-million-dollar lawsuit by Curb against McCarthy.

During his second term, Jerry continued to be a trailblazer in appointments. He appointed Stephen Lachs to the Los Angeles County Superior Court in 1979, making Lachs the first openly gay judge in the United States. In 1981, Brown appointed Mary C. Morgan to the San Francisco Municipal Court, making her the first openly lesbian judge in the United States. In all, Brown appointed five openly homosexual persons as judges. Brown cited the 1978 Briggs Initiative as raising his awareness of gay rights. The Briggs Initiative, which would have banned homosexuals from employment in California public schools, was the brainchild of John Briggs, a conservative Republican state senator from Orange County. It was opposed by Mike Curb, Gerald Ford, and Jimmy Carter. Curb worked with gay San Francisco supervisor Harvey Milk in the successful campaign to defeat the initiative.

Brown made *Apollo 9* astronaut Rusty Schweickart an adviser and later appointed him to the state energy commission. Tom Hayden, an anti–Vietnam War activist and then-husband of Jane Fonda, was appointed as California's representative on the Southwest Regional Border Conference. Hayden later won election to the Assembly and then the state Senate from a Santa Monica–based district. A former Buddhist priest, Brian Victoria, ran the governor's intern program. But by far the most colorful of Democrat Brown's second-term appointees was a conservative white male Republican named B.T. (Brien Thomas) Collins. Collins had lost an arm and a leg while serving as a Green Beret captain in Vietnam. Returning to the United States, he earned a BA and a JD from Santa Clara University, where Brown had gone to school for a year.

Collins entranced Jerry Brown. He was blunt, charming, intelligent, irreverent, thoughtful, and energetic. He had a wide circle of friends of all political ideologies in Sacramento, and whenever a friend, acquaintance, or adversary had a birthday or other significant event, he or she received a handwritten note from Collins. Brown appointed Collins head of the California Conservation Corps in 1979, where he coined the CCC motto: "hard work, low pay, miserable conditions." Collins later became Brown's chief of staff, succeeding Gray Davis.

Republican governor Pete Wilson later appointed Collins as director of the California Youth Authority, a place Collins once described as eighty-six hundred of the most vicious people he'd ever seen outside the Legislature. At Wilson's urging, Collins ran for the Assembly as a Republican in a special 1991 election and won. He was reelected to a second term from his suburban Sacramento district and died in 1993 at age fifty-two. Witnesses said both Wilson and Brown were fighting back tears when they appeared together at Collins's memorial service. "B. T. Collins was the greatest man I ever knew," conservative *San Francisco Chronicle* columnist Debra J. Saunders said. Twenty-eight years after his death, Saunders told me, "Just thinking of B. T. makes me smile."

Brown's stream of out-of-the-box thinking continued in his second term. In what would not be regarded as particularly unconventional today, he proposed the purchase of a state space satellite for emergency communication. He also suggested the establishment of a state space academy, an idea that did not achieve liftoff.

The fact that the governor was in his 30s and a bachelor caused speculation up and down California about his love life—or lack of it. But while women may have taken a backseat to ambition in Brown's life, they were present.

Associated Press political writer Doug Willis inadvertently made a bit of news himself when he sought to sidestep the issue delicately in a speech:

> There were rumors and questions among reporters and others during the 1974 [gubernatorial] election about whether Brown was straight or gay, because he was 32 and never seen with a girlfriend.

I recall one event during the 1974 campaign when Brown aide Llew Werner was joking among reporters that Brown's campaign was the only campaign he ever heard of in which the staff was spreading stories about which women the candidate was sleeping with.

I recall another occasion in 1975 when I was guest speaker for a local publisher at his Rotary Club. After my prepared remarks, the first question came from an elderly Rotarian: "I just have one question: Is our governor a fag?"

There were a couple of local reporters covering my speech, and I didn't want to say anything quotable. So I gave an answer which I thought was too long and too convoluted to quote: "For starters, I don't have any firsthand knowledge either way. But I can recall a few informal interviews with Brown, and an attractive woman has passed by, and I have clearly lost his attention for a few seconds. So I am inclined to think that his interests are similar to mine, and I have a wife and three children."

I thought my nonanswer had cleverly avoided any problems until I got a phone call a few weeks later from Lou Boccardi, then editor and president of AP, asking me what I thought I was doing speculating about our governor's sex life.

It turned out that one of the reporters liked my roundabout answer so much that he made it the lead paragraph of my story, and that one of the then-commonplace low-budget celebrity magazines did a front-page profile of Jerry Brown, and that my quote was in the third graf.[6]

The Jerry Brown Archives at the University of Southern California reveal a bittersweet exchange of letters between Brown and a young woman named Karen. Well after the end of what apparently was an intense relationship, Karen, who had a new man in her life, sent Brown a birthday card in 1971 declaring, "A few months ago—you gave something to me that I needed very much at that time—Because of that and because you are what you are—I'll never forget you. I think of our time together with sadness that it is over—but mostly remember the happy times and how we almost made the pieces fit.... I think of you often, Jerry—I hope that we'll all be happy."

In his immediate typewritten reply on April 17, 1971, Brown told Karen, "Your card meant a lot—and if nothing else produces tears. I have been thinking of you less. I realized how remote it all is as I read over your card tonight. You seemed far away and together we seemed even further. And I thought to myself that's good and cried." The letter concluded with "I care about you and I always will."

Of the letter's five paragraphs, two were devoted to Jerry's new job as California secretary of state. In part, Brown told Karen, "The world is so shaky and what we do in this country could make quite a difference. And there are so many jerks running things.... Within a year or two I'll have this place doing as much as it will ever do for the state. After that and the next president is elected, then the real fun begins."

Brown's nickname "Governor Moonbeam" originated with his long-time (post-Karen) girlfriend, singer Linda Ronstadt, who affectionately and publicly called him "Moonbeam." *Chicago Sun-Times* columnist Mike Royko picked up on it, dubbing Brown "Governor Moonbeam." Royko later said that he regretted pinning the name on Brown, since he eventually found him as grounded as any other politician. But by then it was too late, and Brown was stuck with the "Moonbeam" label for decades to come.

Linda Ronstadt was the pretty and highly intelligent brunette daughter of a successful machinery dealer in Tucson, Arizona. She had come to Los Angeles at age eighteen in search of a career and met Jerry in 1971 at El Adobe Café, a restaurant across the street from the Paramount lot in Los Angeles. Both were young, idealistic, talented, and ambitious. There was chemistry; over enchiladas, the two bonded. At the time, Linda Ronstadt was a rising star, on the cusp of becoming a superstar in the world of rock music. Her break-through album, *Heart Like a Wheel,* was to come in 1974, but she had already achieved a reputation as a folk-rock singer and country-and-western performer. In 1969, she had become the first female singer to release an alt-country album, *Hand Sown... Home Grown.* Eventually, her career would encompass genres ranging from Mexican folk songs to *The Pirates of Penzance,* and she would win eleven Grammys. When she and Jerry began their relationship, she was far better known than the man occupying the then-obscure office of California secretary of state.

Illustrating the tangled, intertwined relationship between show business and politics in California, Ronstadt early in her career was a featured singer with the Stone Poneys, a singing group that Mike Curb helped launch.

In April 1979, while Jerry was preparing his second presidential run, he and Ronstadt took off on a highly publicized trip to Africa. *Newsweek* magazine featured them on the cover of the April 23 issue with the headline "The Pop Politics of Jerry Brown." The couple petted wild animals while photographers snapped pictures. Jerry met with various African leaders and talked about the environment while Linda stayed back in camp, drinking beer with reporters and talking about the state of the music business. The tents and cottages had twin beds, a waiting world was informed.

According to those who saw them together, Ronstadt was probably the best thing to happen to Jerry Brown until his marriage to Anne Gust. Brown blossomed when Linda was around, happily emerging from his usual serious, almost dour persona. Jerry's sometime-adversary, sometime-ally Willie Brown reported, "They really like each other. He's a different person when he's with her. There's a side the public never sees. He's flirty, flippant and very funny. And he's as interested in her physically as I'd like to be."[7]

Possibly because of career demands on an ambitious politician and an equally ambitious entertainer, the intense, long-term relationship never reached the marriage stage, despite the happiness each felt in the presence of the other.

Jerry's 1980 bid for the presidency did not come nearly as close as did his 1976 try and probably accelerated the decline in his political fortunes that marked the last two years of his second gubernatorial term.

This time around, he was attempting to unseat an incumbent president in the Democratic primaries. Jerry's platform had three main planks: a call for a constitutional convention to ratify a balanced budget amendment, a promise to increase funds for the space program, and opposition to nuclear power. The last was Jerry taking political recognition of the 1979 Three Mile Island accident, still in the public mind.

He announced his candidacy before the National Press Club in Washington on November 8, 1979, saying, "My principles are simple: Protect the Earth, serve the people and explore the universe."[8]

In passages that would resonate among liberals today, Jerry declared: "Now is the time for people to exercise greater, not less, control over multinational oil companies and banks." And "Obsolescence, waste and pollution have often provided jobs, but they now must give way to an economy of efficiency, of caring, of quality, not mere quantity."

He also said, "We explore the universe by giving full vent to our creative minds.... I see a future where we reach out into space itself and bring with us other nations, so that at last we begin to sense our unity in the Spirit on this small speck of universal time." Even though Jerry's vision was essentially correct, and Russia, Japan, and other nations have launched joint space ventures in the intervening years, "unity in the Spirit on this small speck of universal time" probably struck hardened Washington reporters and voters as a bit too visionary.

Jerry did not do well in the Iowa caucuses or in the Maine primary and won only 10 percent of the vote in the New Hampshire primary. He pinned his hopes to a last-stand comeback in the Wisconsin primary, but a thirty-minute televised appearance in Madison, created by famed director Francis Ford Coppola, turned into a fiasco. The sound kept going out intermittently, and the visuals were garbled. The campaign had been effectively dead before Wisconsin, but it was the coup de grâce.

In addition to the poor showing in New Hampshire and the difficulty in Wisconsin, his effort was overshadowed by the insurgent—but also unsuccessful—candidacy of Massachusetts senator Ted Kennedy. President Jimmy Carter was easily renominated, going on to lose the presidency to Ronald Reagan.

The second try for the presidency did not go over well in California. An April 1980 Field Poll showed that 56 percent of respondents disapproved of Brown's running for the presidency, while 36 percent approved. A *Los Angeles Times* poll in early May gave Brown a 33 percent "favorable" rating as against 65 percent "unfavorable."

One of Brown's more embarrassing moments came in January 1980 when, during his state-of-the-state speech to assembled legislators and shortly before he left for another campaign swing through Iowa and New England, he hypocritically admonished them, "We must subordinate our own ambitions and our own individual egos to a much larger purpose." What followed has been variously described as laughter, suppressed laughter, and titters.

As it became increasingly obvious that Brown's try for the presidency was going nowhere, editorial writers began to state the obvious. "He has, in fact, pursued his candidacy so far beyond the point of conceivable returns that he seems not even a candidate so much as a presidential junkie," intoned the *Sacramento Bee* in an editorial below the headline "Jerry Come Home!"[9] This commentary wasn't confined to California. Across the country in North Carolina, Ed Williams, the editor of the editorial page of the *Charlotte Observer*, had earlier written that Brown's "glib but vague" phrases had "spread like laughing gas through our TV sets, threatening national amnesia."[10]

While Jerry was off campaigning for president in 1979–80, the day-to-day running of the governor's officer fell to Brown's chief of staff, Gray Davis, an efficient, detail-oriented, nuts-and-bolts manager who harbored large political ambitions of his own but never swerved from his devotion to making the Brown administration an effective one.[11] With Jerry out of the state for long periods, Davis was, in effect, acting governor during part of the 1979–80 presidential campaign season.

Davis arrived as the top staff person with a young-man-with-a-future aura. He had graduated from Stanford with honors and then from Columbia Law School. He won a Bronze Star during service in Vietnam. He was careful, cautious, almost scientific in his political calculations, and had a reputation among some as being aloof.

Davis later served in the Assembly from 1982 until 1986, then as state controller from 1987 until 1995, and then lieutenant governor from 1995 until 1998. He was elected governor in 1998, reelected in 2002, and recalled in 2003, becoming the second governor to be recalled in American history.

As Jerry's administration entered its final months, the Medfly nightmare of 1981 tested the governor's ability to make, and stick to, decisions. The destructive Mediterranean fruit fly lays its eggs under the skin of fruit, causing billions of dollars in crop damage around the world. It had infested fruit crops in Santa Clara County and was threatening to spread to other parts of the state. Agricultural interests in California and the U.S. Department of Agriculture Animal and Health Inspection Service urged Brown to authorize airborne spraying of malathion to kill the insects, saying billions of dollars in agricultural losses could result if there was no aerial spraying. On the other hand, environmentalists said the spraying would threaten human health by cloaking suburban homes in an insecticide whose effects on humans were unknown.

During the height of the controversy, Brown's post–Gray Davis chief of staff, the irrepressible B. T., summoned reporters to watch him drink a glass of water laced with malathion to prove that the pesticide was harmless to humans. Both sides were vocal and emotional. There was no way to reach a compromise. Brown first sided with the environmentalists and refused to authorize spraying. In a public statement he declared that the spraying threatened the well-being and security of half a million residents, including pregnant women and children.

Forty-six hours after making that statement, he had to reverse himself. U.S. secretary of agriculture John Block had threatened to quarantine California produce, which would have meant an enormous loss to California farmers. Brown authorized ground spraying at first but was then forced to approve aerial spraying on a large scale. Fleets of helicopters flew at night, spraying malathion, while the California Highway Patrol set up checkpoints to confiscate huge quantities of fruit heading out of state, even without the USDA carrying through on its threat. Authorities also released millions of sterile male Medflies in an attempt to disrupt the flies' reproductive cycle. The Medfly threat was finally ended but not until millions of dollars in crops had been lost.

Brown's standing had already plummeted, with the respected Field Poll putting his approval rating at 38 percent in 1980, a steep plunge from his highest approval rating, 69 percent in 1976. He was philosophical about his diminished standing, however. "People are looking for a scapegoat for the medfly, and I'm the logical target," he told reporters.[12]

Battered and bruised as his administration wound down, Jerry made one more attempt to enter the national stage. Rather than run for a third term as governor, which he could have done in those days before term limits, he decided to try for the U.S. Senate. Among his primary opponents was the author and commentator Gore Vidal.[13] Brown easily won the Democratic nomination, receiving 50.6 percent of the votes, well ahead of Vidal's second-place 15.1 percent. His general election opponent was San Diego mayor Pete Wilson, who had finished dead last in the 1978 Republican gubernatorial primary. Wilson got 51.5 percent of the vote, and Brown received 44.7 percent.

During the past eight years, Jerry Brown had conducted a very public romance, run twice for president, once for the U.S. Senate, brought previously excluded minorities into state government, lectured his fellow citizens on the virtues of austerity, won new rights for farmworkers, presided over one of the most unconventional administrations in California history, and become the closest thing California ever had to a philosopher-prince. But his philosophical pronouncements on living life and governing were no longer fashionable. He had somehow not suffered from his 1976 try for the presidency after a mere fifteen months in office, but the 1980 run raised eyebrows among voters and made him a quixotic and perhaps even slightly ridiculous figure. Voters began to remember his earlier position against Proposition 13 before he was for it. His relationship with the Legislature, where he was regarded as aloof and cold, had never been cordial. Jerry's impatience with the ordinary courtesies and protocols of state government had caused resentment and bruised feelings across a wide swath of Sacramento's political community, many of whom had not had their telephone calls returned or returned very late.

Although previous governors had all had great political ambition (Warren, for instance, had run for president and vice president before settling for chief justice of the U.S. Supreme Court), a number of them, such as Warren, Pat Brown, and Goodwin Knight, had regarded the governorship as a chance to make the state a better place for people by improving its infrastructure—building freeways and bridges, opening new university campuses, and moving water to where it was most needed. By contrast, Jerry Brown in the 1970s regarded the governorship as a mechanism for realizing two things: his idealism and his ambition. He furthered his idealism through his trailblazing push to appoint more women and minorities to high state office, to win labor rights for farmworkers and state workers, to protect the environment, and to lift the vision of Californians beyond the mundane. He wanted people to be aware that the planet had finite resources, that life should mean something more than the constant struggle to acquire more and more material goods, that daily living should have a spiritual side.

Such an outlook might have come more easily to Brown, the son of a well-to-do family who has never had real worries about money throughout most of his life, than to the offspring of a carpenter or hardware store clerk who had to struggle to acquire a three-bedroom, two-bath home in the suburbs. But it was nonetheless an unusual, one might even say altruistic, stance for any politician to adopt.

Jerry's idealism ran parallel with his ambition. He used the governorship of the nation's most populous and glamorous state as a perch to run for president twice and, when that didn't work out, to run for the U.S. Senate. He seemed to be constantly on the lookout for the next office, the next political victory, the next bit of political sleight-of-hand that would boost his fortunes. But as his second term came to its end after years in office, fairly or not, he was no longer considered a fresh face who would clean up Sacramento. It was time, at least temporarily, to explore other options.

CHAPTER FIVE

Back and Forth

Zen and Politics

For those small minds that slavishly adhere to foolish consistency, their irrelevance is their best reward.

Jerry Brown, speech to high school students, 1979

Out of statewide office for the first time in twelve years, defeated in two presidential bids and one try for the U.S. Senate, Jerry Brown in 1983 contemplated a future that seemed to hold little promise of a political comeback. The unsuccessful Senate campaign against Pete Wilson was a strong indication that Brown had simply gone out of fashion. Fickle voters had grown weary of Moonbeam.

The new governor, George Deukmejian, was in some respects the anti-Brown. He had defeated Los Angeles mayor Tom Bradley by waging a successful law-and-order campaign against retired policeman Bradley. Deukmejian, in fact, had conducted law-and-order campaigns since being elected to the Assembly in 1962. He became a state senator in 1967 and quickly climbed up the legislative ladder to become majority leader in 1969. He finished fourth in the Republican attorney general primary in 1970 but won the job in 1978, while Jerry was piling up his landslide over Evelle Younger. Deukmejian was an advocate of the death penalty and as attorney general had himself photographed on Northern California raids against marijuana plantations. Deukmejian heralded a return to normalcy, at least what was regarded as normalcy in the state Capitol. With the ascent of sobersided, probusiness, law-and-order George Deukmejian, wingtip shoes and solid, business-oriented Republicans were in; Brownian intellectual meanderings were out.

Most major politicians who have strategized and hoped over the course of campaign after campaign and who have spent twelve years in office—eight of them as governor—and then find themselves sidelined spend their time in profitable private-sector occupations while plotting a comeback. Brown did not. Now he could think about Big Things. He was free to exercise his intellectual curiosity and idealism with no hindrance from schedules, legislators, lobbyists, or conflicting staff recommendations. He could roam the world and explore, freed from the sometimes grubby demands of governing.

For the next five years, displaying the baked-in, central contradiction that makes his life so fascinating, this politician son of a politician, who had never met an elective office he didn't like, gave rein to his always-present spiritual side. He wanted to think about the world—the universe—and humankind's place in it. He wanted to develop more insight into what it means to be human. Was gaining elective office the best way to improve the human condition? Or would it be better to become a world traveler and lecturer for causes he felt were important, such as the elimination of the death penalty? How could he best speak out? What could he bring to the table as an experienced politician with intellectual aspirations who presumably could get things done?

The famous ex-governor was almost, but not completely, out of the public eye between 1983 and 1988. He returned, partially, to the Jesuit fold, traveling to Jesuit Sophia University in Tokyo to seek a spiritual reawakening. Sophia was the first Catholic university in Japan, opening in 1913 and graduating its first class of nine students in 1918. The university has historically been welcoming to international students, with a motto of "men and women for others, with others."

Brown spent six months in Japan, studying Zen meditation with Zen master Yamada Koun and Father Hugo Lassalle, who in addition to being a Jesuit was a Zen practitioner. Father Lassalle, a German, had arrived in Japan in 1929 as a missionary and become interested in Buddhism. He was severely wounded in Hiroshima when the atomic bomb was dropped on August 6, 1945. He later was the force behind the construction of a cathedral in Japan dedicated to world peace. As a Jesuit and practitioner of Buddhism, he had the right combination to be an ideal spiritual and intellectual guide for the questing California politician.

Brown spent his time in Japan methodically rebuilding and recharging himself mentally, shedding the habits of thought that had accumulated in Sacramento over the past twelve years. He meditated for two hours a night and once a month participated in a retreat, where there would be more intense meditation and reflection.

In addition to his extended stay in Japan, Brown lectured, practiced law in Los Angeles, studied Spanish in Mexico, practiced yoga, and traveled to Bangladesh as a CARE ambassador of goodwill during the devastating floods of 1988 that inundated more than half the country and claimed three thousand lives.

Perhaps the most attention Brown received during his overseas travels was the month-long visit he made in 1987 to work with Mother Teresa in her Home for the Dying in Calcutta. Mother Teresa, even during his short visit, had a major impact on Brown. He emerged from his time in Calcutta even more thoughtful about the relationship, or lack of it, between politics and the plight of the less fortunate. And, on the cusp of turning fifty, he thought about his own development as a human being: "Politics is a power struggle to get to the top of the heap. Calcutta and Mother Teresa are about working with those who are at the bottom of the heap," he observed later. "And to see them as no different than yourself, and their needs as important as your needs. And you're there to serve them, and doing that you are attaining as great a state of being as you can."[1]

The years traveling and engaging in Zen meditation probably made Brown a deeper and more thoughtful person, but they did not extinguish his thirst for the wheel and clash of California politics. In 1988, after returning from Bangladesh, a mentally refurbished and less impulsive Jerry Brown went back to practicing not only politics but politics of the grittiest kind—chairmanship of the California Democratic Party. Zen-student and Mother Teresa–helpmeet Jerry Brown jumped into the chairmanship contest late and shoved aside Steve Westly, the heir apparent. Investment banker Westly, the vice-chair of the party and a grassroots party activist, had been working to secure support for weeks before Brown's announcement and was thought to be a shoo-in for the chairmanship. But Brown's name recognition and perceived qualities as a political heavyweight carried the day.[2]

Brown proved adept at bringing more money into the party, expanded get-out-the-vote drives, and improved grassroots organizing. But he scorned heavy campaign television advertising, just as he had in his 1974 gubernatorial race against Houston Flournoy. Oddly, for a political practitioner of his acumen and one who had mastered the art of simpleminded political symbolism, Brown had difficulty believing that elemental, broad-brush television spots could really influence voters, whom he thought were much too judicious, informed, and thoughtful to be swayed by television commercials. Democrats lost several races in 1990 that some felt could have been won had the party put up more television ads.

In 1991, Brown abruptly resigned the chairmanship, saying he had become weary of raising money to support Democratic incumbents regardless of their worth. He also wanted to run again for the U.S. Senate to replace retiring Democrat Alan Cranston. But then another chance at the presidency appeared on the horizon, and ever the political optimist, Brown thought he had a realistic shot. So despite good poll numbers for the Senate race—it is entirely possible that he would have won a U.S. Senate seat—Brown abandoned his senatorial campaign and declared he would instead run in 1992 for the Democratic presidential nomination. This would be his third try. The desire to be president had smoldered through all the time of spiritual questing and meditation.

It was a brash move, but not as wild a notion as it seemed at first blush. The incumbent president, George H. W. Bush, was vulnerable. Bush had seen his approval ratings soar after the eviction of Iraqi forces from Kuwait but then lost popularity because of a falling economy. When Bush visited a store and innocently professed curiosity about bar codes—something American shoppers had been familiar with for years—he seemed out of touch with average people. Furthermore, there were only two other major candidates vying for the Democratic nomination: Governor Bill Clinton, the leading Democratic contender, was from Arkansas, a small state, and had been plagued by accusations of womanizing; the second-ranking candidate, Senator Paul Tsongas, of Massachusetts, had health problems.[3] Brown, at age fifty-three, could still be seen as an iconoclastic, forceful man from a glamorous state.

But first there were the primaries, and Jerry was a late arrival, officially making his candidacy announcement on October 21, 1991, at Independence Hall in Philadelphia. "The leaders of Washington's Incumbent Party—both Democrats and Republicans—have failed their duty," he declared. "Placing their own interests above the national interest, they have allowed themselves to be trapped and to varying degrees corrupted by the powerful forces of greed. It is time for them to go." With admirable alliteration, he promised to "take back America from the confederacy of corruption, careerism, and campaign consulting in Washington."[4]

As almost all politicians had done during the previous forty years, he criticized the Washington establishment. Brown styled his effort as a people's campaign, reviving his 1970–76 California theme of acting on behalf of the common man against entrenched, uncaring power. "You and I must deliver a message to those who run the United States of America like a private club that we are going to work change," he declared.[5] To dramatize his common-man motif, he said he would not accept campaign contributions of more than one hundred dollars and used an 800 number to raise money.

The Brown presidential platform was a mosaic of liberal and conservative stances. He favored term limits for members of Congress, called for campaign finance reform, and opposed the North American Free Trade Agreement. At one time or another, he called for the elimination of the federal Department of Education and advocated a flat tax. His blue-and-white placards read "Take Back America."

Brown won endorsements from filmmaker Michael Moore, author Gore Vidal, former adversary Willie Brown, and writer Christopher Hitchens. Ironically, one of his primary opponents was Eugene McCarthy, the former Minnesota senator for whom Jerry had worked in 1968. (McCarthy finished near the bottom of the pack.)

Although Brown was unable to afford television commercials, which he had decried in the past anyway, he waged an impressive low-budget, scorched-earth campaign against front-runner Clinton. Brown also became a bit of a pioneer in political communications during that third bid for the presidency, chatting with supporters and would-be supporters on the then-new Internet. That session came at the behest of the campaign media adviser, Joe Trippi.

There were eleven debates between November 11, 1991, and April 6, 1992, and Brown pulled out all the stops, at one point accusing Clinton of fiscal chicanery involving Clinton's wife, Hillary. He said of Clinton, "He is funneling money to his wife's law firm for state business." An angry Clinton rejoined, "I don't care what you say about me, but you ought to be ashamed of yourself for jumping on my wife; you're not worth being on the same platform with her!"[6] Clinton told reporters, "I feel sorry for Jerry Brown."

On March 26, 1992, not long before the final debate, Democratic national chairman Ronald Brown issued an unusual statement in a news release rebuking Jerry Brown for what had become a series of personal attacks on Clinton. The chairman said Jerry Brown had "crossed the line in terms of inappropriate attacks" against Clinton.

During his debate with Brown on March 15 and in his own attack mode, Clinton had accused Brown of turning a state surplus into a deficit, raising taxes, and taking credit for Proposition 13 after first opposing it. "He doesn't tell people the truth," Clinton said. Brown's campaign said Clinton had relied on faulty numbers from a CNN report to make the charge that Brown had raised taxes.

Jerry did not do well in the Iowa caucuses or in New Hampshire but won in Colorado, Alaska, Vermont, and Nevada. He received a strong third-place showing in the Illinois primary on March 17 and then defeated Tsongas for second place in the Michigan primary, forcing him from the race. He cemented his position as a major threat to Clinton when he managed a narrow win in a bitterly fought Connecticut primary.

All eyes now turned toward the primaries in Wisconsin and New York, both held on April 7. Brown, the only surviving major candidate whose name was not Clinton, then committed a disastrous gaffe. He told a group of Jewish leaders in New York that he would consider African American preacher-politician Jesse Jackson as a running mate. The remark did serious damage. Jackson had made what were widely regarded as anti-Semitic remarks in 1984, while running for president himself, and they had not been forgotten in New York. Jerry lost Wisconsin by a narrow margin, 37 percent to 34 percent, but was crushed in New York, where Clinton won 41 percent and Brown had only 26 percent. Brown was not deterred. He told cheering supporters in Manhattan, "I'll see you all over this country tomorrow, tomorrow and tomorrow."[7]

However, Brown's last-ditch stand in his home state of California was not successful, effectively ending any real possibility of his becoming an insurgent Democratic nominee. He lost by a margin of 48 percent to 41 percent. Because of his earlier primary victories, however, Brown had 596 delegates and still harbored a slight hope of stalling a Clinton victory on the first few ballots, triggering a brokered convention from which, somehow, he might emerge as the nominee. It didn't happen. As the last act of a bitter campaign against Clinton, Brown managed to speak at the convention, again garnering a brief spot before a national television audience, but otherwise it was back to the sidelines.

This time, the sidelines were in Oakland rather than Japan or Calcutta. Brown built a $1.8 million live-work loft near the Jack London Square area and created the We the People Foundation, which described itself as a nonprofit corporation "dedicated to strengthening the practice of democracy and the ability of people to shape the places where they live."[8]

Asked why he had picked Oakland as his new home, Brown said he was attracted by "cheap land," also declaring, "I wanted to live in a grittier place than San Francisco."[9] It may also have been the idea of a clean slate in a new location and the possibility that Oakland would be wide open for political adventures at some point. He would have a more difficult time seeking political office from his former residences in Los Angeles and San Francisco, crowded as they were with ambitious, able political hopefuls.

The recent chairman of the California Democratic Party also renounced party politics and re-registered as a "Decline to State"— California's nomenclature for an independent voter. "I freely admit my disenchantment with the current state of the Democratic Party," he wrote in a *San Francisco Chronicle* op-ed. "The very nature of partisan politics in America is now grounded in corruption, both intellectual and functional."[10]

If a computer programmer with too much time on her hands were ever to decide to write a program of mathematical variables to ascertain those most unlikely to be close confidants of major political figures, she might very well come up with a program that would select Jacques Barzaghi first and foremost. "It is Mr. Barzaghi who, behind the scenes, puts the frost on the California Flake," said the *New York Times*'s Alessandra Stanley.[11]

Barzaghi is a French-born former filmmaker, veteran of the French Army during the Algerian War, and former merchant marine sailor. He claimed to have loved every minute of combat in Algiers, found Hollywood filmmaking inefficient, and declared that his friend Jerry was merely expressing himself when he ran for elective office. Barzaghi also claimed that he had lived for three years in a solar-powered hut in an Australian rain forest, which he ultimately found too rainy, had delivered his first child himself at home (he described the experience as "godlike"), and had been on the barricades during the 1968 student uprisings in Paris.[12] He met Brown at a party when Brown was serving as secretary of state, and the pair quickly struck up an unlikely friendship. Not long after Brown would eventually marry, at nearly seventy, Barzaghi was to be married for the sixth time. Brown paid little attention to clothes; Barzaghi was always carefully attired in black pants, black jacket, black boots, and round wire-rimmed glasses, all topped off by a black beret on his bald head.

But both Brown and Barzaghi were interested in the unusual and esoteric, and both were devotees of Zen mysticism and meditation. Both liked to break the boundaries of the conventional. Brown could count on Barzaghi as a sounding board, intellectual companion, campaign scheduler, speaking coach, and general factotum. Barzaghi was in charge of staging Brown's public appearances and, when Brown was in danger of speaking too long, would make a cutting gesture with his finger across his throat as a signal to wrap it up.

In a statement that would have interested Bill Clinton, Barzaghi argued that Brown's pursuit of elective office was not so much a matter of ambition as it was an exercise in personal growth, akin to his work with Mother Teresa and Zen meditation. Barzaghi is remembered among California political reporters for a remark he made during Brown's 1992 campaign for president. It was later fondly enshrined as "the ultimate spin quote." Talking with reporters about the Brown campaign, Barzaghi said, "We are not disorganized. Our campaign transcends understanding."

Barzaghi was a living example of Jerry's quirkiness. Others could have fulfilled the roles that Barzaghi played in Brown's personal and political life, but Barzaghi filled them all, at the same time meeting some unarticulated need within Brown's psyche. Some described Barzaghi as Brown's closest friend; others, less admiringly, spoke of him as Brown's only friend.

Jerry also began exploring various philosophies of living as the sponsor and host of Research by the People, a live-in program in which invited guests over a six-week period would offer lectures, discussions, seminars, and reading groups on such subjects as the difference between space and place and ways in which humans can manage themselves rather than be managed by experts. The name was later changed to the Oakland Table. The events were conducted in a spacious loft apartment that Jerry had built on Harrison Street in Oakland and that had become sort of an intellectual commune. In a way, it was a continuation of the salon that Brown had run for eight years in the governor's office, where a wide variety of thinkers and celebrities had visited for conversations with him.

Some insight into one facet of Jerry Brown's mid-1990s view of humankind and the world can be gained through his admiration for Ivan Illich, one of the Oakland participants. Illich was a Catholic priest who had achieved an international reputation as a rebel and critic of the Vatican, automobile transportation, the industrial state, and "do-gooders" who visit developing nations, among many other artifacts of modernity. Born in Vienna in 1926 of a Croatian father and a Sephardic Jewish mother, Illich was a brilliant scholar who spoke Italian, Spanish, French, and German from an early age. He later learned Croatian, the language of his father, along with ancient Greek, Latin, Portuguese, Hindi, and English.

Illich received his formal education at the University of Florence, the Pontifical Gregorian University at the Vatican, and in Salzburg, where he studied medieval history. Despite, or perhaps because of, that kind of background, he became a critic of institutionalized education. Illich advocated a system of self-directed education, fluid and free from stultifying institutional restrictions. He was also a critic of formal international development programs, arguing that they merely imposed a kind of Western industrial hegemony on the developing world.

Illich achieved the height of popularity in the 1970s, becoming especially revered among the French intelligentsia for his criticism of modernization and the corrupting impact of institutions and for his celebration of free human beings, unshackled by political, economic, and social conventions. Here's what he had to say to an audience of youths volunteering to serve in developing countries in a speech titled "To Hell with Good Intentions": "Next to money and guns, the third largest North American export is the U.S. idealist, who turns up in every theater of the world: the teacher, the volunteer, the missionary, the community organizer, the economic developer, and the vacationing do-gooders. Ideally, these people define their role as service. Actually, they frequently wind up exacerbating the damage done by money and weapons, or 'seducing' the 'underdeveloped' to the benefits of the world of affluence and achievement."[13]

Brown had first met Illich in 1976 and had been entranced by his somewhat mystical philosophy and indifference to material goods. Jerry said of his friend:

> When I try to understand Ivan Illich, I am forced back upon my experience in the Jesuit Novitiate in the 1950's. There, I was taught Ignatian indifference to secular values of long life, fame and riches. It is only through that mystical lens that I can grasp the powerful simplicity of the way Illich lived. He had no home of his own and relied on the hospitality of friends. He traveled from place to place with never more than two bags. He refused medical diagnosis, any form of insurance and gave away whatever savings remained at the end of each year.
>
> Among the serious thinkers I have had the privilege to meet, Ivan Illich alone embodied in his personal life as well as in his work, a radical distancing from the imperatives of modern society.... [He] bore witness to the destructive power of modern institutions that create needs faster than they

can create satisfaction, and in the process of trying to meet the needs they generate, they consume the Earth.[14]

Illich influenced Jerry Brown's philosophical outlook during the time in Oakland prior to Brown's becoming mayor. Illich represented a side of Brown that fueled his imagination and broad ethical values, but he didn't influence Brown's unerring sense of realpolitik in the public arena or what Brown sought to accomplish while holding elective office. It was as if Brown had separate compartments in his psyche—one for idealistic if somewhat offbeat philosophies, the other for the world of cut-and-thrust politics and what one could achieve in elected office.

While Illich advocated uninstitutionalized education, Brown established two charter schools in Oakland, one of which is a military academy. Brown also pushed for downtown development in Oakland and courted business. He was the principal advocate of a Navy–Marine Corps exercise in Oakland dubbed Operation Urban Warfare—all of which would seem to fly in the face of Illich's values. It seems much more likely that Brown, fond of intellectual playthings, appreciated Illich's philosophical outlook, but as a pragmatist in politics, he realized it was not something one would incorporate into day-in-day-out matters of importance when one had actual responsibilities for governing a city or a state.

Brown touched on his own internal development during this period in a 1994 speech titled "Political Consciousness and Transformative Action," made before the International Transpersonal Association:

> I want to start with my own growing consciousness about the world of politics: just to say that word is nasty, yet it is very important because each of us is a political being. Politics comes from the word polity, polis. Aristotle used the phrase "political animal"—*zoon politicon*. We are not just by ourselves. We are not just in a little group, but are part of a larger community. And when you have more people, you need some rules. You need some basis for making decisions, and that is at the heart of politics.
>
> Now between that and what we have today is a large gap. We are in a degenerate state of self-government. In fact, even to use the words self-government is not only an exaggeration, it's a lie. It's is a big lie! I hope I

can convince you of that, but not depress you. I don't want you to feel good after this talk, but I don't want you to feel so bad that you rationalize not doing anything. Because you do have power. And as much as I dislike politics, I have devoted my life to it—out of some form of enlightened masochism—or some other deep motive that I have not yet been able to plumb. But I am not sick of it, and I am not cynical about it—but I'm not naive about it.[15]

Illich fell out of fashion among the international academy in the 1980s, and by the time he died in Germany on December 2, 2002, his international fame had dwindled to a band of devoted admirers. Brown says that for the last twenty years of Illich's life, he had left untreated a cancerous growth on the side of his face. Illich called the growth "my mortality."[16]

On January 31, 1994, Brown entered the increasingly crowded and mostly right-wing arena of talk radio by launching a two-hour-long call-in program, *We the People,* on the Talk America Radio Network. Talk America syndicated the program to about thirty stations, most of them in small markets. Brown later switched to noncommercial, left-leaning Berkeley radio station KPFA, saying KPFA was more aligned with his message. KPFA made the program available to other noncommercial stations. KPFA was one of the first listener-supported broadcast outlets in the nation when it went on the air on April 15, 1949. Its mission statement declares, in part, that KPFA was created "to promote cultural diversity and pluralistic community expression" and "to contribute to a lasting understanding between individuals of all nations, races, creeds and colors."

Broadcast five days a week from the Oakland loft, Brown's program sought to do all those things, with the former governor conducting interviews with a wide variety of thinkers, such as Allen Ginsberg and Barbara Ehrenreich, on such topics such as protecting the environment, politics, and philosophy. Despite his previous experience in radio appearances during his numerous campaigns, hosting a talk show was

something new and challenging. Along with politics and the environment, callers wanted to discuss everything from incinerator emissions
to how "hemp technologies" could lessen the need to chop down trees.
Brown said it was like going to graduate school.

"I just feel it's a lot of work, to have a lot of knowledge, to keep
talking," he told interviewer Paul D. Colford.[17] "But I appreciate the
value of the talk-show format. Ideas are complicated. The quickie
newscasts distort and simplify the issues, but a talk show allows you a
few hours to really explore the issues. There's a narrative in the talk-
show format whereas the mainstream media is like acupuncture of
entertainment and isolation. Your brain is agitated, but your mind is
not engaged."

In the same interview, Brown even expressed admiration for fellow
talk-show host Rush Limbaugh, declaring, "When Limbaugh has a
project, he does it justice and it's not glossed over.... He certainly
pounds home an idea. It's pretty incredible.... I basically define him as
a tall-storyteller of rightist perspective."

Perhaps more vividly than any other period of his life, Brown's back-
and-forth among Zen Buddhism, care for the dying in Calcutta, and
politics between 1983 and 1999 illustrates the paradoxes and contradictions of his nature—deep concentration on a life of the mind during
spiritually centered Zen retreats in Japan interspersed on the other side
of the world with repeated hyperambitious, down-and-dirty political
combat in pursuit of elected office. The contrast is striking. Brown is a
man capable of attending a Zen retreat and on the return trip home
plotting a campaign that involves the brutal ending of another politician's hopes and dreams. Ending rival politicians' hopes and dreams is
standard political practice, of course, and frequently may be a good
thing to do, but never before in California history has it been done by a
politician who has done it to advance his own fortunes while truthfully
claiming that as a Jesuit seminarian, "I was taught Ignatian indifference
to secular values of long life, fame and riches."

Plate I. The Brown family *(left to right):* Jerry, Pat, Kathleen, Bernice, Barbara, and Cynthia (undated). Photo courtesy of the Bancroft Library at the University of California, Berkeley.

Plate 2. Jerry Brown and family at the governor's mansion in 1959. AP Photo.

Plate 3. In this photograph *(left to right)*, Edmund G. "Pat" Brown, Jerry Brown, Colusa rancher Wally Lynn, and former California governor and Supreme Court chief justice Earl Warren pose after a duck-hunting outing on Lynn's Colusa County ranch (undated). Photographer unknown. Photo courtesy of Dan Walters/*Sacramento Bee.*

Plate 4. The Brown family with singer Nat "King" Cole (undated). Photo courtesy of the Bancroft Library at the University of California, Berkeley.

Plate 5. Present-day Magellan Avenue in the Forest Hills neighborhood of San Francisco, where young Jerry Brown grew up. The upper-middle-class area has remained mostly unchanged over the decades since Brown's birth. Photo by author.

Plate 6. Governor-elect Jerry Brown in Los Angeles on election night, November 5, 1974 (note Jerry Brown for President sign in background). Photo courtesy of Dick Schmidt/*Sacramento Bee.*

Plate 7. Governor Brown leads members of the Capitol Press Corps up the twisting iron staircase between the inner and outer Capitol domes on May 28, 1975. Photo courtesy of Dick Schmidt/*Sacramento Bee*.

Plate 8. Brown walks to work across Capitol Park on January 31, 1976. The apartment building where he lived is in the background. Photo courtesy of Dick Schmidt/*Sacramento Bee*.

Plate 9. Singer Linda Ronstadt and Jerry Brown stand with members of the Eagles rock group during a concert in Maryland in 1976. AP Photo/Karin Vismara.

Plate 10. The "Taj Mahal" governor's mansion in suburban Sacramento, which Brown refused to occupy (undated). AP Photo by Kim D. Johnson.

Plate II. Colton Hall in downtown Monterey, where the first California constitution was written in 1849. Photo by author, courtesy of the City of Monterey.

Plate 12. The 1877-vintage governor's mansion in downtown
Sacramento, where Brown studied for his second try at
passing the California bar examination. The mansion is now
an unlived-in historic site. Photo by author.

Plate 13. Brown in the kitchen of his Brown-for-mayor headquarters in Oakland, March 24, 1998. Photo courtesy of Dick Schmidt/*Sacramento Bee*.

Plate 14. California gubernatorial candidates Democrat Jerry Brown *(right)* and Republican Meg Whitman *(left)* exhibit outward goodwill on stage with California governor Arnold Schwarzenegger during the Women's Conference on October 26, 2010, in Long Beach, California. AP Photo/Matt Sayles.

Plate 15. Brown is sworn in for his third term as governor of California on January 3, 2011, by his wife, Anne Gust. AP Photo/Rich Pedroncelli.

Plate 16. Governor Brown, his wife, Anne Gust, and their corgi, Sutter, walk to the Capitol in Sacramento on January 4, 2011, the day after his third inauguration. AP Photo/Rich Pedroncelli.

Plate 17. While his wife, Anne, looks on, Brown confers with Gray Davis, his former chief of staff and former California governor, at an inaugural event at the California Railroad Museum on the evening of Brown's third inauguration. AP Photo/Rich Pedroncelli.

Brown has seemed undisturbed by these seemingly contradictory themes running through his life and in fact has given every appearance of enjoying their interplay. References to St. Ignatius and Buddhism have repeatedly cropped up in his speeches and interviews. He told interviewer Fred Branfman, "The [Zen Buddhist] training of zazen aims at emptiness, emptiness being a space without illusion. Since politics is based on illusions, zazen definitely provides new insights for a politician. I then come back into the world of California and politics, with critical distance from some of my more comfortable assumptions."[18]

Comfortable assumptions have always been foreign to Brown. He was never part of a Golden State dream that envisioned a three-bedroom, two-bathroom home with a nice lawn in a suburb, even though it was part of the life aspirations of millions of post–World War II Californians, including millions who voted for him. For most of his life, Brown has believed that people should not make assumptions. They should explore alternatives and question what they have been told by authority figures. By loudly challenging conventional wisdom and what is perceived to be an elite and uncaring power structure and the public figures attached to it, he has managed to be a populist figure, even as he has sat atop the political power structure in Sacramento. He has spoken directly in campaign appearances, giving him an aura of blunt simplicity despite his fondness for abstract intellectual pursuits far removed from the concerns of the common man he seeks to help.

"Jerry Brown is like one of those crystal balls that hang over the dance floor," said Gray Davis when he was Brown's chief of staff in his first term. "He's a man with many facets and interests, and as they become apparent to others, they may think it's a shift in policy. But what is occurring is that different aspects of the man are being revealed. The media get confused because they focus on one idea at a time, rather than the whole mosaic of leadership Brown is creating."[19]

Brown has never tried to hide his enjoyment of intellectualism and his interest in the spiritual, even as he has advocated for the common man and even at the risk of alienating those voters who would prefer their politicians to be down-home people one could have a beer with. He has frequently mentioned life lessons he has learned from his religious and philosophical studies and once told biographer Orville Schell, "Government is constantly faced with value questions in education, about people imprisoned in mental hospitals and prisons, the way we allocate our funds, the way we deal with our forests, parks, rivers, oceans and farmlands. The ethical value questions are very important to the political process, and to the extent that religious traditions have something to say, I'm interested."[20]

Just as in the case of Illich, Brown's spiritual quests in Japan and around the world during these out-of-office years seemed not to have had a discernible effect on his subsequent day-to-day political practice. The Zen student Brown is a clever, opportunistic, and intelligent politician, with an almost uncanny ability to gauge voter reactions to events and take advantage of them. He is a master at creating crowd-pleasing symbolic gestures.

"Jerry Brown is an intelligent man with a genuine love of ideas and an intuitive grasp of left-coast culture. If he's more likely than most politicians to say something deeply silly, he's also more likely to say something deeply right," writer Jesse Walker declared in *American Conservative* magazine.[21]

Has Brown's lifelong fondness for intellectual pursuits made him a better public servant? At least some of the people who have worked most closely with him are convinced that it has. Steve Glazer, who managed Brown's successful 2010 campaign for the governorship, spoke of Brown's "rigor" in tackling issues.[22] Former press secretary Doug Faigin said, "He's one of the smartest, if not *the* smartest, person I've ever met."[23]

In sum, the out-of-office years in Oakland were a continuation of the things that were characteristic of Jerry Brown's first eight years as governor: his exploration of new intellectual frontiers and his love of the unconventional. In various nongovernmental forums, he continued to advocate for environmental protection, better opportunities for those left out of the economic and political mainstream, governmental reform, and personal lifestyles with less emphasis on the acquisition of material goods.

And despite his supposed dislike of politics, he was alert to opportunity. And now opportunity was ahead, right there in Oakland.

CHAPTER SIX

The Governor-Turned-Mayor and Marriage

Oakland government was not working. We had process
paralysis. The insider group needed to be shaken up—the
friends getting jobs for friends. People voted for change, and
that's what they're getting.

Jerry Brown, salon.com interview, 1999

Brown in 1998 saw a golden pathway ahead for a return to elective politics. Elihu Harris, the two-term incumbent mayor of Jerry's adopted hometown of Oakland, had decided to run for the Assembly, where he had previously served for six terms.[1] There was an opening, and Jerry seized it.

Political observers around San Francisco Bay recognized that Brown's ambition was always simmering below the surface, even when he was not a candidate and even when he was engaged in intellectual exploration. "His community involvement seems to have revolved entirely around his plan to run for mayor... in part, to give himself the political stage he's been lacking since he left the governor's office," the *San Francisco Bay Guardian* declared. But it also called Brown Oakland's "best bet."[2]

Brown's decision to run for mayor of Oakland followed a pattern of campaigning for office, retiring—not always willingly—from the political wars to recharge his intellectual and spiritual batteries, and then picking an opportunity for a return. There was probably not a step-by-step plan. Oakland was not a statewide platform. Few people in Los Angeles, San Diego, or even San Francisco cared about what was happening in Oakland. But being mayor of Oakland returned Brown to elective office—a place he craved throughout his adult life. And it was a perch as mayor of a major city from which he could observe the California political scene. Who could tell what might happen? Being mayor might prove to be a springboard. Oakland was opportunity.

The city that Jerry Brown adopted is a curious amalgam. It is described as "gritty" when it is not being described as "working-class" or as a city that has never lived up to its potential. Some detractors have described Oakland as "Newark West." There is an enormous social and economic divide between the Oakland Hills, where homes sell for as much as $2.5 million or more, and the flatlands below, with depressed and depressing swaths of tired bungalows, liquor stores, and battered parks. But the flatlands are occasionally brightened by streets of well-kept homes of an emerging African American middle class.

The city has high crime rates; depending on the source, Oakland has been ranked the fourth or twenty-fourth most dangerous city in the nation. In October 1966, Huey Newton and Bobby Seale, reacting to what they perceived as white police persecution in crime-riddled areas of the city, founded the Black Panther Party for Self-Defense.[3] On New Year's Eve and the Fourth of July, police patrol cars and ambulances on duty in some areas of Oakland customarily park under freeway over-crossings for brief times before and after midnight to protect against descending bullets fired into the air by celebrating Oakland residents.[4]

It was a minority-majority city. When Brown decided to run for mayor in 1998, Oakland had a population that hovered around four hundred thousand, made up of roughly 35 percent African Americans, 31 percent Caucasians, 21 percent Hispanics, and 15 percent Asians. In 2011, it was the eighth-largest city in California. And into this city of sidewalks, sometimes littered with broken glass and abandoned couches and tarnished by abject poverty pockets and high crime rates, came mayoral hopeful Jerry Brown—son of a governor, himself a former governor, Zen student, talk-radio host, and creator of a think tank and an intellectual commune.

Brown ran on a platform that emphasized crime reduction, education, and a revitalization of the downtown, declaring he would bring ten thousand additional residents to that area of the city (the "10K" program). Although the downtown revitalization had been started by Elihu Harris, Brown emphasized it, which went over well. He held out a vision of a sparkling, vital, cosmopolitan city—one that Oaklanders could be proud of.[5] He also finessed the powerful African American coalition of ministers and community activists who would not normally be expected to support a white candidate, although a group of activists appeared outside his live-work loft to shout "*We're* the People!" The demonstration did not deter Brown's campaign.

Jerry faced ten other candidates but easily won 58.7 percent of the vote, obviating the need for a runoff. His campaign contributors included singer Helen Reddy, actor-producer-activist Rob Reiner, and Berkeley restaurateur Alice Waters. The Brown name had worked its magic once again, only this time it was not because Pat Brown's son was on the ballot. This time it was because Jerry Brown, two-term celebrity governor, was running. Oakland voters, whether white, African American, or Asian, were flattered that a man who had been governor had decided to become mayor of their hard-luck city.

"People like Jerry. His approval ratings when he was mayor were through the roof. He took Oakland by storm," said Chip Johnson, who covered Oakland for the *San Francisco Chronicle* through his twice-weekly column.[6]

Although more than a third of Oakland's residents were African American, Jerry became the first white mayor of Oakland since 1977. He threw himself into his new job, displaying no evidence that he considered being mayor of Oakland a demotion from the governorship. After his triumph in the primary, Brown was able to put through a "strong mayor" initiative in the general election. It gave the mayor real power, making the person a chief executive rather than the somewhat ceremonial head he or she had been previously. At Jerry's insistence, the measure also imposed term limits—the mayor could serve only two terms.

When Brown began his new job, it was apparent that "Moonbeam" was over. Jerry was interested in filling potholes, spurring economic growth, creating a downtown renaissance, and doing something about Oakland's horrendous public schools. "Governor Moonbeam has become Mayor Pothole," the *Wall Street Journal* declared.[7]

"Oakland opened his eyes," Chip Johnson said. "Jerry recognized that he wasn't an everyday man. I remember there was a going-away party once at a bar that cops and reporters used to go to. We were having a few pops, and Jerry wanders in from where he was living, only a few doors away. He's like, 'Hey, what's going on?' and we tell him—and then he says, 'Why don't you all come to my place?' I think more than anything else, he wanted to relate to these guys. He realized he was coming to a blue-collar town."[8]

Ignacio de la Fuente, who had been an electoral opponent of Brown's, became a fan. "I'll tell you a story," he said. "On election night, about 8:30, already knowing I'd been beaten by Jerry, I was looking out the window of the two-story building where I had my campaign headquarters, and I see this man down there, alone, waiting for the light to change so he could cross the street. I recognized Jerry Brown. So I go down to meet him, and he says, 'Well, it looks like I've won, and I just wanted to come and see you and tell you that I want to work with you.' Think about that—what kind of a guy is that?"[9]

Brown had scarcely settled into his new office after his January inauguration when in March he faced a major controversy. The Navy and the Marine Corps wanted to stage an urban warfare exercise in Oakland involving hovercraft landings and flashbang grenades, among other things. The "Urban Warrior" exercise was to be held at the defunct Oakland Army Base and at the closed Oak Knoll Naval

Hospital. Access had earlier been denied at the Presidio, in San Francisco, as a result of Bay Area residents' protests of the exercise. An organization called the Coalition against Urban Warrior also staged protests, including the picketing of Brown's home and a brief takeover of Brown's office by high school students. Brown, a former foe of the Vietnam War, had invited the three-day exercise, arguing that it would bring millions of dollars to the city. He called the protests pathetic. The exercise went ahead.

Brown has been able to point to a number of praiseworthy achievements during his eight years as mayor. One of the most publicized was restoration of the Fox Theater, built in 1928 in downtown Oakland as one of the grand West Coast movie palaces featuring talkies. The twenty-eight-hundred-seat theater was a fanciful pastiche of Middle East architecture, with terra-cotta moldings, gold accents, and a tiled dome. It had fallen into neglect since the '60s, with a leaky roof and mushrooms sprouting from the decayed old carpets. The city bought the theater for three million dollars in 1996, hoping it could be resurrected. Some of the restoration work began in 1999, before Brown took office. Later, under his stewardship, a complete restoration project was financed through a complex mixture of private fund-raising and government grants. Although the theater didn't reopen until February 2009, after Brown had left the mayor's office, he did shepherd the work, making sure that it was not derailed. He had viewed restoration of the grand old theater as a key part of his effort to revitalize Oakland's downtown.

Despite his admiration for the ideals and philosophy of his friend Ivan Illich, who scorned institutional education, Brown established two educational institutions during his years as mayor. The Fox Theater building now houses the Oakland School for the Arts, a charter school founded by Brown in 2000, which by 2011 had a waiting list for admission. The school says its mission is to "provide students with intensive conservatory-style training in the arts while maintaining a rigorous college-preparatory curriculum." In 2006, the school was able to boast that 100 percent of its first graduating class had been accepted at four-year colleges.

In 2001, Brown founded the Oakland Military Institute, another charter school with a 2009–10 enrollment of 605 students from Oakland's lower economic strata. Although it has seemed a far cry from the type of educational institution Zen student Jerry Brown might begin, the school does reflect his fondness for self-discipline and study. It is designed to give a leg up to students who might not do well in a regular public high school. Nearly 80 percent of the student body is "economically disadvantaged," according to the school's records. Twenty-eight percent of the enrollment is African American, 42 percent Hispanic, 19 percent Asian, and 3 percent Caucasian.

The school's Web site declares, "We understand that some of our cadets enter OMI performing below grade level standards, and we support these students by providing extra opportunities to accelerate learning, i.e. Saturday school, after school classes, or study hall. It is our expectation that each cadet will take advantage of these opportunities, and through hard work, determination, and a positive attitude do whatever it takes to meet OMI's academic standards."

Brown was less successful in efforts to improve Oakland public schools. Thanks to a feckless school board and administration, the district found itself thirty-five million dollars in the red in October 2002 because of overspending and accounting errors. The board then laid off 330 teachers and counselors and 260 support staff in May 2003. The state took over the district's management, naming Randolph Ward as the state administrator in June 2003.

The mayor of Oakland had little direct control over the school district, but Brown nevertheless attempted to improve things. He allied with state senator Don Perata to raise money to put Measure D on the 2000 ballot and get it passed, allowing Brown to appoint three additional board members to what would become a ten-member board. The board then split into two factions—Brown supporters and those who backed Superintendent Dennis Chaconas. Brown was never able to gain support from a sufficient number of board members to put reforms into effect. He said later his attempts to improve Oakland's public schools were foiled by the district's bureaucracy and were largely "a bust."

Even in later years, among some families in Oakland's better-off neighborhoods, it became routine to call the movers after elementary school. In December 2010, the *San Francisco Chronicle*'s education writer, Jill Tucker, reported, "One of every four Oakland students—including 40 percent of its highest achievers—fled the district's public schools after finishing fifth grade in the spring, shunning the city's middle schools."

Jacques Barzaghi for a time continued to play a major role in Brown's life. He remained the mayor's confidant and adviser, constantly reminding everyone inside and outside city hall that this was an administration with a difference. He once encouraged Brown to bring a Sufi choir to a prayer breakfast. "Without that creative approach, government tends to reproduce itself in an unimaginative way," Brown said. "Jacques is a catalytic element in the mix of advisers I have. I understand that he's not everybody's favorite person, but he's quite remarkable."[10]

Although his contributions to the Brown administration may have at times been esoteric, Barzaghi could also ring in with insightful political advice of a practical nature. When some of Brown's advisers urged him to attend the funeral of a slain child, Barzaghi demurred, pointing out that the murderers were possibly the child's parents, and that Brown would then be embarrassed. That later proved to be the case. Barzaghi's advice had avoided a political land mine.

But Barzaghi himself became a potential land mine for Jerry Brown. In 2001, the city paid fifty thousand dollars to settle a sexual harassment case triggered by a female city hall employee's complaint against Barzaghi. Additional women then came forward to voice accusations. Barzaghi was suspended for three weeks and ordered to undergo counseling. In July 2004, after police were called to quell a domestic disturbance involving Barzaghi and his sixth wife, Brown fired Barzaghi, ending a close friendship that had endured for more than thirty years. At last report, in early 2011, Barzaghi was running a yoga studio in Paris.

In March 2002, Brown was reelected to a second term in a landslide over Wilson Riles Jr., the son of the former state superintendent of schools. Riles Jr. was a former member of the city council and had served for three terms, but his two previous tries at being elected mayor, like the try against Brown, were unsuccessful. Riles picked up just 24,611 votes, while Brown cruised with 42,892 votes. It was a bigger margin of victory than the one that had originally put Brown in the mayor's office.

Brown's legacy as mayor of Oakland is generally a good one. Although he failed to upgrade Oakland's subpar public schools, he began two charter schools, boosted the existing "10K" program to bring more residents into downtown Oakland, and oversaw the continued successful restoration of the Fox Theater. But in addition to these specific achievements, Brown did more. His very presence in Oakland's city hall boosted citywide morale. Oaklanders felt that with a former governor and a national political celebrity as mayor, their city had regained a place in the major leagues, a feeling that had not been present since the Oakland Athletics had won three World Championships in a row from 1972 to 1974 and then again in 1990.

Ignacio de la Fuente, the Oakland city council member who ran against Brown in 1999, praised Brown's record in office, saying, "Overall, he was a good mayor." He said that Brown's years as mayor changed him significantly, but that Brown, ever flexible, was open to change if it would help him succeed: "Absolutely he changed. Jerry Brown at first was in the clouds. He changed dramatically. We used to take walks in some of the toughest neighborhoods. No bodyguards, nothing. He learned the realities of people living in those neighborhoods. It changed him. . . . I've seen him change from a total liberal to a more conservative person."[11]

Steve Glazer, a longtime acquaintance who managed Brown's 2010 gubernatorial campaign, had a similar assessment, saying, "It is true the mayorship of Oakland made him very pragmatic."[12]

The Oakland years did more than transform Brown from Moonbeam to pragmatic civic booster. For the first time in his adult life, Brown felt ready to commit formally to a romantic connection that had existed for a decade and a half. In Anne Gust, he had found a woman who was an intellectual companion, a confidante, and a savvy political adviser.

Jerry Brown, sixty-seven-year-old balding bachelor and former Jesuit seminarian, married Gust on June 18, 2005. The new Oakland first lady was a lively forty-seven-year-old powerhouse lawyer who had been Brown's longtime companion. The two had met at a party in San Francisco and had discovered an almost instant affinity for each other fifteen years earlier, when Brown was chairman of the state Democrats.

Gust grew up in Bloomfield Hills, Michigan, graduated from Stanford, and then the University of Michigan Law School. She had been the general counsel and then chief administrative officer for the GAP clothing chain, headquartered in San Francisco, but resigned a few months before the wedding. She had told reporters earlier that she had been a registered Republican, an independent, and a Democrat. Like her husband, Gust had politics in the family during her growing-up years. Her father, Rocky Gust, had been the 1962 Republican candidate for lieutenant governor in Michigan.

Without exception, Brown's friends and acquaintances say that Gust has been good for him on a personal and professional basis. They describe Gust as lively, intelligent, and—as did Linda Ronstadt years earlier—someone who brings out the humor in Brown. "Being involved with Anne for so long has been great for him," says Faigin, the former Brown press secretary.[13]

Friends say Gust has the added ability to get Brown to focus and set priorities, something Brown had notoriously failed to do sufficiently during his first two terms as governor. "I think she's very well organized," Brown told reporters. "She's very insightful, very quick, sizes up things very quickly, and so in that sense she's a very good partner and has lots of great ideas."

The guest list of nearly six-hundred was a roster of California Democratic luminaries. The ceremony was conducted by U.S. senator Dianne Feinstein in downtown Oakland's Rotunda Building, close to city hall. On hand were former governor Gray Davis, who had served as Brown's chief of staff when Brown was governor; Willie Brown, now a friend of Jerry's; Gavin Newsom, the mayor of San Francisco who was destined to become a gubernatorial rival of Brown's briefly and then lieutenant governor; Bill Lockyer, the attorney general who was to become state treasurer; then-state-senator Don Perata, a political ally of Brown's who was to face a surprising loss in a campaign for mayor of Oakland; Kamala Harris, the San Francisco district attorney who would become attorney general; and old friend Tony Kline, now a district appeals court judge.

There were readings from the Old and New Testament, Gregorian chants, and a brass fanfare. Brown was beaming and outgoing. *San Francisco Chronicle* columnist Leah Garchik reported that Brown had earlier inspected the diamond in his fiancée's wedding ring with a jeweler's loupe before purchase to make sure it was flawless.

In 2007, the newlyweds settled into a five-level home in the wooded Oakland Hills, with views of San Francisco Bay and the Golden Gate Bridge. Married life didn't change Gust's continuing role as a political adviser and intellectual resource to Brown. She was never interested in being a decorative appendage or in pushing her own, first-lady-appropriate projects. She remained part of the mainstream Brown operation and his closest political adviser, managing his 2006 campaign for attorney general. In the last few years, especially during his gubernatorial run in 2010, Gust played a principal role in Brown's political strategy and tone. Many regard her as Brown's not-so-secret weapon in his public life.

Political ambition—the desire for the next step up—had never left Brown. Buoyed by his lopsided victory over Riles that had given him his second term as mayor, Brown began thinking harder about statewide office. While he continued to make appearances as mayor of Oakland, close observers thought the intensity of his absorption with the job had lessened. "No question about it. Particularly in the last two years of his term, he wasn't anywhere near as visible a presence as he had been earlier. The lights were on, but no one was home," said *San Francisco Chronicle* columnist Johnson.[14]

But where was the opening? The logical reentry was attorney general. Bill Lockyer, the incumbent, had for years hankered to become governor. He had been elected to the Assembly in 1973, then to the state Senate, where he had become the president pro tempore. Still climbing the ladder, he had been elected attorney general in 1998, succeeding Republican Dan Lungren, who had left the office to make a hopeless run for governor. Near the end of his two terms, Lockyer was on his way to being termed out as attorney general, and in 2005 he announced he was running for governor. In about four months, it was apparent that the Lockyer gubernatorial campaign was not electrifying voters. Lockyer decided to run for state treasurer instead. (He was easily elected treasurer in 2006.) But the attorney general job was open, with no incumbent.

Declaring himself a Democrat again, Brown filed candidacy papers to run in his readopted party's 2006 primary election for attorney general. He faced formidable opposition from Rocky Delgadillo, the Los Angeles city attorney. Delgadillo had two things going for him: he was well financed, and Brown had a high-profile record of opposing the death penalty.

California law specifies that the attorney general contests criminal appeals, including appeals of death sentences. As an undergraduate at Berkeley, Jerry had urged his father to grant clemency to Caryl Chessman and had stood vigil in 1967 outside the gates of San Quentin when Aaron Mitchell, screaming, "I am Jesus Christ!" was executed in the pale green gas chamber for the killing of a Sacramento policeman. In 1977, during his first term as governor, Brown had vetoed death-penalty legislation, but the veto was overridden by the Legislature.

Brown insisted that his near half-century of opposition to the death penalty was a nonissue and that he would enforce the law in death penalty cases regardless of his personal feelings. In repeated meetings with reporters as he campaigned across the state, Brown insisted that he was willing to fight appellate cases and see that the death sentences approved by juries were carried out. But some voters remembered that Brown's idealistic opposition to the death penalty had caused him to appoint Rose Bird to the state Supreme Court, and she had manifestly not enforced the law regardless of her personal feelings.

Delgadillo himself had a mixed record. He had pushed civil injunctions designed to prevent gang activities in designated areas of Los Angeles. He had won praise for implementing a program that put city attorneys in each of the city's police divisions. He had overseen the prosecution of actor Paul Reubens, known as Pee-Wee Herman, for misdemeanor possession of pornography.[15] The charge was settled for a hundred-dollar fine. Delgadillo was involved in another high-profile settlement in a case involving a firefighter who had charged racial harassment. Delgadillo had wanted to offer a $2.7 million settlement, but the strategy was vetoed by Mayor Antonio Villaraigosa. The city finally settled the case for $1.49 million, but legal fees pushed the final figure to $2.84 million. In addition, Delgadillo's wife, Michelle, had been involved in an accident while driving with a suspended license in a city-owned vehicle, and Delgadillo had charged the city for the repairs. He later paid the $1,222 bill.[16]

Delgadillo was a graduate of Harvard University and Columbia University Law School. He compared his upbringing in northeast Los Angeles and his university education through scholarships with Brown's background as the son of a governor. Standing on the steps of the state Capitol, Delgadillo told reporters, "I am not an ex-governor or the son of a governor. I haven't run for president. My name is Delgadillo, not Brown."[17]

Delgadillo won endorsements from public employee unions in Oakland representing firefighters and teachers. Both had feuded with

Brown during his two terms as mayor. But Brown won endorsements from Dianne Feinstein, the Sierra Club, and—despite his opposition to the death penalty—the statewide California Police Chiefs Association, which declared Brown would be "a tough on crime attorney general." Brown also made much of his endorsement from the Oakland Police Officers Association.

Delgadillo hammered at Brown's record as a crime fighter and said Brown was soft on defending women's abortion rights. As the June 6 election day drew near, Delgadillo poured more than $2.5 million into television, outspending Brown by more than 6 to 1. Well ahead in the polls and with plenty of money, Brown again shunned last-minute television, confining himself to biographical cable spots rather than a TV counterattack. This time, Brown's reluctance to use last-minute television did not result in a tight finish. On June 6, 2006, he won the nomination easily, defeating Delgadillo, 63 percent to 37 percent.

Brown now faced Chuck Poochigian, a popular Republican state senator from Fresno who had won his party's primary with no opposition. Poochigian had worked in future governor George Deukmejian's 1978 campaign for attorney general; Deukmejian had appointed him to the California Fair Employment and Housing Commission, then as the chief deputy appointments secretary. Deukmejian's successor, Pete Wilson, promoted Poochigian to appointments secretary. Poochigian had won election to the Assembly from a Fresno district in 1994, then was unopposed when he ran for the state Senate in 1998. He was reelected in 2002, again without opposition. Poochigian was generally respected for his work in the Legislature, although he was condemned in liberal circles for his unabashed opposition to equal rights for bisexual, gay, lesbian, or transsexual persons.

The Brown-Poochigian campaign was one of the most vigorously contested of 2006. Brown attacked Poochigian for his record on the environment; Poochigian painted Brown as a "Moonbeam" politician who had allowed crime rates to soar in Oakland. On October 5, the two clashed in a rancorous one-hour televised debate, sponsored by the *San Francisco Chronicle,* during which Poochigian called Brown "the least qualified person to be attorney general in all of California" because of Brown's opposition to the death penalty. Brown accused Poochigian of spreading "disinformation," saying, "This man is not to be believed." The offended Poochigian said he had never before been called a liar. Brown replied that his record on crime had been distorted by Poochigian, adding, "That constitutes a fabrication, misrepresentation, and where I come from, we can call that a lie."

Poochigian also sought to embarrass Brown by bringing up the Barzaghi matter, saying that the city of Oakland had been forced to pay fifty thousand dollars in taxpayer money to settle the 2001 sexual harassment claim because of Brown's friendship with Barzaghi. He said that Barzaghi had been fired only when Brown had begun seriously considering a run for attorney general and did not want to be handicapped by his aide's background.

The Brown-Poochigian campaign was a trendsetter in at least one respect. A conservative Republican with roots in the rural Central Valley, hundreds of miles from that other valley famous for technical innovation, pioneered the use of an emerging technology in an attempt to win votes. Although he did not seek to raise campaign funds by blasts of e-mails to hundreds of thousands of potential donors, as Barack Obama did so successfully more than a decade later in his own pioneering 2008 fund-raising, Poochigian used YouTube for at least one campaign spot. A campaign pitch by Poochigian, lasting two minutes and twenty-five seconds, could still be seen on the Web in 2011.

Several weeks before ballots were to be cast, Brown's eligibility for the attorney general's office was challenged in court. The lead plaintiff was Tom Del Beccaro, the Republican Central Committee chairman of Contra Costa County and vice-chair of the Republican state party. The plaintiffs argued that Brown was ineligible because he had not been admitted to practice before the California Supreme Court for the required five-year period before the election. Brown's response pointed out that he was eligible to practice law within the technical meaning of the statute, because he had been admitted to practice law since 1965, and although he was on voluntary inactive status, he was nonetheless a member in good standing of the California bar, and that was all that was required. The suit was eventually thrown out.

Despite Poochigian's strenuous efforts and Republican lawsuits, the outcome was never much in doubt. Brown rolled to a lopsided victory, picking up 56.4 percent of the vote to 38.2 percent for Poochigian.[18]

Brown's first year as attorney general was primarily concerned with environmental issues, or at least with shaping a perception that the attorney general was a guardian of California's environment. Of the seventy-six news releases issued by the attorney general between January 23 and December 20, 2007, twenty-seven had to do with environmental issues, ranging from tailpipe emissions to climate change. He challenged supervisors in California's fifty-eight counties to "combat global warming through green buildings, alternative energy and wise land use rules" and urged the federal Environmental Protection Agency to adopt strict greenhouse gas regulations for oceangoing vessels.[19]

Only one of the seventy-six releases had any connection to the death penalty. Brown announced on April 30, 2007, that a death row investigator had pleaded guilty to perjury, forgery, and falsifying documents while defending four death row prisoners. The investigator "crossed the line from vigorous defense to unethical and illegal conduct, which cannot be tolerated," Brown said in the news release.[20]

In June 2008, Brown and a number of other state attorneys general sued Countrywide Financial. Brown's news release accused the lender of using unfair and deceptive practices in marketing its loans, claiming that the company was "a mass-production loan factory, producing ever-increasing streams of debt without regard for borrowers."[21] In October 2008 the suit was settled after Bank of America acquired Countrywide. The settlement required Countrywide to offer payments to eligible borrowers, as well as a loan modification program and relocation assistance for homeowners whose homes had been foreclosed on. Countrywide was also sued by the Federal Trade Commission, which charged that the company imposed excessive fees, made false claims about the amounts owed by homeowners in bankruptcy, and did not tell people in bankruptcy that new fees were being added to their loans. The FTC settlement announced on June 7, 2010, included a $108 million consumer redress fund.

Brown's political iconoclasm was on full display during his tenure as attorney general when he was in the headlines over gay marriage. The state Supreme Court had ruled against gay marriages in August 2004, observing that they violated state law.[22] But on May 15, 2008, shortly before Brown sued Countrywide, the same state high court in a separate legal action ruled 4 to 3 that marriage was a fundamental right for all under the state constitution, and therefore existing laws banning gay marriage were unconstitutional. The court also said that any state law discriminating against gays and lesbians because of their sexual orientation was unconstitutional.

As might be expected, the ruling set off a furor. Opponents of single-sex marriage had already started collecting signatures to place an initiative on the November ballot to amend the California Constitution to ban gay marriage, and the ruling stirred their efforts. The result was Proposition 8, which declared that marriage under the state constitution was limited to marriage between a man and a woman.

The ensuing campaign was loud, emotional, and expensive, with the Mormon and Catholic Churches prominent in their opposition. Backers and opponents of Proposition 8 spent a combined total of more than eighty million dollars on their campaigns, making this pro-and-con campaign one of the most expensive in national history. Proposition 8 backers said they were protecting the institution of marriage; opponents said it was a question of equal rights for all. On November 4, 2008, voters approved Proposition 8 by a margin of

52.2 percent to 47.7 percent. It was the most high-profile dispute over a California ballot measure since Proposition 13, in 1978. Even though the attorney general is expected to defend California law and in spite of his earlier pledges to uphold the death penalty regardless of his personal feelings, the former Jesuit seminarian Brown refused to defend Proposition 8 when it was challenged in federal court. The refusal meant that the law would have to be defended by a group of private lawyers instead of the attorney general's office. Brown was joined in his refusal by Governor Arnold Schwarzenegger, another opponent of Proposition 8. When federal judge Vaughn Walker ruled on August 4, 2010, that Proposition 8 was unconstitutional under both the due process and equal protection clauses, Brown hailed the decision, declaring in a formal statement: "In striking down Proposition 8, Judge Walker came to the same conclusion I did when I declined to defend it: Proposition 8 violates the equal protection guarantee of the Fourteenth Amendment of the United States Constitution."[23] In late 2012, Proposition 8's backers were successful in getting the issue before the U.S. Supreme Court.

Of the last thirteen California attorneys general going back to Earl Warren, at least nine have harbored gubernatorial ambitions, and four of them have won the governorship.[24] The job puts its occupant in a prime position to run for governor, should he or she desire to climb further up Benjamin Disraeli's greasy pole. It is a job that lends itself to publicity, if the occupant is so inclined, and most of them are. Moreover, it is publicity of the best kind, frequently depicting the attorney general as a crusader against crime—ideal for reassuring voters that they would be in good hands if the attorney general were to become governor. Attorney General Brown issued a constant stream of news releases describing his actions in cracking down on fraud, gangs, and despoilers of the environment. A particular target was the federal Environmental Protection Agency, which Brown felt under the Bush administration was not doing enough to protect the environment.

Just as he had more than three decades earlier, Jerry Brown, his idealism and opportunism still intact, was moving aggressively to take advantage of an elective office that carried with it the opportunity to move up the political ladder. Attorney General Jerry Brown, blazing an unprecedented comeback trail, was poised to reclaim the office he had held more than three decades earlier. He would be part of one of the most remarkable campaigns in American political history.

CHAPTER SEVEN

The Remarkable Election

My mother had the good sense to name me after my father.
Jerry Brown, on more than one occasion

Jerry Brown had at least four significant advantages as he embarked on his 2010 campaign to regain the governor's office. First, his Democratic Party held a robust plurality of registered voters and favorable demographics. The California secretary of state's office reported that as of September 8, 2010, there were 16,993,075 registered voters in the state. Democrats had about 7.6 million registrants, or 44.08 percent; Republicans, 5.3 million, or 31 percent; and "decline to state" or independents, slightly more than 3.4 million, or 20.25 percent. Minor parties made up the rest.[1]

A longtime and astute student of state politics, California state treasurer Bill Lockyer observed in a January 2011 postelection analysis, sponsored by the University of California's Institute of Governmental Studies, that Republicans have been at an extreme demographic disadvantage in California for years:

> Democrats continue to win substantial majorities of women, Latinos, African-Americans, Asians, younger voters, gay and lesbian voters, coastal voters, liberals, and college-educated voters. You combine that coalition with the majority of moderate and DTS (Decline to State) voters who express their preference for Democratic candidates in almost every election and you have to ask, "Who the hell is left to vote for the Republicans?"

Simply answered, Republicans are the party of older white voters from inland California, a base too small to win in 21st Century California. These demographics have been with us for 20 years now and show no signs of changing.[2]

Brown's second advantage was name recognition. In a state of more than thirty-seven million people, candidates without high name recognition are forced to spend tens of millions of dollars in statewide races just to let voters know they exist. A candidate such as Jerry Brown, at least vaguely known to most voters even though his last term as governor ended more than three decades earlier, could save those millions for other uses, such as attacking the opponent.

The third advantage was lack of formidable primary opponents. Brown had no significant opposition on the June ballot, so he could save money for the general.

The fourth advantage, related to the third, was linked to the dynamics of the primary system itself. Because Brown faced no opposition in the Democratic primary, which attracts the more left wing among the faithful, he didn't have to toe the line for advocates of liberal purity. Instead, he could remain moderate (and less potentially alienating to the all-important independents) during the primary season.

In 2010, the problem of wooing the base while attempting to retain some attractiveness to the general electorate was particularly acute for Republican Party strategists. They had to deal with a party electorate that seemed to be increasingly congealing around principles that, more and more, did not conform to the beliefs of the majority of voters in blue-state California.

Two multimillionaire Californians, Steve Poizner and Meg Whitman, both fifty-three years old, found themselves in early 2010 facing each other in what was to become a bitter, expensive, and damaging Republican campaign for the right to face Jerry Brown in the general. Both sides were trying to figure out what would win the hearts and votes of conservative Republican primary voters without alienating the larger electorate. For better or for worse, their campaigns were to illuminate starkly what professional strategists in 2010 believed would motivate California Republican voters.

Poizner, born in Corpus Christi, Texas, on January 4, 1957, had come to California in 1978 to attend Stanford Business School and had gone on to great success in his adopted state. He founded SnapTrack, a Silicon Valley firm that invented GPS tracking for cell phones. He sold the company for one billion dollars in 2000. With his fortune made, Poizner turned his attention to education and community service. He served as a volunteer teacher at Mount Pleasant High School in San Jose, teaching twelfth graders about American government. He served as a White House fellow in 2001–2, and in 2003 Poizner was one of the cofounders of the California Charter Schools Association. He ran for the California Assembly in 2004, winning the Republican primary only to be defeated in the general by Democrat Ira Ruskin. But Poizner was unopposed when he ran in the Republican primary for state insurance commissioner in 2006, going on to defeat Lieutenant Governor Cruz Bustamante, a Fresno Democrat who had served earlier as speaker of the Assembly.

Poizner was one of a number of talented and relatively young multimillionaires who had decided to enter politics after success in Silicon Valley enterprises. Two others were Steve Westly and Meg Whitman. Westly had been defeated by Jerry Brown in 1988, when Brown had decided he would like to be chairman of the California Democratic Party. Westly served one term as state controller and in 2006 ran unsuccessfully for governor. He was defeated in the Democratic primary by state treasurer Phil Angelides, who went on to lose to Arnold Schwarzenegger.

Republican Meg Whitman was born on August 4, 1956, on Long Island, New York, and graduated from Princeton University and Harvard Business School. She served as an executive in the Walt Disney Company, DreamWorks, Procter & Gamble, and Hasbro before becoming the CEO of eBay in 1998. When she arrived, the company had thirty employees and four million dollars in annual revenue; when she left in 2008, eBay had grown to more than fifteen thousand employees and eight billion dollars in annual revenue.

Over the years, many students of California have argued that it is really two states—Northern and Southern California. But Whitman's, Poizner's, and Brown's strategists and their colleagues had long realized that politically the divide was really between eastern California and western California. While "Yes We Can" Obama bumper stickers can be found in Modesto and "Impeach Obama" signs can be found in San Francisco, the coast is primarily Democratic, and the interior is mostly Republican, as pointed out by Lockyer. The two wealthy Silicon Valley hopefuls therefore had to win the votes of a Republican Party that had the bulk of its strength in the rural far northeast, the southeast inland empire, and the great Central Valley. The small-business people and farmers in those areas were a world removed from the corporate cultures that abided within the sleek glass headquarters of coastal Silicon Valley high-tech firms. Strategists for both Republican candidates had to find themes that would resonate with those voters to win primary votes.

In thrall to their strategists, both Poizner and Whitman unleashed incendiary strategies that were probably not the low points of twenty-first-century American politics so far but certainly came close. The campaigns were united in several assumptions. The first was that California voters, especially Republican voters, were convinced that Sacramento was ineffective, dysfunctional, and too expensive. Second was the assumption that Republicans knew in their hearts that Sacramento was not working because it was being run by sybaritic politicians, not businesspeople who knew how to wring the most value out of every hard-earned taxpayer dollar. The third strategic foundation was based on a supposed voter conviction that huge sums were being wasted on things that weren't really needed and that the state's budget ills could be cured by eliminating waste, fraud, and abuse. Finally, the strategists believed that Republicans had convinced themselves that liberals were allowing thousands of dusky illegal immigrants to swarm across the border from Mexico, which was causing some of California's economic ills in addition to being morally wrong.

Whitman and Poizner were not far apart on the issues, and that proved disastrous for the Republican Party. Both advocated tighter border security to guard against illegal immigration; both were against useless bureaucracy; and both wanted the state to be run on a more businesslike basis (even though businessman-actor Arnold Schwarzenegger had held the exact same positions and had seen his approval numbers plunge in the last year of his governorship). But because Poizner and Whitman had few major disagreements on the issues, and strategists had to find some way to differentiate between the two, the race immediately became personal.

Jarrod Agen, Poizner's communications director, said the nature of the Poizner-Whitman exchange over immigration rebounded to the benefit of Jerry Brown and the detriment of Republican hopes in the general: "If we'd gotten into the general, it would have been a policy debate between Steve and Governor Brown on the policy issue of immigration. Jerry Brown would have had one stance on immigration, Steve would have had the other. But it would have been a policy discussion on immigration.... What ended up happening, though, was immigration turned into a character issue and that is what ultimately hurts the Republican Party hugely is if immigration is a character issue."[3]

Duf Sundheim, the former Republican state party chairman, said the campaign was too nasty. "As Republicans, we were really concerned as the primary went on because since they were so close on the issues, it was really going to come down to a very nasty, personal fight," he told the University of California at Berkeley Institute of Governmental Studies postelection conference.[4]

Robert Naylor, a former Republican leader in the state Senate, was more blunt, declaring, "When the dust settled in the primary, the Whitman campaign was over."[5] Steve Glazer agreed, saying the savage primary between Whitman and Poizner, with Whitman flooding the airwaves with negative campaign spots, was instrumental in Brown's win. "It was a harsh campaign to win by fifty points," he said. "The primary made it more difficult to warm up to her in the general."[6]

Since Poizner was an incumbent Sacramento officeholder, Whitman's people felt they had an opening. Whitman ads accused Poizner of being "just another liberal Sacramento politician." That attack was aimed at scoring two points: Poizner was a "liberal"—something thought to be detested by Republican voters—and, since he was the state insurance commissioner, he was a "Sacramento politician," which made him an equally odious creature in another sense. "Steve Poizner—way more liberal than he says he is," one Whitman ad declared. She accused Poizner of receiving a 100 percent approval rating from Planned Parenthood and of donating ten thousand dollars to the 2000 Al Gore recount effort in Florida.

When she wasn't attacking Poizner, Whitman was promising California voters that she would clean up "the mess those politicians [presumably including Poizner and Jerry Brown] have made in Sacramento." She would end the deficit by getting rid of forty thousand state workers.[7] She said she was tough enough to stand up to the power of state employee unions. Her radio commercials were works of art, hitting on every single issue that focus groups and polling had told her campaign team would resonate with voters, especially denouncing a bloated state workforce and those "Sacramento politicians."

But if Whitman's Republican primary ads were deceptive and simpleminded, some of the Poizner ads were even more calculatedly contemptuous of Republican voters' intelligence. One particular low point was a May 17 television spot labeled "Adults Only," which said that under Whitman's leadership eBay had created a separate division solely devoted to pornography and that it had become one of the largest sites on the Internet. Another Poizner ad, more high-minded, accused Whitman of failing to vote for twenty-eight years. "She didn't vote for Ronald Reagan; she didn't vote for George Bush; she didn't vote for Pete Wilson," the ad's female voiceover said in accusatory tones.

Whitman also stood accused of "supporting the Obama amnesty plan for illegal immigrants" and of supporting, as well, Democratic senator Barbara Boxer. One of Poizner's ads featured him saving a car (representing California) from going over a cliff.

In retrospect, the ads look unbelievably phony and deceptive, and they were. But they were also designed to catch the attention of tired, overworked, and worried voters, not to meet the standards of pundits or political science professors. If a Republican voter could be left with a vague idea that Whitman was in favor of allowing hordes of Mexicans to cross the border and take Californians' jobs, that was all that was required. If an ad left a Republican voter with the impression that Whitman was a little soft on pornography, that, too, was effective, never mind nuance. Campaign media experts are aware of the "sleeper effect"—a voter may see an ad over and over again saying that Poizner is dishonest, crafty, and liberal, and dismiss it as mudslinging. But weeks later, in the polling booth, the harried voter may forget everything except that there was something about Poizner being dishonest— and vote against him and for Whitman.

As the campaigns proceeded, and the Brown camp looked on in (mostly) silent glee, it became clear that immigration was becoming the primary field of battle. Each candidate tried to outdo the other in rhetoric about cracking down on illegal immigration. Poizner, who had endorsed Proposition 187, a 1994 California law created by an initiative that denied education and health services to illegal immigrants but was ruled unconstitutional by a federal court, tried to outflank Whitman on the right by saying he supported an Arizona law that allowed police to investigate the immigration status of persons they stopped, announcing in a news release that he totally supported what they were doing and considered it good for the people of the state of Arizona.

By running ads that were certain to offend much of California's Latino population, both the Poizner and the Whitman campaigns appeared to effectively write off Latinos as potential supporters in a general election. Their strategists' operating principle was to surmount the immediate hurdle—the Republican primary—and worry about the general election later. A strategy of writing off the fastest-growing ethnic group in the state in hopes of appealing to Republican voters, however, does not appear to be an advantageous plan for a party's long-term political success. The Public Policy Institute of California reported that Latinos in 2010 constituted 18 percent of likely voters, an increase of 4 percent over the 2006 figure. The share of white voters went down during that same period—from 72 percent of likely voters to 66 percent.[8]

On June 8, Whitman blew past Poizner, winning 1,101,528 votes, or 64.2 percent, versus Poizner's 461,823 votes, or 26.9 percent. Because of the high-visibility, high-spending contest in the Republican primary, the turnout was almost as high as the Democrats' in sheer numbers and much higher in the percentage of registered voters who showed up at the polls. There were 2,377,079 total Republican votes, a 45.5 percent turnout, versus 2,395,287 total Democratic votes, a 31.7 percent turnout.[9]

Combined, Whitman and Poizner spent more than $127 million savaging each other, rewriting spending records. Whitman spent $99,866,607, or $65.29 per vote, and Poizner spent $27,621,775, or $43.64 per vote.[10] By contrast, Jerry Brown, with no significant opposition, spent $774,476 in his primary, or $.38 per vote.[11] Whitman's spending "created its own center of gravity," said Jim Bognet, Poizner's campaign manager.

Jerry Brown, meanwhile, had maintained a relatively low, money-saving profile, letting the two Republicans try to drive up each other's negatives. Brown had briefly faced a potential high-profile challenge in the Democratic primary from Gavin Newsom, the young mayor of San Francisco who had championed gay marriages and had the endorsement of former president Bill Clinton, a Brown opponent in the 1992 Democratic presidential primary. But Newsom's campaign failed to catch fire, and he abruptly withdrew, even before Brown had announced his own formal candidacy. In a statement, Newsom declared, "With a young family and responsibilities at city hall, I have found it impossible to commit the time required to complete this effort the way it needs to—and should be—done."[12] Newsom then found time to run for lieutenant governor instead. Against seven unknowns, Brown took 84.4 percent of the vote, with a low turnout of 31.7 percent.[13]

Over on the Republican side, the defeated Poizner did not immediately endorse Whitman, and when he did, it was not an exclusive. Poizner waited until September 7 to issue a six-paragraph statement through the state Republican Party that endorsed both Whitman and Republican senatorial nominee Carly Fiorina. "Our ticket is led by successful business women who know that if there is to be a viable public sector, there must be a vibrant private sector," Poizner said. "They know that the best, most reliable job is one created by the private sector. They understand that governments, like families and businesses, must live within their means."

The electorate that Jerry Brown and Meg Whitman contemplated in June 2010 was large—some seventeen million registered voters—and more sharply divided than it had been when the last gubernatorial election had been held, in 2006. Democrats had increased their registration by 3 percent, to 44.5 percent of registrants, while Republican registration had declined 3.5 percent, to 30.8 percent. Independents were up a slight 1.5 percent, to 20.2 percent of registrants. The Republicans had moved rightward. A survey by the Public Policy Institute of California showed that among likely Republican voters, 73 percent viewed themselves as conservative, up 8 percent from 2006. Among likely independent voters, the percentage regarding themselves as conservative had climbed five percentage points between 2006 and 2010, from 26 percent to 31 percent. There was also a slight shift in 2008 toward a preference for lower taxes and fewer services—48 percent preferring higher taxes and more services versus 43 percent preferring a decrease, compared with the 2006 totals of 49 percent preferring higher taxes and more services versus 44 percent preferring a decrease.[14]

The staff-size disparity between the Whitman and Brown campaigns was dramatic. Whitman had a staff of sixty-six at the beginning of the general election campaign, including a number of consultants, and that number almost doubled by the time the campaign was over. Brown's paid staff never exceeded eighteen, supplemented by volunteers.

The roots of Whitman's campaign, and to a somewhat lesser degree Brown's, can be traced to a style of stainless-steel politicking perfected in California and practiced by its politicians for more than seventy years. It began in 1933, when Clem Whitaker and Leone Baxter formed Whitaker & Baxter ("Campaigns Inc.") in San Francisco. In the Whitaker & Baxter formula, campaign utterances were packaged, tied into an overall strategy, and thoughtfully designed to resonate with the fears, ignorance, and prejudices of voters. Before anyone else did, Whitaker & Baxter achieved success by realizing that the average voter did not want to be educated but wanted rather to be entertained. Campaigns Inc. melded advertising, public relations, and, whether they knew it or not, sociology into a nuts-and-bolts operation designed to win.

David McCuan, a political scientist at Sonoma State University who is writing a book on the firm, says Whitaker & Baxter's influence can be felt into the twenty-first century because of what today's political gurus learned from them: "They worked BOTH sides of the aisle.... Those they defeated in one election often hired them in subsequent elections. They, in a word, made Karl Rove, James Carville, Lee Atwater, and so many others. Whitaker & Baxter served as a bridge from the torchlight parades and party activities of yore to the modern-day sophistication of today's social media politics blending media, message, and then repeat. Selling politics and selling shampoo were inexorably linked forever."[15]

Jerry Brown had learned the California lessons of media, message, and repeat well over the years and used them in all his campaigns, including the 2010 gubernatorial effort. His message to the voters was disciplined, clear, and winning. Whitman waged a campaign that adhered to the Whitaker & Baxter formula even more slavishly—or tried to—but she lost, probably because she and her advisers didn't know when to stop.

With a huge war chest and a candidate who had never run for public office before, Whitman's people did what campaign textbooks advised: use the money to buy as much television and radio as possible, and limit public exposure to carefully controlled events with little give-and-take with reporters. The idea was to keep absolute control over the campaign message, Whitaker & Baxter style, and limit the possibility of a gaffe from an inexperienced candidate. Whitman's public appearances were mostly at events sponsored by her campaign. The tactic outraged political reporters, but their protests were met with indifference from Whitman's campaign strategists. Brown, with less money, had to appear at events sponsored by outside organizations. That limited his ability to be a full-throated, red-meat Democrat, but among independents, that could be seen as an advantage.

Awash with money and with Poizner out of the way, Whitman hardly paused in her television barrage, seeking to set the campaign dialogue early on and define the seventy-two-year-old Brown as a weary old pol with a history of failure. She unleashed wave after wave of attacks on Brown, putting his campaign on the defensive.

Speaking at the annual Women's Conference in Long Beach on October 26, Brown offered to pull his "reasonably defined" negative campaign spots and run only positive ads if Whitman would pull hers. "If we do it together, no problem," he said in response to a question from moderator Matt Lauer, a coanchor of NBC's *Today* show. The Whitman campaign refused, saying it was necessary to make Brown's record known to voters. The Brown camp issued news release after news release defending against the attacks. A typical news release headline was "Desperate and Flailing, Whitman Throws Kitchen Sink, Oven and Blender at Brown."[16]

Even though Brown's campaign was forced onto the defensive by the sheer volume of the Whitman attacks, it never went underwater for long. He won the endorsements of the *San Francisco Chronicle*, the *Los*

Angeles Times, the *Sacramento Bee,* and the *San Jose Mercury-News,* the last of which said in a glowing editorial, "Jerry Brown offers California exactly what it needs in its next governor: a mature politician who can get things done in Sacramento and who brings good ideas, strong principles and a reputation for telling the truth."[17]

To remedy the anti-immigration sentiment so prevalent in the Republican primary, Whitman started running ads on Spanish-language radio and television stations. It did little good. *La Opinion,* the state's leading Spanish-language newspaper, endorsed Brown, declaring in an editorial, "California is at a crossroads. Our state's future is threatened by the gigantic budget deficit, by a series of crises from the pension system to the prison system, and by the needs facing both education and infrastructure. To address this challenge, we need an experienced person capable of battling all the forces vying for power. Jerry Brown is the right person for the office of governor at this time."[18]

On August 3, Whitman ran into trouble when she opened a campaign office in heavily Latino East Los Angeles. A crowd of a hundred protestors with picket signs shouted and banged drums. Whitman said the protests had been arranged by Democratic operatives. Sheriff's deputies had to clear a way for her to exit after brief remarks on schools and job creation.

Brown, with twenty-three million dollars on hand, remained mostly silent, conserving his resources. The Brown campaign early on had only a smattering of union-sponsored anti-Whitman television and radio ads, causing some Democrats to worry that Whitman would overwhelm Brown and define the issues while he was silent. But Brown preferred to keep his funds in reserve until the last stages of the campaign, since he could not hope to match Whitman's firepower. "She's advertising every day, and I gotta wait because I don't have the same kind of money. I'm not a billionaire," Brown told an interviewer on Los Angeles television station KTTV.[19]

Brown's people also had hopes that the Whitman campaign would strangle itself on its own huge supply of dollars. Glazer told reporters after the election that his greatest single fear was that Whitman would "go dark," with no television after the primary, not start advertising again until Labor Day, and thereby give voters some relief after the nastiness of the primary. But the Whitman barrage went on unabated. In the minds of some strategists not involved in the campaigns, Whitman became the woman who wouldn't get off people's television sets.

Overshadowing the campaigns was the state's fiscal crisis. California's economy had suffered because of the national recession, and on November 19, 2009, the legislative analyst's office said the state's budget would have a projected 2010 deficit of nearly $21 billion. Because of what it called California's "painfully slow economic recovery," the analyst's office boosted that estimate to $25.4 billion by November 10, 2010, just a few days after Brown won the election. That total was 29 percent of the total state general fund budget.

During the campaign, Brown said that he would not raise taxes to solve the crisis without voters' approval. "No new taxes without a vote of the people," he declared over and over again. He said he would help create five hundred thousand clean-energy jobs and would speed up permitting for wind- and solar-power plants. He said he favored sales tax reductions for businesses that buy manufacturing equipment and that he would ask voters whether to cut programs or raise taxes if lawmakers couldn't agree.

Whitman said she would solve the situation by bringing businesslike practices to state government, slashing payrolls and waste along with cutting bureaucratic red tape to unleash the economic power of the state's businesses. She said she would cut taxes, including capital gains, and reduce regulations to create two million jobs. She vowed to cut spending on welfare, negotiate lower pension benefits for existing workers, and put future employees into a 401(k)-like savings plan to trim state spending.

Ironically, the politician who, like no other, had blended idealism and ambition throughout his career told voters this time around that at this stage in his life—age seventy-two—he had no ambitions beyond repairing California. He styled himself as an experienced hand at the helm, as someone wise to the devious ways of politicians in Sacramento and prepared to handle them on behalf of the people. In a year when incumbents suffered nationally, Brown won by touting his experience. In addition, voters had been targeted by so many Whitman television commercials that when the relatively poor Brown campaign finally went up with its television ads, he somehow appeared to be refreshingly new—a relief from Whitman. Even Jim Brulte, another former state Senate Republican leader who became a political consultant-strategist, said that because of Whitman's overexposure, Brown, who was governor when Brulte was in high school, was the fresh new face.[20]

Brown was also helped by an amazing decision on the part of the Whitman high command to accuse him of being a tax-and-spend liberal. That gambit ignored what Californians knew about Jerry Brown if they knew anything: he was a skinflint in both his personal and his political life. In retrospect, it is astonishing that managers of a major political campaign had so little feeling for an electorate that they would employ an accusation so disconnected from voter perceptions. The approach was the result of formulaic thinking—Brown was a Democrat, so let's do the traditional thing and paint him as a tax-and-spend liberal. Brown's campaign manager, Glazer, defended the Whitman campaign strategy, however, saying it was not as inept as has been painted. "It's a simplistic view," he said. "Remember, they were *ahead* on Labor Day. They were winning in a Democratic state. It's impossible to say they ran a disastrous campaign."[21]

A tradition in politics is that the candidate's relatives, especially the spouse, create problems for professional campaign managers. Anne Gust was a dramatic exception, said Glazer. "It has sometimes been difficult in campaigns, but not this time. No one has a better relationship with Jerry than her. The problem in any campaign is 'how do you get the most out of the candidate—how do you make sure that the candidate performs at his or her best?' And that's what she did."[22]

Another somewhat amorphous factor in Brown's favor was his deft tongue. As Mario Cuomo once remarked, "You campaign in poetry; you govern in prose."[23] Whitman campaigned in prose; her campaign rhetoric was never lyrical. While her radio commercials were well designed, her speeches were prosaic compared with Brown's idealistic and more personally genuine style. Whitman's campaign reeked of pragmatism and anger, because all the information her strategists possessed indicated, accurately, that Californians were worried and uncertain about the future. It was a logical tactic. But Brown's campaign tapped into a deeper chord. Despite his onetime calls to lower expectations, for the millions of older Californians, who habitually voted in higher-than-average percentages, his name conjured up, factually or not, memories of a happier, burgeoning state that was on its way every day to further greatness. The millions more California voters who had no real memory of the Brown political dynasty nonetheless gravitated toward Brown because, formidable eyebrows and severe personal style aside, he still seemed to be a more genuine person than the careful construct that was Meg. Perhaps also the faint aura of past idealistic stances and actions lingered, but to the millions of voters who made decisions on the basis of their gut reactions, he seemed more in tune with what they wanted in a chief executive.

In their first face-to-face debate on September 28 at the University of California's Davis campus, Whitman went on the attack, declaring, "The labor unions and Jerry Brown have been joined at the hip for 40 years. Putting Jerry Brown in charge of negotiating with the labor unions around pensions, around how many people we have in state government, is like putting Count Dracula in charge of the blood bank."

"As far as unions, I'm the only governor that ever vetoed the pay raises for all public employees," Brown replied. "I did it once. I did it twice. I'll do it again if I have to."[24]

Whitman said spending her own money on her campaign made her independent of special interests—unlike Brown, who would be indebted to public employee unions. "I have invested a lot of my own money in this campaign," Whitman said. "I don't think you can buy elections. I think Californians are too smart."

Onlookers afterward thought that Whitman performed credibly, sticking to her preplanned talking points and responses and proving herself a good student of her handlers. Brown was looser, more informal, self-deprecating, and seemed to be having a good time. Whitman seemed determinedly cheerful.

In an October 2 debate at California State University, Fresno, sponsored by Univision, the Spanish-language television network, Whitman sought to repair the damage her primary campaign did to the potential Latino vote. She reminded the audience that she had not favored the Arizona law. She said she would revive California's economy and that would mean more opportunity for Latinos. "I can really deliver for Latinos.... I can deliver on jobs and education. I know more about the needs of small business."[25]

Whitman attacked Brown's record as mayor of Oakland, claiming that "crime soared" during his tenure. The claim was not accurate. Between the time Brown took office and the time he left, the number of crimes reported to police had declined by more than 13 percent from the year before he came into office. The number of murders did soar— from 72 in 1998 to 145 in 2006, according to the FBI's Uniform Crime Reports. The rise in murders, however, was more than offset by drops in rapes, assaults, larceny, and burglaries, creating an overall decline.

But all of the charges and countercharges, the heavy advertising, and the contrasting strategies fell aside in the wake of Nickygate. While Whitman sought to keep on the offensive throughout the campaign, she suddenly found herself on the defensive when Los Angeles attorney Gloria Allred charged that Whitman had continued to employ a maid, Nicky Díaz Santillán, when she knew the maid was an illegal immigrant and fired her only when she decided to run for governor. With the tearful ex-employee of Whitman at her side, Allred told a news conference the maid had been made to feel "exploited, disrespected, humiliated, and emotionally and financially abused."[26]

Whitman's attorney, Tom Hiltachk, told reporters that the maid had filled out all the requisite forms for employment, including immigration forms that stated under penalty of perjury that she was a lawful resident.

As a Republican, Whitman had already started the race with a disadvantage among Hispanics. Proposition 187, prohibiting illegal immigrants from receiving social services such as public education and health care, had saved Republican governor Pete Wilson's 1994 reelection campaign (against Jerry Brown's sister, Kathleen), but resentment of it among Hispanics proved to be a handicap for future Republican candidates. In addition, Whitman had opposed the DREAM Act, allowing permanent residency to illegal immigrants meeting certain conditions, and she did not want to allow the children of illegal immigrants to attend public institutions of higher education under any circumstances. She had said repeatedly during the primary that she would be "tough as nails" on illegal immigration.

After the Allred news conference, Whitman tried lamely to turn the situation to her advantage, declaring at the CSU, Fresno, debate: "Jerry, you know, you should be ashamed. You and your surrogates put her deportation at risk, you put her out there and you should be ashamed for sacrificing Nicky Diaz on the altar of your political ambitions."

Brown called the charge "incredible," adding, "You have blamed her, blamed me, blamed the left, blamed the unions, but you don't take accountability and you can't be a leader unless you're willing to stand on your own two feet and say, yeah, I made a mistake and I'm going on from here." Both candidates ducked the moderator's question as to whether they would take a lie detector test.

In the end, none of it mattered very much. The combination of favorable demographics and voter registration with the Whitman campaign's ineptitude was too much. Brown won an overwhelming victory, capturing 5,428,458 votes, or 53.8 percent, over Whitman's 4,127,371, or 40.9 percent. Total voter turnout was 10,300,392, slightly more than 59 percent of registered voters.[27] Brown won the remarkable campaign in what was the most expensive nonpresidential race in American history. Whitman's campaign spending reports showed she spent $178.5 million, with $144 million of that total coming from her own pocket. By contrast, Brown spent $36.7 million.[28]

Republican and Democratic strategists not allied with either campaign and political reporters seemed to agree afterward that Whitman's loss was due to two factors: first, Brown's campaign was brilliant while her campaign was inept, with her strategists unable to see beyond the dollar signs, and, second, California's demographics made it tough for any Republican to win a statewide race regardless. Conservative columnist Debra Saunders, like Lockyer, thought it was probably all in the demographics, presciently telling readers a few days before voters went to the polls, "In the punditry biz, we have a tendency to overplay the importance of campaigns. In California, 44 percent of registered voters are Democrats and 31 percent are Republicans. In a wave year that sends Republicans to the polls while Democrats stay home, the tide could propel some Republicans into statewide office. Any other year, the Democratic primary winner has to really mess up to lose in November."[29]

Brown did not mess up. His campaign was disciplined, nimble, frugal, focused, and demonstrated a feeling for California politics missing from the blunderbuss Whitman campaign. Some analysts argued that voters felt Whitman suffered because she hadn't "paid her dues" by serving in any lower elected office before trying for the top job. But neither Ronald Reagan nor Arnold Schwarzenegger had served in elected public office before running, and neither had suffered electorally because of it.[30] However, both were familiar faces to voters before beginning their campaigns, whereas Whitman, politically speaking, had come out of nowhere. Illogically or not, to many voters her candidacy seemed presumptuous.

"Jerry supplied the comfort level that voters needed. Jerry hit just the right tone," said Robert Naylor, the former state Senate Republican leader. "The most brilliant line of the campaign was 'at this stage in my

life.' 'At this stage of my life' was genius."[31] Republican Brulte said
Brown ran "a picture perfect campaign."[32] He added that Brown had
also adroitly managed to use the attorney general position to consistently create favorable headlines for himself—a use-the-office-
to-advantage Brown strategy that dated back to 1969.

In their defense, Whitman's strategists realized that they had little
going for them besides money. The demographics were grim, and their
candidate had started as an unknown; why not exploit the breathtaking
monetary advantage they had to its fullest extent? Critics with 20–20
hindsight, however, would argue that they did not exploit it as effectively as they might have. "Campaigns need to be focused and when
you have that many big-name, big-money political consultants telling
you what to do, it's hard to keep your campaign focused on just one
theme, just one message," said the UC San Diego political science
professor Thad Kousser.[33] Glazer disagreed with the ineptitude charge,
arguing that the Whitman campaign was not as unfocused and
scattershot as some had suggested. "It was not scattershot at all. Most of
it was behind three ads," he said.[34]

Brown's victory was remarkable not only because he overcame an
opponent with vastly more money to spend but also because he and his
fellow Democratic candidates won in what was otherwise a Republican
election cycle. Republicans nationally gained sixty-three seats in the
House, six in the U.S. Senate, and picked up five governorships. In
California, Democrats had a firewall against the Republican triumphs
elsewhere across the nation. They won the governorship, lieutenant
governorship, and the offices of attorney general, state controller, state
insurance commissioner, and state treasurer. All Democratic House
candidates won, and the Democrat incumbent Barbara Boxer won
reelection to the U.S. Senate over Republican Carly Fiorina.

California had once again proved it was its own idiosyncratic place.
In a year that was rough nationally for incumbents, the idealistic, ambitious, and opportunistic Jerry Brown, the most "incumbent" politician
in California, had again proved he knew what would work and what

wouldn't work with California voters, no matter what might be happening elsewhere. The son of a governor, the most experienced major politician in California, was the fresh new face.

And then, when most people his age were well into retirement and some were contemplating hip replacements, Jerry Brown faced the daunting prospect of putting his unhappy, uncertain, and perhaps ungovernable state back on track.

CHAPTER EIGHT

Difficult Choices

Wherever I look, I see difficult choices.
   Jerry Brown, January 31, 2011, state of
   the state address

It was not always articulated precisely, but from taxicab drivers in Long Beach to computer programmers in Silicon Valley, there was a question on the minds of Californians as they and their governor entered the second decade of the twenty-first century: Can we ever get this end-of-the-rainbow place back on track? Jerry Brown and his constituents had little to cheer about. The Golden State was tarnished. Its economy was limping, its people were uncertain, and its deeply polarized politics resembled theology more than civics.

Poll after poll showed heavy majorities believing their state was in decline. The Field Poll reported in September 2010 that only 12 percent of respondents thought California was moving in the right direction, while 81 percent thought it was headed in the wrong direction. In February 2011, Californians rated their quality of life at its lowest point in two decades, with only 39 percent of respondents considering the state "one of the best places to live." In 1985, by contrast, 78 percent had given their state its highest rating as a place to live.[1] People were worried about the economy, and had reason to be. In June 2001, California had a seasonally adjusted unemployment rate of 5.2 percent. Ten years later, in June 2011, the unemployment rate had more than doubled, to 11.8 percent.[2] The respected Anderson Forecast released in June 2011 by the University of California at Los Angeles predicted an unemployment rate averaging 11.7 percent during the year amid "a continuing period of slow growth."

Along with its economic difficulties, the state had a governance structure that did not meet the needs of the twenty-first century. The overarching reality was that Californians did not trust their Legislature. In March 2010, the Legislature's approval rating was 9 percent among likely voters. The Legislature did better a little more than a year later, when its approval rating among likely voters soared to 17 percent, according to a survey from the Public Policy Institute of California (PPIC).

The Legislature created by the California Constitution signed at Monterey's Colton Hall in 1849 has seen its relevance eroded over the past thirty-plus years. A 2011 survey by the PPIC showed that voters believed they could make better decisions via the initiative process than could their elected representatives in the Capitol. "Californians not only think it's a good thing they can make policy at the ballot box, but six in 10 adults (62%) and likely voters (62%) also think that decisions made this way are probably better than decisions made by the governor and state Legislature," the PPIC reported. Californians' mistrust has been constantly reinforced by political campaigns that every two years attack the supposedly evil and profligate ways of "Sacramento politicians." Thad Kousser, the UC San Diego professor of political science introduced earlier, said that in addition to the constitutionally embedded three branches of government—executive, legislative, and judicial—California has a fourth branch: the initiative.[3]

It has not always been thus. The years of Earl Warren and Pat Brown saw a partnership between business and state government, with the state providing the freeways, education, and the giant California Water Project, with which business and agriculture were able to expand and flourish. Californians could depend on the state to do its best to help.

That all ended with the election of Ronald Reagan, who in essence campaigned against Sacramento and all that went on there. State government within the space of a few years changed from partner to scorned adversary. Reagan, an amiable, wealthy movie star and a political junkie, was brilliantly presented as a citizen who, with a sigh, felt it his duty to leave civilian life and take up the onerous burdens of public office. Following student unrest at Berkeley and riots in Los Angeles, his backers had sensed that voters were ready to become resentful. They took full advantage of it.

There are a number of reasons why the California Legislature has been held in increasing contempt, even post-Reagan. Term limits have removed much of the Legislature's institutional memory and ended the reign of longtime legislators who had developed expertise in one or more subject areas. These limits have also led to newly arrived lawmakers sometimes finding themselves heading committees or taking even more important positions. Democrat John Perez, for instance, became a member of the Assembly in December 2008 and took over as speaker of the Assembly on March 10, 2010, only fourteen months after he had arrived.

The idea that legislators would fulfill a civic duty for a limited time in Sacramento—à la the Reagan myth—and then return to the insurance agency in Tracy or the hardware store in Glendora has proven to be mostly a fairy tale. Lawmakers have spent their time instead plotting ways of somehow, somewhere, staying in elected office. There is constant scrambling, if not for reelection, then for election to another office higher on the political ladder, or sometimes even lower on it.[4] The result has been less time for thoughtful legislation and more posturing.

Furthermore, for decades the now-abandoned two-thirds majority required to adopt a state budget had enabled a minority of Republicans in either the Assembly or the state Senate to block passage at least temporarily, causing embarrassing, well-publicized, and harmful delays. The habit of failing to approve a budget until well past the deadline damaged the state's fiscal credibility, along with threatening hardship for vendors, state employees, and the supermarkets and shoe stores that counted on them as customers. In the past, the Republicans who held out on the adoption of a budget had been wooed back into line by promises from governors or legislative leaders to provide bridges, highway interchanges, or more money for law enforcement in their districts. That cooperation did not happen, however, until newspapers up and down the state had days of headlines shouting "Crisis!" while editorialists scolded lawmakers for not doing their jobs. It all reinforced the idea that the Capitol was infested with irresponsible people not deserving of public trust.

The supermajority requirement was ended when voters approved Proposition 25 in November 2010, giving Democrat Brown a better chance at getting his proposed state budgets approved on time. The proposition's chances of passage were enhanced by a provision that lawmakers would not be paid for every day that a state budget went unpassed beyond the June 15 deadline. Without that appeal to populist sentiment, junking the supermajority requirement is much less likely to have won approval, its civic virtue notwithstanding.

The Legislature has also been viewed by voters as ineffectual because any attempt to address a major issue has frequently proved harmful to one or more powerful interest groups. Although special interests cannot always get their most visible and important bills passed, they can usually kill visible and important bills put forth by other, competing interest groups. The result has been LobbyLock, to use the phrase of the onetime California Medical Association lobbyist Jay Michael. Given LobbyLock, frustrated special interests with ample financial resources turn to the initiative process to get what they want, making the Legislature increasingly irrelevant to major public policy decisions.

Finally, legislators require money, frequently in the hundreds of thousands of dollars, to run their reelection campaigns, and the best place to get it is from lobbyists. Influencing twenty-two hundred legislators and staffers in Sacramento is an industry; interest groups spent

$539 million lobbying state government during the 2009–10 legislative session. Sacramento lobbyists themselves are part of a big business: The secretary of state's office reported in January 2012 that total payments to California lobbyists amounted to a stunning, and record, $285 million during 2011. That was a jump of 6 percent over the previous year and a bit more than the previous record of the nearly $282 million spent in 2008. When a lobbyist and an ordinary citizen are waiting to see a legislator, the chances are the lobbyist is going to get in first to present his or her case if the legislator wishes to continue in office, and they almost always do. That political fact of life contributes to a Capitol culture seen as remote from the concerns of ordinary citizens, who lack the ability to make large campaign contributions, and it intensifies the sense that Sacramento is an arcane and foreign place.

There has been hope that a revamped primary system can produce a legislature with less stonewalling partisanship. The top two vote-getters now face each other in the general election regardless of party. Legislative district lines have been drawn by an impartial citizens' commission,[5] rather than by the legislators themselves, but no one is sure this will work. Doubters point out that voters tend to cluster into like-minded communities, so in many areas of strong Democratic or Republican voter majorities, the main contest would still come in the primaries anyway, regardless of redrawn, less incumbent-friendly districts.

Doug Willis, who for thirty years covered the California Legislature and politics for The Associated Press, has been one of the doubters, declaring,

> A better hope is that the new top-two primaries could produce a few general election races in both Republican and Democratic districts between moderate and Tea Party Republicans and between moderate and ultraliberal Democrats. I doubt if any of these changes, either individually or all together, are going to produce an overnight shift from gridlock to a new golden age of compromise and bipartisan good will. But if there is just a small infusion of a desire to compromise it might begin to change the Legislature's poisoned atmosphere of distrust and demagoguery.[6]

Willis argued that if there is such a change, Brown—even in the face of his unsuccessful 2011 negotiations with Republicans over allowing voters to decide on tax extensions—will be able to revive the diplomatic skills he demonstrated more than three decades earlier, when he shuttled between groups to hammer out California's farm labor law. "He has the potential to prove government can still be made to work successfully," Willis said. Nonetheless, in 2012 there was even hope among some Democrats that there could be a two-thirds Democratic majority in both legislative houses after 2012, presumably making Brown's life easier.

Those advocating big changes in California governance have said it is necessary because the eighteenth-century ideas of the Founding Fathers are no longer a good fit for twenty-first-century California. While they had important differences among themselves, the Founding Fathers all had a common culture. There were no Asians, Hispanics, Samoans, and certainly no African Americans among them; they were all white male landowners, so the checks and balances—the diffusion of power—worked. "Transpose that structure to a state as big and diverse as California, with many cultures. When you apply that structure to this kind of society—hey, folks, it doesn't work," said longtime *Sacramento Bee* columnist Dan Walters.[7]

The advocates of change can be divided into two groups—incrementalists, who believe that gradual, step-by-step change, such as redrawn legislative districts and top-two primaries, will get the job done over time; and the Big Bang advocates, who would like to see a constitutional convention convened to make wholesale changes. The Big Bangers have faced an uphill task. Because of the peculiarities of the state constitution, a difficult two-step initiative process is required to create a constitutional convention. The first initiative would allow citizens to call a convention on their own, without requiring permission from the Legislature to do so. The second initiative, which could appear on the same ballot, would actually call the convention and specify its duties and any restrictions on its scope.

In late 2011, events favored the incrementalist approach. The last effort to call a constitutional convention had foundered in early 2010, when Repair California, the organization sponsoring the drive for a convention, ran out of money, thus postponing, if not killing, the prospects for a convention. California Forward, a separate reform organization, has pushed for legislation that would, among other things, establish a two-year budget-writing process that would require lawmakers and governors to adopt more long-range fiscal thinking, allow programs to be created only if funding is found, evaluate state agencies against a set of objectives, and give local governments more power to raise their own revenue and provide services. California Forward's plans did not call for initiatives that would create a constitutional convention.

Jerry Brown: incrementalist or Big Banger? Given his temperament and background, he's an incrementalist, said Walters:

> He wants to rescue the Brown name. He wants to undo the reputation he once had—Moonbeam and all that—and I think it's a sincere desire. But I don't know if he wants to throw it all on the table and take that kind of a chance [of getting behind a wholesale Big Bang restructuring of California governance and then failing]. The question is, is Jerry willing to look into the abyss and say, "Things have to change"? He's not the person to do that. Maybe in an intellectual way, he understands it, but I don't think he has the guts to do it.[8]

The University of Southern California's Sherry Bebitch Jeffe, one of the more acute observers of California and its politics, pointed out that, regardless of his desires, Brown has fewer dollars at his disposal and must deal with a polarized legislature. "This Jerry Brown is far more hampered than the Jerry Brown who took office in 1974," she said. "I don't see any governor being able to accomplish big, bold projects. There's not a whole heck of a lot any governor can do, given the situation—just look at the terrain."[9]

As Brown began his third term in January 2011, he was indeed a far different person from the one he had been nearly thirty years earlier and in a far different terrain from the one existing then. His eight years as mayor of Oakland had made him more pragmatic, less interested in pursuing intellectually stimulating projects with questionable immediate value, and more philosophical about the fact that other people had ideas and priorities that he would have earlier dismissed as idiotic.

"He's a little softer around the edges," said Doug Faigin, the former press secretary. "He's still got that fire, the concerns, but at the same time I think he's been able to expand his view of life. He's more aware of the concerns of the people around him. Earlier, he was so intent on what he was doing. Being involved with Anne for so long has been great for him."[10]

Bebitch Jeffe agreed: "I see him as mellowing quite a bit over the years. The sharp edges that were once there are gone. He is no longer Governor Moonbeam. He's learning that there are parameters and that he pretty much has to stay within those parameters. He's far more grounded. Anne has been good for him. Sutter Brown [the Browns' corgi] has been good for him."[11]

When Brown was governor between 1975 and 1983, he operated with a legislature that was open to compromise, with Republicans and Democrats usually finding some way to resolve their differences, even if unhappily, on a piece of legislation. Now it was different, but there was a question as to whether Brown fully realized how different the Capitol had become, even though he had spent the previous four years in statewide elected office as attorney general.

The most-cited example of how disconnected Brown had become by the start of his new administration was his decision to negotiate with Republicans in an effort to close the gap in the state's finances, not realizing how ideologically rigid Republicans had become. Brown spent several frustrating months attempting to get legislative approval for a statewide vote on extending some taxes so that the state budget could be balanced without gimmicks. Republicans stonewalled him, he said in numerous interviews, and he was not successful. He was given no arrival-in-office honeymoon. As in past years, a state budget that was finally adopted depended on chimerical revenue increases that might or might not appear, but probably would not. But the budget was approved on time.

Brown himself seemed to agree that he was unprepared for the deep polarization of the Capitol. "What is shocking to me coming back here after 27 years is the hyper-partisan quality of debate," Brown told Michael J. Mishak of the *Los Angeles Times*. "There's not a thread of common purpose."[12]

It shouldn't have been all that surprising, said Walters: "The truth is the place is so much different now than it was then—much different. Much, much different. Jerry should have known that," Walters argued. Walters added that governors—all governors—arrive with an inordinately grandiose vision of their influence. "Politicians like to think, 'I'm here—things will change.' Well, things don't change.... This is a very, very complex society. It's difficult to make public policy. That means that with any issue—ANY issue—there are multiple stakeholders.... It's very, very easy to stop something. To get it through, you have to tweak it to satisfy all the stakeholders, and by the time you've satisfied all the stakeholders, you have a monster."[13]

Barbara O'Connor, emeritus professor of political communication at California State University, Sacramento, said the intellectually agile Brown was nonetheless adjusting to the new reality: "Now he's regrouping. He knows the way now is, he's going to have to force it down people's throats. It runs against his core. He's pivoting from 'I can persuade them' to 'I have to force it down people's throats.' It will be much more hardball. I think he can do it. I think he will get there. He can do that better than anyone on the planet. Given his skill set, if he takes a deep dive on something, he can persuade people."[14]

Brown's 2010 campaign manager, Steve Glazer, the cool and analytical strategist who has more than once seen Brown meet daunting political challenges, believes that Brown's inherent intelligence—his ability to take that deep dive—will see him through. "He will approach the challenges the way he has in the past," said Glazer. "He will develop an approach that will make him the smartest person in the room on the substance of any issue. He commits to a thoroughness to the issue—an appreciation for a wide range of perspectives. You can see there is a pattern of intellectual application to these problems. It's like learning Latin—if you know the roots, you know the language. He has a rigor of analysis greater than any I have known in my professional life. He does require rigor in his staff."[15]

Darrell Steinberg, the president pro tem (leader) of the California Senate, agreed that Brown does engage intellectually with whatever he's required to study or whatever captures his attention. "He's unique. It's taken me a little while to get used to him—engage with him," Steinberg said. "If you ask him to look at an issue, he will take the time. I asked him to take a another look at an education bill I carried that I heard he wasn't too fond of, and he spent four hours that very day studying it."[16]

Jerry Brown in his third term is indeed a different person from the Jerry Brown of thirty-plus years ago, but some traits remain, said Jerry Roberts, the former political editor, editorial page editor, and managing editor of the *San Francisco Chronicle.*

> I think his temperament is significantly different than when I covered him as governor first time out (which actually was his second term). He's still sardonic, prickly, and intent on proving he's the smartest guy in the room. But he's also more candid, in public settings, than he was previously. The biggest example has been his championing of tax increases, even though with the caveat that they be tied to a public vote. I think he was an important part of beginning to change the national discussion of taxes— Democrats seem more emboldened, both in California and in Washington, to put the notion out on the table, which is quite different than the past thirty years; they haven't succeeded yet of course, but it feels like the narrative is beginning to change.... The other thing that's striking, that goes to the question of his background, is his absolute mastery of the details and nuances of policies and programs; he's been through this stuff so many times and at so many levels of government that it's almost impossible for anyone to get anything by him; I recall he had some kind of "what we should we do to fix California" roadshow shortly after winning this time

out and heard from some local officials in Southern California; I don't remember the details now, but some mayor or supervisor or something started complaining about the state not financing something for locals, and Brown went chapter and verse through the history of the program, which he may even have signed into law. When Phil (Trounstine) and I interviewed him in March or April of '09, which was his first big interview about the governor's race, I was struck by his comments about how there were "too many laws," in the way that it sort of broke him out of the "Got a problem? Here's a bill" mind-set of Sacramento. To some extent, of course, it's always been thus with his iconoclastic view of politics, but again during his first stretch as governor, he was more likely to point to something he'd done or sponsored legislatively as important solutions, and he now is much more skeptical that a lot of stuff that gets churned out of the Capitol has much value to people at all.[17]

In at least one respect Brown has not changed. He is still the master of the grand, headline-grabbing, symbolic gesture of frugality. A few days after his inauguration, he ordered forty-eight thousand state workers to turn in their cell phones, saying he wanted to cut in half the total of ninety-six thousand phones used by state employees. "It is difficult for me to believe that 40% of all state employees must be equipped with taxpayer-funded cell phones," Brown said in a statement. "The current number of phones out there is astounding." He said he was turning in his own phone as well. His office estimated the savings would amount to twenty million dollars.

Brown also eliminated the office of the secretary of education and eliminated funding for the state First Lady's office. He gave back nearly all the money that had been earmarked for the transition to his new administration.

Jerry Brown's history and temperament show him to be a man bold in some areas, cautious in others. During his first governorship, as we've seen, he appointed unprecedented numbers of women and minorities to high positions in state government, introduced collective bargaining for state employees, brought environmental concerns to the fore, and blazed a trail for farmworkers, using his gubernatorial bully pulpit to publicize their treatment in California's fields. He signed landmark legislation that gave farmworkers, too, collective bargaining rights. But while doing that, Brown ignored the plight of California's middle class, who were paying higher and higher property taxes. He sponsored no large, fundamental remake of a tax structure that threatened to drive some Californians from their homes, despite the manifest need. To be fair, the California Legislature, then regarded as one of the best in the nation, ignored the situation as well. Because of their collective neglect, Proposition 13 was put on the ballot and won easy approval from voters, who had grown more and more disgusted with Sacramento. Their contempt endured and grew through successive decades.

The intense budget negotiations behind closed doors meant that Brown maintained a mostly low profile during the first six months in office. He said he wanted to get the state's fiscal house in order before tackling any other major issues. Nonetheless, if he was not becoming a Big Banger, there were repeated signs of at least some stirring during the last half of 2011. Brown said during an August appearance in Fresno that he would support a ballot initiative in 2012 to raise more state revenue, although the exact nature of such an initiative was not specified. More jobs would come, Brown said, by generating confidence that California's finances were on sounder footing.

Surprisingly, he also told reporters in Fresno that he favors California's much-criticized hundred-billion-dollar high-speed rail project, a throwback to the think-big days of Pat Brown, designed to eventually connect San Francisco and Los Angeles in two and a half hours. Brown said he is "really getting into" the project, adding, "I'm doing the best I can to keep this train running."[18]

Brown also said he would have a plan for a peripheral canal or another way to move water through or around the Delta to Central Valley farms and Southern California sometime in 2013. He was waiting to see the outcome of the Delta Conservation Plan, which seeks to provide adequate water for agriculture and cities while meeting environmental concerns—a very tall order that depends on the willingness of stakeholders to compromise. And in a flat contradiction to his decades-earlier mantra about an "era of limits," Brown declared in Fresno, "I would like to be part of the group that gets America to think big again."[19]

Earlier, Brown acted like a state cheerleader in his January 31, 2011, state-of-the-state address. While he acknowledged, "Wherever I look, I see difficult choices," he went on to deliver a ringing endorsement of his native state, one that could have been delivered by Pat Brown:

> But I also see a bright future up ahead and a California economy that is on the mend....
>
> We have the inventors, the dreamers, the entrepreneurs, the venture capitalists and a vast array of physical, intellectual and political assets. We have been called the great exception because for generations Californians have defied the odds and the conventional wisdom and prospered in totally unexpected ways. People keep coming here because of the dream that is still California, and once here, their determination and boundless energy feeds that dream and makes it grow.[20]

Did all that mean that the former seminarian and apostle of austerity Jerry Brown is seeking to become head cheerleader for his native state? "No," said Barbara O'Connor, a Brown observer for thirty-five years. "He's interested in being the Messiah, meaning the savior. He knows exactly what he needs to do. He just needs to sell it. And he can do that better than anyone. He lived through what many people regard as California's Golden Age of the '50s and early '60s. His father was the architect of it. And now he's watching it being dismantled."[21]

But at that point there were no signs that Brown was moving to seek bold and fundamental reform of a governmental structure that was failing to meet the needs of the people, or that he was even interested in doing so. He appeared to be concentrating on being a prudent manager during difficult economic times, despite his occasional outbursts of Big Thinking. And despite his out-loud ruminations about high-speed rail and the declaration that he would unveil some sort of proposal attempting to solve California's perennial water problems in 2013, Democrats who want someday to become governor or senator began tossing veiled jabs at Brown during the summer of 2011, hinting that he was not doing enough to move the state forward.

Los Angeles mayor Antonio Villaraigosa, in an August speech before the Sacramento Press Club, challenged Brown to take on the third rail in California politics—revisions to popular Proposition 13. Under current provisions in the law, businesses are not reassessed as often as homes are, thereby escaping the escalation in assessed property value that produces correspondingly higher taxes for homeowners. Villaraigosa said Brown should push for a separation of assessments on businesses from homes so that business property would also reflect current property values:

> Governor Brown, I say, we need to have the courage to test the voltage in some of these so-called "third rail" issues, beginning with Proposition 13. We need to strengthen Prop. 13 and get it back to the original idea of protecting homeowners.
>
> Prop. 13 was never intended to be a corporate tax giveaway, but that is what it has become.... Not only have we suffered the long-term consequences of disinvestment in public education and public infrastructure Prop. 13 has had the unintended effect of favoring commercial property owners at the expense of homeowners.[22]

Gradually lifting the Proposition 13 cap for businesses could raise between $2.1 billion and $8 billion a year—money the state could invest in education and lower property taxes for homeowners, according to Villaraigosa's calculations.

A few days later, Brown rejected the idea during his appearance in Fresno, adding, however, "I certainly welcome the debate."[23]

And that caution is exactly what's wrong with Brown's approach, according to Walters. If Brown wants to make a real difference and leave a legacy of achievement, he must advocate for big change, Walters argued. "If you want to accomplish something, you've gotta get out and change the system. He's a smart guy, but he has his limits. He's not an original thinker. He's a synthesizer. He can't get his mind around the fact that this thing called California is different than it used to be." For one thing, Walters said, Brown must recognize that, unlike what happened in past years, there will be no dot-com upswing and no big dollars from the Pentagon to rescue the California economy. "It's difficult to do things in this state without some sort of artificial injection of capital," Walters said, and if the state is left to its own devices, there is no reason to think it will recover from the economic downtown in the foreseeable future.[24]

Brown himself has admitted the state suffers from a "governability crisis" but has displayed little interest in defusing it. "We're allocating the less here instead of handing out the more," Brown said in an interview. "There's a lot of work to be done not in just promoting new things but managing what's already on the table." He has argued that the state cannot afford ambitious policy ideas. He told Mishak of the *Los Angeles Times* he viewed himself as a fiscal caretaker, keeping a sharp eye on bills sent to his desk that involved spending money.[25]

George Skelton, the political columnist for the *Los Angeles Times*, argued that, contrary to the beliefs of many pundits, California remains a state that is governable. "Absolutely. It's a question of leadership," he said. Skelton argued that Brown should have negotiated a straight-up tax hike with Republicans in the Legislature, instead of negotiating whether to put a tax increase on the ballot. Failure to do that, Skelton said, was a major strategic blunder.[26]

A counterargument is that Brown, campaigning, thought the state needed to have a tax hike to bail it out of its fiscal crisis. But he couldn't campaign on a platform of "elect me, I'm for a tax hike." He chose instead to pave the way for a tax increase with a campaign slogan of "No tax hike without a vote of the people," and that required, as a first tactical move, negotiations with legislators about placing a tax increase on the ballot.

"Thirty years ago he preached the era of limits and now he's got it," said Peter Schrag, a former editorial page editor of the *Sacramento Bee*, columnist, and author of several well-regarded books on California and its problems. "Frankly, I don't think he cares all that much about making California into a great state again.... He doesn't like big institutions. A great state was his father's thing. The only things that might get his juices going are the growing social and economic gaps and the image of kids getting screwed, but so far he hasn't shown anything like it. Instead he's behaved very much like Obama, trying to get compromises with a cult of rigid ideologues."[27]

Former governor Gray Davis, who was Brown's first chief of staff, worried that Brown was perhaps letting his best opportunity for major achievement slide away early in his new term. "The first year is the best opportunity to make change," he said. "It's best to seize the moment."[28]

Even Republicans joined the call for Brown to become bolder: "The idea of a caretaker governor just doesn't cut it for a nation-state with a cosmic-size ego—especially when we see what other big-state governors are achieving, while our guv seems stuck in neutral," wrote Bill Whalen, a research fellow at Stanford's Hoover Institution and former speechwriter for Republican governor Pete Wilson, in an opinion piece in the *Sacramento Bee*.[29]

While Brown has faced criticism that he isn't thinking big enough, there also has been evidence that the three-time presidential candidate has not lost his fondness for the national political stage. He made an August appearance on CNN's *State of the Union* to give President Obama campaign advice.

Lieutenant Governor Gavin Newsom, who, like all lieutenant governors, hankers for the state's top job and was briefly a potential gubernatorial rival of Brown's, unveiled his own thirty-page jobs plan in August 2011, declaring that it "marks the beginning of a statewide conversation about how we can win again." The proposal, "AN ECONOMIC GROWTH AND COMPETITIVENESS AGENDA FOR CALIFORNIA," frantically titled with all caps, urges the consolidation of economic development agencies, the streamlining of business regulations, and an expansion of manufacturing. Almost immediately, Brown announced that he was appointing former Bank of America executive Michael E. Rossi as an unpaid state jobs czar. A Brown news release said Rossi would "streamline and invigorate the state's economic development infrastructure" and advise the governor on regulatory, legislative, and executive actions to stimulate job creation.

Kevin Starr, one of California's more insightful historians and certainly the best known, said Brown represents a fusion of liberal and conservative leanings that can be understood only in view of his background of growing up in blue-collar, idiosyncratic, open-minded, "high provincial" San Francisco in the '30s and '40s, coupled with his background as a Jesuit seminarian. Rather than through direct confrontation, Brown will seek to achieve his goals through indirection and negotiation, Starr said. Brown has a "temperamental disaffinity" for grand, empire-building adventures, Starr maintained, so "he will run a very minimalist, very prudent administration," and it would take a near-death experience economically or politically or both to move Brown off those moorings.[30]

Starr is probably right. Despite Brown's occasional utterances about high-speed rail, tackling the water problem, appointment of a jobs czar, and "the dream that is still California," there was a consensus among the most knowledgeable of California observers whom I contacted that Brown would not engage in a large-scale effort to remake his native state, crestfallen though it may be. Brown has limited faith in the ability of government to do that, and anyway such an effort is not in the nature of one who has preached the virtues of austerity all his life. In the unlikely event that Brown were ever to preside over the opening of a new freeway, the dedication would probably be accompanied by a Sufi chorus and a Brown speech emphasizing prudent speed and minimal consumption of gasoline.

A legacy of skinflint fiscal management during difficult economic times may not be thrilling to those who recall a California of golden new beginnings and Big Thoughts, where all things seemed to be possible, if not right around the corner. But it may be the best that can reasonably be expected of any governor, given the straitened circumstances of the early twenty-first century.

I would add one caveat to the mixture of thoughts seen above, however. On April 7, 2011, Jerry Brown became seventy-three years old. Despite his apparent superb physical condition, he took office as a man who by most definitions is elderly. With most of his life behind him, and presented with a last chance for glory in the history books, he may not be content to be regarded by future generations as a mere caretaker, an apostle of austerity, or a good manager. He is above all a politician—a thoughtful politician, but a politician nonetheless. And politicians of all stripes like to leave legacies beyond "he kept things on an even keel."

The most convincing evidence of that is Brown's persistence in talking up California's proposed high-speed rail system during the latter part of 2011 and early in 2012. Conceivably he could view it as his principal legacy. Skelton said that Brown does indeed view high-speed rail as his legacy. "He wants a legacy—he wants high-speed rail as his legacy," Skelton said. "That's New-Age stuff; it's groovy."[31]

Some evidence of legacy-yearning came in Brown's state-of-the-state address on January 18, 2012, when, in another cheerleader speech that again might have come from Earl Warren, Goodwin Knight, or Brown's father, he repeated his August 2011 endorsement of high-speed rail more emphatically and—in what certainly appeared to be a return to his Fresno utterances about Big Thinking—declared,

> California is still the land of dreams—as well as the Dream Act. It's the place where Apple, Intel, Hewlett-Packard, Oracle, QUALCOMM, Twitter, Facebook and countless other creative companies all began.
>
> It's home to more Nobel Laureates and venture capital investment than any other state. In 2010, California received 48 percent of U.S. venture capital investments. In the first three months of last year it rose even higher—to 52 percent. That is more than four times greater that the next recipient, Massachusetts. As for new patents, California inventors were awarded almost four times as many as inventors from the next state, New York....
>
> California also leads the nation in cleaning up the air, encouraging electric vehicles and reducing pollution and greenhouse gases. Our vehicle emissions standards—which have always set the pace—now have been adopted by the federal government for the rest of the country.[32]

Whether anything will come from Brown's retro-rhetoric remains a question. Much of the uncertainty rests on how much follow-through

Brown will demonstrate. Skelton said of Brown, "He's got a very short attention span," and in addition, Skelton said, Brown is unlikely to take any political chances: "He really doesn't do anything that's not good for him politically."

The situation in 2012 was different from that of 1958. Peter Schrag, the longtime and insightful observer of California's political scene, pointed out that Californians were used to bold infrastructure adventures fifty-five years ago but were not as favorably inclined in 2012: "In the days when Pat Brown was building—water systems, university campuses, freeways, schools, parks—there was still a powerful sense of common purpose, much of it left from World War II. Voters sometimes needed to be recalled to it, but it didn't need to be created, as it does now. That makes it hard for any latter-day governor to be Pat Brown."[33]

The speech and the August 2011 remarks in Fresno are nonetheless a marked departure from the "Era of Limits" mantra of Jerry Brown's first two terms as governor and could mark yet another iteration of California's quirky, unpredictable chief executive. There may yet be major initiatives—aimed at leaving California a different and better place, complete with a Jerry Brown project of some sort aimed at legacy building.

"He is now a much more practical governor now than maybe 30 years ago," said state senator Ted Lieu, a Democrat. "But he is still a dreamer. High-speed rail is very evocative and is one of those things that I think he would like to be part of his legacy."[34]

But all of the speculation, back-and-forth arguments, and suggestions for Jerry Brown's future course of action or inaction, legacy or lack of one, have been conducted by a tiny elite of knowledgeable people. Although most Californians say they follow the news of politics and government with some regularity, those of a growing minority have said they do not. The Field Poll reported in June 2011 that 25 percent of voters admitted that they follow governmental matters "only now and then" or "hardly at all." In 1979, the poll reported, only 16 percent of voters did not follow politics and government very closely.[35]

It has become clear that any large remake of California governance, no matter how badly needed, or whether begun by Brown or someone else, will come only as the result of an enormous, probably expensive, broad-brush public campaign designed to appeal to voters' mostly unarticulated fears and aspirations. Neither the governor nor the Legislature appears even remotely interested in leading the charge, and good-government groups lack the resources to mount their own campaign. If there is to be a movement for wholesale change, it will in all likelihood have to come from somewhere outside Sacramento.

O'Connor pointed to the Silicon Valley: "A large part of any remaining sense of California exceptionalism is in Silicon Valley and small businesses. It's driven by discrete groups. The Silicon Valley is emerging as a California thought leader, not just in technology, but the culture as well."[36] Steinberg, the state Senate leader, agreed with the general idea, declaring, "Major reforms come when elected officials work with outside groups." Wealthy Silicon Valley entrepreneurs, such as the Republicans Meg Whitman and Steve Poizner, along with the Democrat Steve Westly, have all run statewide campaigns and maintained an interest in matters beyond Internet commerce and the etching of smaller circuits on microchips.[37]

The ignorance and apathy of voters and the attempts of politicians to con and gull them have been central facts of politics in the United States for the last 175 years or more. It's not the voters' fault. They watch football on television, they mow the lawn, they take the kids to the park. They work hard, frequently at soul-numbing, sweaty jobs. They do their best in most areas of their lives, but their precious free time is not usually going to be devoted to a judicious consideration of who might be the next speaker of the Assembly or whether the state constitution should be revised. Going into that little canvas booth or filling out the mailed ballot once every two years or so is, for most, almost their only haphazard, direct contact with the political process. When they cast that vote, they are sending a plea to those enigmatic names in black typeface on the ballot: "Try to make things better for me somehow. At least don't screw it up any more than it is now."

The measure of an elected official in our land is how well, after the campaign and its deceptions, he or she tries to fulfill that mute hope—with honesty for the ignorant and uninterested as well as the knowledgeable and sophisticated.

Throughout his public life, Jerry Brown has tried to meet that test, but always on his own terms. He has sought ways to meet the aspirations of those who for reasons of race and gender have been shut out of mainstream California. He has wanted to make politics an instrument that connects voters with reality, an almost-unheard-of characteristic of anyone who wants to get ahead in this most ruthless of vocations. He has sought, not always in conventional ways, to bring a higher level of well-being to that great mass of people who shun politics. At the same time, he has charged off in attractive intellectual flights of fancy on occasion and sometimes neglected the mundane, or even distasteful, tasks that come with the territory of high office.

Showy, idealistic, and contradictory, California has never before seen a governor who was such an contrasting amalgam of religious questing, down-and-dirty politics, and consistent, fervent ambition. He has sought to advance the cause of those formerly relegated to the back of the bus; he has traveled the world seeking spiritual insight and plotted strategies that would achieve his political goals; he has repeatedly sought the national spotlight, sometimes quixotically. At the end of his third term as governor, he will have spent more than one-third of his lifetime in elected office. He has spent all of his lifetime trying to be the smartest guy in the room.

As he has worked his way through his old/new governorship, Brown's legacy, whatever it ultimately might or might not be, has been a work in progress. One large part of it, however, is already on the record. Quirky, contradictory, and smart, in so many ways a reflection of his native state, Jerry Brown has been a political phenomenon the likes of which Californians are unlikely ever to see again.

AFTERWORD

By the early morning hours of November 7, 2012, the word had spread among California political types still awake: Jerry Brown had scored a huge personal political triumph, perhaps the biggest in his long political career outside his repeated campaigns for governor. Proposition 30, the six-billion-dollar sales and income tax increase measure he championed against heavy odds, had won. Not only had it won, but it had won decisively by a 53.9 to 46.1 percent margin. The man who had flip-flopped on Proposition 13 in 1978—the master of the empty, crowd-pleasing gesture—had made a daring gamble on what many saw as an idealistic, even quixotic, quest to save California education. Cynical California voters, witness for decades to political ads decrying "those Sacramento politicians," had put their trust in Brown, giving him a resounding vote of confidence.

It was all Jerry. He put his own political capital on the line to become the most visible and ardent champion of Proposition 30. Defeat would have been catastrophic and seemed quite possible. Conventional wisdom said that if a California ballot initiative did not build to at least a 60 percent favorability rating before balloting began, it would fail. Proposition 30 had been declining in popularity during the fall of 2012, with late polls showing it hovering at a mere 50 percent approval rating on the eve of the November 6 balloting. But Brown rocketed around the state in the final days, visiting five cities from San Francisco to San Diego on election-eve Monday, campaigning furiously on behalf of the measure. And, as he had so often done in the past, Brown turned conventional wisdom on its head, to his own political benefit. Tax-adverse California had approved a quarter-cent raise in the sales tax for four years and a slight increase in state income taxes over seven years for those with annual incomes of more than $250,000. Brown had made good on his 2010 campaign promise of "No new taxes without a vote of the people."

Despite an announcement on December 12 that Brown was being treated for "localized prostate cancer," as 2012 drew to a close, he was riding high. His schedule remained busy, his doctor said his prognosis was "excellent," and he contemplated what he might do with his height-ened political power. A headline in the November 8 *Los Angeles Times* told readers: "Prop. 30 win gives Jerry Brown major boost: Victory on his tax measure offers the governor more clout to tackle other issues he cares about." But what were those issues? The two most prominently mentioned continued to be high-speed rail, which the governor backed, and peripheral tunnels in the California Delta that would move North-ern California water to the south. Midway through his third term as governor, however, there was still a question as to what the always-sur-prising Jerry Brown would do with his renewed stature.

One thing appeared certain: Brown would seek a public role as the grown-up on the Sacramento playground. The stage was set by two events. In addition to the Proposition 30 triumph, it appeared that California's Democratic governor might also have a two-thirds super-majority of Democrats in the legislature. Republican Party registration in the state had dropped below 30 percent. Few governors, in California or elsewhere, had enjoyed such a commanding situation. But speculation about possible schisms within the ranks of the triumphant Democrats began to appear almost immediately. Hours after the results were in, a few emboldened Democrats began to talk of increasing funding for various state programs that had suffered earlier cuts. With a legislative supermajority that would enable them to increase taxes without Republican approval, might Democrats mount a renewed push for tax hikes of one kind or another, following hard on the heels of the passage of Proposition 30? A November 10 *San Francisco Chronicle* headline read "Dominance in Legislature could cause Dem clashes." Brown, however, had been quick to head off talk of a post–Proposition 30 Democratic spending spree and to reinforce his carefully nurtured reputation for governmental frugality. He told a morning-after news conference of something he recited to himself during his months of Zen meditation in Japan: "Desires are endless. I vow to cut them down." Nonetheless, if the Democratic caucus held together, and the Democrats held onto their putative two-thirds majority, Brown's vetoes could be overridden, including vetoes of tax hikes.

A new factor emerged from the 2012 balloting: Jerry Brown was born when Franklin Roosevelt was in the White House, most automobiles had running boards, and television was a curiosity seen by few. Yet in another one of the oddities that have marked his life, Brown's Proposition 30 victory could boost the 74-year-old governor's standing among the state's youngest voters. He had stood in the way of threatened six-billion-dollar cuts to state programs, including hefty reductions in funds for the University of California, the California State University, and the states's 113 community colleges. If Proposition 30 had not entirely eliminated the likelihood of tuition increases, to some degree it promised to hold such increases in check. Twenty-eight percent of those who cast ballots on Proposition 30 were between the ages of eighteen and twenty-nine, according to exit polls conducted for The Associated Press and a consortium of television networks, and, with self-interest at stake, two-thirds of them supported Proposition 30.

Optimists said approval of Proposition 30 marked the beginning of a California renewal, a move led by Brown away from a crabbed, sour attitude toward state government, which had persisted for decades and, coupled with systemic dysfunction, had caused some to brand the state as ungovernable. A few political liberals even declared it amounted to a repudiation of the 1978 tax revolt that saw the passage of Proposition 13. Others saw the possibility of a nationwide trend toward tax increases for the rich as a result of Brown's Proposition 30 victory in the nation's most populous state. But whatever conclusions the pundits drew, whatever the mood of Californians, and whatever lay ahead for this diverse, restless, and enterprising place, political 2013 in the Golden State began on one salient point: Jerry Brown had done it again.

APPENDIX ONE

THREE INAUGURAL ADDRESSES

FIRST INAUGURAL ADDRESS OF CALIFORNIA'S
THIRTY-FOURTH GOVERNOR (DEMOCRAT)

Delivered: January 6, 1975

Thank you, Mr. Speaker, Mr. President, Members of the Judiciary, friends. I probably won't come again to this rostrum for a while. As a matter of fact, I wasn't sure I was going to make it. My father thought I wasn't going to make it, either. But here I am.

Well, this morning I'm not going to give you a formalistic address. I just want to tell you what's on my mind. And what my hopes are for the people of California in the coming year.

First, I think we ought to put this whole thing into perspective. We have all come through an election, and what have we learned? More than half the people who could have voted, refused, apparently believing that what we do here has so little impact on their lives that they need not pass judgment on it. In other words, the biggest vote of all in November was a vote of no confidence. So our first order of business is to regain the trust and confidence of the people we serve.

And we can begin by following not only the letter, but the spirit of the political reform initiative, the biggest vote-getter of all in the

181

primary election. The provisions of Proposition 9 will not always be easy to follow. But I honestly believe that they are the surest and most certain path to a government beyond reproach.

But an honest government is not enough. We also have to be effective. Today, unemployment in this state is well above the national average. That is not just a statistic, it is a reality. Men and women whose futures are uncertain, whose families are anxious, look to us for answers. I know much of the solution lies at the federal level, but I also know that California is the most influential state in the nation. What we do here will not only help our own citizens, it will provide a model for the entire country.

Very shortly I will sign an Executive Order requiring every state agency and department to actively participate in federally-funded public service employment programs.

Before the month is out, hundreds of men and women who are on unemployment or welfare will be performing meaningful jobs. My administration will work closely with the federal government.

We are going to use to the fullest the millions of dollars available to put Californians back to work. We are going to cooperate with local government and industry to create as many new jobs as humanly possible. And as we do we will not ignore the role of women in our work force and the special need for additional child care centers.

Both men and women will have equal opportunity to obtain every available job. In this I look to the legislature for assistance and guidance. I look to the state employees to make this program a reality. Finally, no employment program will be successful without the help of labor and business. The private sector still is, as it well should be, the principal source of employment. For our part, the state must cut through the tangle of overlapping environmental and land use rules which often delay needed construction. In the long run, the air, the water and the land will be protected. But only by clear rules which are fairly enforced and without delay. Just as critical as unemployment is inflation, the cruelest tax of all. Again, major initiatives are required at the national level. But nothing prevents us from doing what we can. And we do that first by keeping the burden of state taxation at a level no higher than it is today.

Avoiding a general tax increase will not be easy. Rising unemployment means reduced state revenues as well as escalating expenditures for health and welfare. But I'm determined to see this year through without asking the people for further sacrifices in the form of new taxes. This means that every branch and department of state government must re-examine itself with a view toward eliminating expenditures not absolutely essential to the well-being of the people. For my part, I propose a flat 7% reduction in my own office budget.

The uncertainty of the economy as well as the need to provide a fair system of school finance make it imperative to keep state expenditures well within current revenues. I also believe it is time to end special privileges once and for all. I will support legislation to eliminate the oil depletion allowance and provide a realistic minimum tax on preference income. In addition I'll support constitutional amendments to remove the home office deduction for insurance companies and the requirement of a two-thirds vote to alter business taxes.

And while we remove the special privileges of the few, we should not overlook the sacrifices of the many. It is time that we treat all workers alike, whether they work in the city or toil in the fields. This year I hope you will give the governor another chance to sign an appropriate bill including farm workers within the protection of unemployment insurance.

I also believe it is time to extend the rule of law to the agriculture sector and establish the right of secret ballot elections for farm workers. The law I support will impose rights and responsibilities on both farm worker and farmer alike. I expect that an appropriate bill that serves all the people will not fully satisfy any of the parties to the dispute, but that's no reason not to pass it.

As we bring collective bargaining to the fields, we should also establish appropriate mechanisms for public employees to choose the bargaining representative of their choice. All workers, whoever they are, and wherever they are, should be strongly represented and have an effective voice in the decisions that affect their wages and working conditions.

It is a big job ahead. The rising cost of energy, the depletion of our resources, the threat to the environment, the uncertainty of our economy and the monetary system, the lack of faith in government, the drift in political and moral leadership—is not the work of one person, it is the work of all of us working together. I ask your help. We have lot of work to do. Let's get to it. Thank you very much.

SECOND INAUGURAL ADDRESS OF CALIFORNIA'S THIRTY-FOURTH GOVERNOR (DEMOCRAT)

Delivered: January 8, 1979

The new year on which we now begin is a year of testing. Once again our economy is careening down the path of inflation that inexorably leads to recession. At such a time, it is right to reexamine our assumptions, state clearly our goals, and work confidently for the future.

1979 is the international year of the child. Those born this year will graduate in the class of 2000. What they inherit will depend on the courage and vision we pass on to them. Whether Californians in that year are up among the best or stagnating in the continuing aftershocks of obsolete technology and pervasive foreign imports, that depends on us.

Today we see the ethos of our moment dominated by "getting and spending" rather than innovation and risk. The depressing spirit of the age ungratefully feeds off the boldness of the past. Where there should be saving for the future, I see frantic borrowing. Where there should be investment in productive capacity, I see frenetic consumption.

California has been called the great exception. From the mystic aura of the name itself to the conquest of outer space, California has inspired greatness among its many immigrant people. Gold, forests, rich agricultural fields, high technology, universities of excellence, the Pacific horizon, diverse ethnic groups—all these have converged to keep our state a dream for the hundreds of thousands who still cross our borders each year. In the last four years, 1.5 million jobs have been created and the proportion of people over the age of sixteen employed in the wage economy has grown from 56 percent to 61 percent, a participation rate matched rarely anywhere in this country or anywhere else in the world. Over 14 million motor vehicles each month set new records in gallons of gasoline consumed and miles driven over our roads.

Our 22 million people produce each year more than the combined effort of the billion people who inhabit India, Pakistan, Indonesia, the Philippines, South Korea, Nigeria, and Zaire. We have the most advanced technology, the most stringent environmental laws, a strong legal commitment to equality, the highest transfer payments to those who depend on government and the most advanced labor laws.

Yet the mistrust of our public institutions and mere anxiety about our future economy are more the order than the exception. Three-quarters of the people do not trust their government. More than half of the eligible citizens in California again decided not to vote in the last election. Why? Why the anti-government mood? I asked this same question four years ago and now I believe I understand. Simply put, the citizens are revolting against a decade of political leaders who righteously spoke against inflation and excessive government spending but who in practice pursued the opposite course.

It is in this fundamental contradiction between what political leaders have said in their anti-inflation and anti-spending speeches and what they have actually done in their fiscal policies that we find the cause of today's political malaise. The ordinary citizen knows that government contributes to inflation and that runaway inflation is as destructive to our social wellbeing as an invading army.

The economists will argue about the fine points but the people know that something is profoundly wrong when 75 percent of government spending decisions are automatically decided by past formulas and not present lawmakers—formulas that ensure that government and its taxes always keep ahead of inflation.

People know that something is wrong when the federal government stimulates inflation and inflation raises the face value of prices, income and property, so that the taxes on each grow higher and higher. This perverse government money machine has created a fiscal dividend for local, state and federal government and allowed all three to expand faster than inflation and faster than real economic growth. These unauthorized dividends are now being cancelled. The tax revolt is being heard.

There is much to learn about the unprecedented primary vote and victory of Proposition 13. Not the least of which is that the established political union, and corporate powers are no match for an angry citizenry recoiling against an inflationary threat to their homes and pocketbooks.

While it is true that the tax revolt has increased the privileges of the few, it has without question inspired the hopes of many. Plain working people, the poor, the elderly, those on fixed incomes, those who cannot keep up with each new round of inflation or protect themselves from each subsequent round of recession, these are the people who are crying out for relief.

But in their name and in the name of misfortune of every kind, false prophets have risen to advocate more and more government spending as the cure—more bureaucratic programs and higher staffing ratios of professional experts. They have told us that billion dollar government increases are really deep cuts from the yet higher levels of spending they demand and that attempts to limit the inflationary growth of government derive not from wisdom but from selfishness. That disciplining government reflects not a care for the future but rather self-absorption. These false prophets, I tell you, can no longer distinguish the white horse of victory from the pale horse of death.

In this decade government at all levels has increased spending faster than the true rate of economic growth, taxes per $100 of income have climbed steadily. The cure for inflation has been administered with a vengeance. Yet most people feel worse, not better, about their government benefactor. The elderly find their fixed income eroding in half; those about to retire fear their future pensions will never keep pace. Ten million California workers see their wages rise but not as fast as prices. Those on welfare obtain larger grants but find more expensive groceries.

It is time to get off the treadmill, to challenge the assumption that more government spending automatically leads to better living. The facts prove otherwise. More and more inflationary spending leads to decline abroad and decadence at home. Ultimately it will unwind the social compact that forms the basis of our society.

Lord Keynes, in whose name many of the false prophets claim to speak, had this to say on the subject:

"By a process of inflation, governments can confiscate, secretly and unobserved, an important part of the wealth of their citizens. By this method they not only confiscate, but they confiscate arbitrarily; and, while the process impoverishes many, it actually enriches some.... There is no subtler, no surer means of overturning the existing basis of society than to debauch the currency. The process engages all the hidden forces of economic law on the side of destruction, and does it in a manner which not one man in a million is able to diagnose." ("The Economic Consequences of the Peace," J. M. Keynes)

Government, no less than the individual, must live within limits. It is time to bring our accounts into balance. Government, as exemplar and teacher, must manifest a self-discipline that spreads across the other institutions in our society, so that we can begin to work for the future, not just consume the present.

I propose that this year the state government lower the amount of taxes it collects per $100 of income to the level of four years ago. This will require a billion dollar tax cut. Such a tax reduction should, on a percentage basis, give the greatest benefit to renters and those at the lower and middle level of the income scale. A flat tax credit combined with an increase in renter assistance will accomplish this goal.

Some might ask, how did the state obtain this billion dollars? Did the state extract it from the new wealth or increase production? Was there a vote of the legislature to levy a new tax? No! Quite simply the perverse money machine of inflation is artificially raising income, poverty, prices, and profits and combining with pre-existing state law to generate a tax windfall. Unearned, unvoted, and undeserved.

Next, I propose that for the first time since World War II, we actually decrease the number of positions in state government. A reduction of 5,000 is reasonable and attainable without significant layoffs. It will mean that in 1980 we will operate government with fewer employees than we did in 1977.

I see this as state government, not working less, but becoming more productive. Jobs in government, education, and health constitute a substantial part of the work done in our state. Yet, it is in these fields where productivity is declining. Each year government employment grows. Each year we spend more money on fewer students. Each year we increase dramatically the amount spent on medical care. Are we better governed? Are we better educated? Are we healthier? Perhaps, but not commensurate with the additional dollars and taxes spent on each. The time has come for California to pioneer and increase productivity in these fields. It is a myth that services such as government, teaching, and curing lay fundamentally beyond those processes which have created our modern agriculture, our electronics, and aerospace. Our higher standard of living comes directly from work that uses the latest tools and the most imagination. Unless we improve the way we learn, the way we heal, and the way we govern, it is inevitable that our standard and quality of life will decline.

We are in the midst of an information revolution that draws its center from the computer and communication industries of California. As the power of the human mind expands through the technology of our own state, the challenge will be to use the new tools to expand learning, to prevent disease and make government leaner as it becomes more effective.

As government makes itself more productive, it must also strip away the roadblocks and the regulatory underbrush that it often mindlessly puts in the path of private citizens. Unneeded licenses and proliferating rules can stifle initiative, especially for small business. Society is more interdependent and our capacity to harm both nature and ourselves is greater than ever. Yet many regulations primarily protect the past, prop up privilege or prevent sensible economic choices.

These are the rules that should be changed in the ongoing self-examination by each department of government. Where economic incentives, instead of rules, can accomplish the goal, they should be tried.

Finally, in order to ensure that we permanently slow the inflationary growth of government, I will support an appropriate constitutional amendment to limit state and local spending. Such measures are difficult to draft but are justified today in order to recapture a sense of the common interest as opposed to the narrow and special interests that combine to push spending beyond what is reasonable.

I will also support the resolution now pending before the legislature calling upon Congress to propose a constitutional amendment to balance the federal budget or to convene a constitutional convention to achieve this goal.

The roller coaster of inflation followed by recession is out of control. In the last 12 years, leaders of both parties have tried in vain to slow its reckless course. At the same time, states compete with each other to extract more and more federal grants that are financed out of the deficits and not the productivity of the nation. It is, therefore, right that these same states join together to demand a constitutional amendment that will serve as the occasion for finally restraining the inflationary spending of the federal government. The nation, no less than the individual states, must eventually balance its books. The excuse that only annual deficits promote full employment is refuted by the continuing decline in productivity and investment which form the only true base of long term employment.

A constitutional convention to propose an amendment to balance the budget is unprecedented, but so is the paralysis that prevents necessary action.

The time has finally come to balance what we spend with what we produce.

To truly achieve this, we must enlist the talent of all the people in our society. This is what I call investment in human capital—an investment we have yet to fully make. Despite the affluence of California, too many still languish in the backwaters of our society.

We encounter each day the paradox of unfilled jobs existing side by side with unemployed or underemployed people. The challenge is to break down the remaining discriminatory barriers and encourage business, labor and government to provide on-the-job training, apprenticeships, and full upward mobility. We can never reach our full capacity unless we liberate the human spirit and enfranchise all the people of our state—whatever their color, their language, their disability, their age or their sex. To more completely achieve this goal, I will support the necessary changes in our Fair Employment Practices Act, to include prohibitions against discrimination based on sexual preference. The diversity of our people can be a cause of hatred and anxiety or the source of strength and continued advancement. The choice is ours.

As we expand the opportunities for those within our borders, we must recognize the affinity that we have with those beyond. No small part of our present wealth or our future possibilities derives from our location on the Pacific rim. The trade and widening exchange with Mexico, with Canada, and with our more distant neighbors in the far east, offer potential still rarely imagined.

After the first Americans and long before most of our ancestors arrived in California, our neighbors from Mexico were naming cities and dividing our lands. For too long we have ignored Mexico. Unless we understand that California and Mexico are linked by history, geography, families and a common future, we will miss one of the great opportunities of the next decade.

Let us also not neglect the other forms of life and natural systems on which we all depend. The soil, the sun, and the water make possible our forests and the wood we take from them, as well as the food that our farmers are able to produce. This timeless beauty will endure only if we have proper reverence and respect for our natural systems. The air can become cancerous, the water polluted, and the soil eroded. It is up to us to so manage growth and technology, that we enhance the quality of our environment, not undermine it to the loss of those who will come after us. Many a civilization has fallen with its forest and eroded with its soil.

I said that 1979 was a year of testing—testing whether these people that fill the freeways of California have the vision to prepare for the year 2000. Is Alexander Solzhenitsyn correct when he says that: "A decline in courage may be the most striking feature which an outside observer notices in the west in our days"? Will we make the sacrifices to protect our land and to create the new energy sources that will power our factories? Will we invest in the information revolution and continue to dominate the conquest of outer space? Will we see beyond the stereotypes and embrace our human diversity?

To all of this I must answer with a resounding yes. California will build for the future, not steal from it. And as we do, we will know in our hearts patriotism is not just defending the country of our fathers, but preparing the land for our children.

THIRD INAUGURAL ADDRESS OF CALIFORNIA'S THIRTY-NINTH GOVERNOR (DEMOCRAT)

Delivered: January 3, 2011

Madam Chief Justice, Governor and Mrs. Davis, Governor and Mrs. Schwarzenegger, esteemed members of the Senate and the Assembly, constitutional officers, distinguished guests, fellow Californians. Thank you for joining me today.

Governor Schwarzenegger, thank you also for your courtesies and help in the transition, and for your tireless efforts to keep California the Great Exception that it is.

This is a special moment as executive power passes from one governor to another, determined solely by majority vote. It is a sacred and special ritual that affirms that the people are in charge and that elected officials are given only a limited time in which to perform their appointed tasks. For me this day is also special because I get to follow in my father's footsteps once again—and 36 years after my first inauguration as Governor, even follow in my own.

Then—1975—it was the ending of the Vietnam War and a recession caused by the Middle East oil embargo. Now, as we gather in this restored Memorial Auditorium, dedicated to those who died in World War I, it is our soldiers fighting in Iraq and Afghanistan, and our economy caught in the undertow of a deep and prolonged recession.

With so many people out of work and so many families losing their homes in foreclosure it is not surprising that voters tell us they are worried and believe that California is on the wrong track. Yet, in the face of huge budget deficits year after year and the worst credit rating among the 50 states, our two political parties can't come close to agreeing on the right path forward. They remain in their respective comfort zones, rehearsing and rehashing old political positions.

Perhaps this is the reason why the public holds the state government in such low esteem. And that's a profound problem, not just for those of us who are elected, but for our whole system of self-government. Without the trust of the people, politics degenerates into mere spectacle; and democracy declines, leaving demagoguery and cynicism to fill the void.

The year ahead will demand courage and sacrifice. The budget I propose will assume that each of us who are elected to do the people's business will rise above ideology and partisan interest and find what is required for the good of California. There is no other way forward. In this crisis, we simply have to learn to work together as Californians first, members of a political party second.

In seeking the Office of Governor, I said I would be guided by three principles.

First, speak the truth. No more smoke and mirrors on the budget. No empty promises.

Second, no new taxes unless the people vote for them.

Third, return—as much as possible—decisions and authority to cities, counties and schools, closer to the people.

With your help, that is exactly what I intend to do. The budget I present next week will be painful, but it will be an honest budget. The items of spending will be matched with available tax revenues and specific proposals will be offered to realign key functions that are currently spread between state and local government in ways that are complex, confusing and inefficient. My goal is to achieve greater accountability and reduce the historic shifting of responsibility back and forth from one level of government to another. The plan represents my best understanding of our real dilemmas and possibilities. It is a tough budget for tough times.

When dealing with a budget gap in the tens of billions, I must point out that it is far more than waste and inefficiency that we have to take out. Yes, government wastes money—and I will be doing a lot about that, starting this week—but government also pays for things that most people want and that are approved only after elected representatives debate their merits and finally vote them into law. They cover the spectrum from universities, parks, health care, prisons, income assistance, tax incentives, environmental protection, firefighting, and much else.

Choices have to be made and difficult decisions taken. At this stage of my life, I have not come here to embrace delay or denial.

In reflecting on our difficulties, my thoughts turned to those who preceded me and what they faced and what they were able to accomplish. My father who took the oath of office as governor 52 years ago. His mother, Ida, born on a ranch in Colusa County in 1878, and her father, August Schuckman, leaving Missouri in 1852, and traveling across the plains to Sacramento.

I tried to imagine the difficulties my great-grandfather confronted as he left Germany and came to America and then across the plains and over the Sierras into California. Let me read from the diary that he kept during his long trek westward:

"On the 26th of June, we came to the first sand desert—it was 41 miles. We went there at night and rode 19 hours in it....

"On the 26th of July, we came to the second large plain—also 40 miles long. Here we lost seven oxen which died of thirst.... Thousands of cows, horses and mules were lying about dead....

"The discarded wagons by the hundreds were driven together and burned. We saw wagons standing that would never be taken out again and more than 1,000 guns that had been broken up. Here on this 40 miles are treasures that can never be taken out again."

We can only imagine what it took for August Schuckman to leave his family and home and travel across the ocean to America and then across the country—often through dangerous and hostile territory—in a wagon train. But come he did, overcoming every obstacle. Yet, he wasn't finished. After a few years, he went back to his homeland and found a wife, Augusta, and brought her with him, sailing around the Horn and up the coast of South America back to California. Their granddaughter, my aunt Connie Carlson, is here with us this morning—this March, she will be 99.

Aunt Connie, could you please stand up?[1]

It is not just my family but every Californian is heir to some form of powerful tradition, some history of overcoming challenges much more daunting than those we face today. From the native peoples who survived the total transformation of their way of life, to the most recent arrival, stories of courage abound. And it is not over.

The people of California have not lost their pioneering spirit or their capacity to meet life's challenges. Even in the midst of this recession, Californians this year will produce almost two trillion dollars of new wealth as measured by our state's domestic product. The innovations of Silicon Valley, the original thinking coming out of our colleges and universities, the skill of our farmers, the creative imagination of Hollywood, the Internet and the grit and determination of small businesses everywhere—all give hope for an even more abundant future. And so do our teachers, our nurses, our firefighters, our police and correctional officers, our engineers, and all manner of public servants who faithfully carry out our common undertakings.

This is a time to honestly assess our financial condition and make the tough choices. And as we do, we will put our public accounts in order, investments in the private sector will accelerate and our economy will produce new jobs just as it has done after each of the other ten recessions since World War II.

As Californians we can be proud that our state leads the rest of the country in our commitment to new forms of energy and energy efficiency. I have set a goal of 20,000 megawatts of renewable energy by 2020 and I intend to meet it by the appointments I make and the actions they take. There are hundreds of thousands of new jobs to be created if California regulatory authorities make sensible and bold decisions. It will also be necessary to make sure that our laws and rules focus on our most important objectives, minimizing delays and unnecessary costs.

I will meet not only with the leaders of energy companies but with executives from a broad range of California business and industry to work on common problems and break down barriers that hold us back. We live, after all, in the eighth largest economy in the world. Over the last decade, California has outpaced the nation in the growth of our gross domestic product and in our productivity per capita.

Aside from economic advance, I want to make sure that we do everything we can to ensure that our schools are places of real learning. Our budget problem is dire but after years of cutbacks, I am determined to enhance our public schools so that our citizens of the future have the skills, the zest and the character to keep California up among the best.

One of our native sons, Josiah Royce, became for a time one of the most famous of American philosophers. He was born in 1855, in a mining camp that later became the town of Grass Valley. I mention him because his "Philosophy of Loyalty" is exactly what is called for. Loyalty to the community, to what is larger than our individual needs.

We can overcome the sharp divisions that leave our politics in perpetual gridlock, but only if we reach into our hearts and find that loyalty, that devotion to California above and beyond our narrow perspectives.

I also mention Josiah Royce because long ago my father spoke to me about his philosophy of loyalty. I didn't really grasp its importance, but as I look back now, I understand how this loyalty to California was my father's philosophy as well. It drove him to build our freeways, our universities, our public schools and our state water plan.

In the coming year, we will grapple with the problems of our schools, with our prisons, our water supply, its reliability, and our environment. We will also have to look at our system of pensions and how to ensure that they are transparent and actuarially sound and fair—fair to the workers and fair to the taxpayers.

Many of these issues have confronted California one way or another for decades, certainly since the time of Governor Earl Warren. It is sobering and enlightening to read through the inaugural addresses of past governors. They each start on a high note of grandeur and then focus on virtually the same recurring issues—education, crime, budgets, water.

I have thought a lot about this and it strikes me that what we face together as Californians are not so much problems but rather conditions, life's inherent difficulties. A problem can be solved or forgotten but a condition always remains. It remains to elicit the best from each of us and show us how we depend on one another and how we have to work together.

With realism, with confidence, with loyalty—in that deepest sense—to California, to my forebearers and to posterity—as our song says:

"California here I come, right back where I started from."

Thank you and God bless you.

AUTHOR'S NOTE ON CALIFORNIA'S CONSTITUTION

Bigger, but Not Necessarily Better

Jerry Brown, in common with all California governors, has had to pick his way through the cumbersome, overly long, and frequently amended document that is the state constitution, a document providing visible proof that California's governance has historically been a case study in good intentions gone awry.

Responding to the call from the military governor of California, Brigadier General Bennet Riley, an oddball assortment of Californios, and a few gold-seeking Anglo adventurers gathered in a large second-story room at Monterey's Colton Hall in 1849 to write the first California constitution, a year before California even became a state.

Riley specified that the thirty-four delegates to the convention would be apportioned among locales, with two from San Diego, four from Los Angeles, two from Santa Barbara, two from San Luis Obispo, five from Monterey, five from San Jose, five from San Francisco, four from Sonoma, four from Sacramento, and four from San Joaquin. The resulting document was partly modeled after the Iowa Constitution, at the time the latest model available. It outlawed slavery and provided for a state Assembly and Senate, a judiciary, and a governor, complete with checks and balances.

A ponderous rewrite came in 1879, but it was a long way from doing the job. During the ensuing decades, the document was amended and amended again—at last tally there were at least 485 amendments and counting. Between 1911, when progressives put citizen initiatives in place, and 1996, when the California Constitution Revision Commission made its count, there were 425 amendments alone.

Through that series of amendments, the California Constitution has become one of the longest in the world. Jerry Brown and the Legislature must work within the strictures of a document that at last count stood at a hodgepodge of 110 pages, some of which contain clearly outdated material. Among other things, it specifies that California teachers must be paid at least twenty-four hundred dollars a year.

There have been periodic attempts to institute a state constitutional convention to write a more compact and functional document, but as of this writing, none has become reality. Californians have been unhappy with the status quo but fearful of change. A constitutional convention, after all, might find a way to raise taxes or limit the ability of interest groups to put initiatives on the ballot under the guise of "People Power." Advocates of People Power initiatives have ignored the pundits and political scientists who point out that initiatives are all too frequently ham-handed, aimed solely at enriching special interests, and impossible to change except through another statewide vote.

Writer Peter Schrag put it succinctly: "Again and again in our distrust, we reduce the legislature's ability to function. Again and again, we complain about gridlock and the legislature's inability to do the people's business, increasing the distrust and bringing yet another round of restrictions."[1]

As of this writing, it appears likely that California's governance will stagger on under the burden of an oversized document that seeks to micromanage state governance, despite the best efforts of reformers. As Mark Twain once famously said of the weather, "Everyone talks about it, but no one does anything about it."

NOTES

INTRODUCTION

1. Davis's first name was misspelled as "Grey" on the document marking his reserved seat. Sic transit gloria.

2. The penultimate line in the inaugural address that followed was "California here I come, right back where I started from."

3. Henry Cleland, "California," in *The Encyclopedia Americana* (New York: Americana Corporation, 1952), 205.

4. The U.S. Conference of Catholic Bishops estimated that 28.6 percent of the state's residents were Catholic in 2008.

CHAPTER ONE

1. Thomas A. Bailey, *The American Pageant*, 2nd ed. (Boston: D. C. Heath and Company, 1961), 389.

2. The quotations are taken from Brown's inaugural address on January 3, 2011, www.gov.ca.gov/news.php?id=16866.

3. Orville Schell, *Brown* (New York: Random House, 1978), 60.

4. Jerry Brown Papers, Regional History Collection. Doheny Memorial Library, University of Southern California.

5. Sally later opened what was regarded as a very good restaurant, the Valhalla, in Sausalito, on the other side of the Golden Gate Bridge from San Francisco. The restaurant had a stunning cross-bay view of the San Francisco

skyline (one would say romantic, if one appreciated irony) and was decorated with mementos and photographs of Sally in her heyday as a famed madam whose clientele included members of the cultured male—"High Provincial," in the historian Kevin Starr's apt phrase—San Francisco establishment. She was a frequent and sometimes successful candidate for the Sausalito City Council and was finally elected mayor.

6. Jerry did, however, show a rare flash of humor at a meeting with Ronald Reagan shortly after Jerry was elected governor. Reagan, famous for having jelly beans around the office, jovially asked the governor-elect what he was going to use as his trademark office snack. "I've been trying to avoid hasty commitments. That decision will have to wait a few days," Jerry replied, parodying his own approach to the governorship.

7. John C. Bollens and C. Robert Williams, *Jerry Brown in a Plain Brown Wrapper* (Pacific Palisades, CA: Palisades Publishers, 1978), 27.

8. St. Ignatius was also the alma mater of the late Leo McCarthy, a fellow Democrat and a 1948 graduate who, as speaker of the California Assembly, tutored Governor Jerry Brown in how to deal with legislators.

9. Robert Pack, *Jerry Brown: The Philosopher Prince* (New York: Stein and Day, 1978), 8.

10. Roger Rapoport, *California Dreaming: The Political Odyssey of Pat and Jerry Brown* (Berkeley: Nolo Press, 1982), 46

11. George Skelton, interview with the author, April 26, 2012.

12. McComb was removed from the court on grounds of senility in May 1977. His removal allowed Jerry Brown to appoint Frank C. Newman as his replacement.

13. Finnegan in 2011 was a San Francisco lobbyist and political activist and has been a longtime political supporter of Brown. Damrell became a federal judge.

14. Jerry was, however, well enough acquainted with events in the outside world to urge his father in 1957 to run for the U.S. Senate, rather than the governorship, on the grounds that Washington, not Sacramento, was where the action was. Jerry apparently still believed this decades later during his three unsuccessful attempts at the presidency and one unsuccessful try for the U.S. Senate.

15. The Three Degrees of Humility may be described most simply as levels of union with the will of God, in ascending order.

16. Rapoport, *California Dreaming*, 57.

17. Pack, *Jerry Brown*, 25. Sacred Heart has become a retirement center for older Jesuits and no longer educates young men for the priesthood. Novitiates are now educated in Culver City, California.

18. In their biography of William Knowland, *One Step from the White House: The Rise and Fall of Senator William F. Knowland* (Berkeley: University of California Press, 1998), authors Gayle B. Montgomery and James W. Johnson report that Knowland was having an affair with an attractive Washington woman, Ruth Moody, while Knowland's wife, Helen, was having an affair with Ruth Moody's husband, Blair, a Washington correspondent who later became a Democratic senator from Michigan. The authors say that when Blair Moody died, Helen Knowland was despondent, upset over Knowland's continuing affair with Ruth Moody, and eager to leave Washington, a city she had never liked. The result was family pressure on Knowland to put Washington and the Senate behind him favor of a new political career in his native state. Knowland acceded. Westward the Course of Adultery takes its way.

19. Rapoport, *California Dreaming*, 78.

20. Tuttle & Taylor closed its doors on November 30, 2000.

CHAPTER TWO

1. Forty-five years after the Free Speech movement made headlines, its leaders are regarded by many as founders of a more humane, logical, and just set of rules governing political activity on University of California campuses. They were not so regarded by a decisive segment of the California electorate in 1964, 1965, and 1966.

2. Robert Pack, *Jerry Brown: The Philosopher Prince* (New York: Stein and Day, 1978), 40.

3. Antonovich was elected to the Board of Supervisors in 1980 and as of 2011 was still serving.

4. Metzger's dismissal was appealed through all levels of the state judicial system; the state Supreme Court finally ordered her reinstated with back pay. She continued to be an active writer and explorer of new ways of approaching life. Ms. Metzger's Web site in March 2011 described her as "a poet, novelist, essayist, storyteller, teacher, healer and medicine woman who has taught and counseled for over forty years, in the process of which she has developed therapies (Healing Stories) which creatively address life threatening diseases, spiritual and emotional crises, as well as community, political and environmental disintegration."

5. Paul Peek, a former Assembly speaker, served the two years—1940–41.

6. A Brown campaign news release, quoted in Pack, *Jerry Brown*, 42.

7. Roger Rapoport, *California Dreaming: The Political Odyssey of Pat and Jerry Brown* (Berkeley: Nolo Press, 1982), 118.

8. Flournoy was not related to Houston Flournoy, who was the successful 1970 Republican candidate for state controller and Brown's opponent in the 1974 gubernatorial election.

9. James Flournoy died in 2009; Jerry Brown called his onetime opponent "a wonderful man and a true gentleman" (*Los Angeles Times,* March 3, 2009).

10. Although impressive, Reagan's margin of victory over Unruh was a little more than half as large as his nearly one-million-vote win over Pat Brown four years earlier.

11. After his defeat, Rafferty moved to Alabama. Rafferty was loathed by liberal Democrats and teachers' unions; a particularly nasty comment that circulated in Sacramento soon after his move declared, "Rafferty's moving from California to Alabama increased the average IQ of both states by 50 percent."

12. James Mills, *A Disorderly House: The Brown-Unruh Years in Sacramento* (Berkeley: Heyday Books, 1987).

13. For a detailed account of legislative maneuvering, see James Richardson's *Willie Brown: A Biography* (Berkeley: University of California Press, 1996).

14. Doug Faigin, telephone interview with the author, May 6, 2011. The Virgin Sturgeon was a (usually) floating restaurant-bar that became a beloved hangout for Capitol reporters, political staff members, and some legislators. It sank at its mooring on the Sacramento River and was resurrected at least once.

15. Rapoport, *California Dreaming,* 121.

16. "Brown Says Top Solons Trying to Cripple Him," *Long Beach Independent, Press-Telegram,* June 17, 1972, A7.

17. Ibid.

18. The late Bill Stall, the correspondent in charge of The AP bureau, later became Brown's press secretary. Dave Jensen, a former UPI and *Sacramento Bee* reporter and editor, also served as a Brown press secretary.

19. This was even before Agnew's own scandal erupted unrelated to Watergate, resulting in his resignation in October 1973.

20. News release, January 1970, Jerry Brown Papers, Regional History Collection. Doheny Memorial Library, University of Southern California.

21. Faigin, interview with the author, May 6, 2011.

22. Pack, *Jerry Brown,* 45.

23. News release, Jerry Brown Papers.

24. James C. Bollens and G. Robert Williams, *Jerry Brown in a Plain Brown Wrapper* (Pacific Palisades, CA: Palisades Publishers, 1978), 71.

25. Post, admired by lawmakers on both sides of the aisle and an accomplished painter, was once described as so controlled that he could eat only one peanut out of a bag of them. He died early in 2011.

26. News release, early 1974, Jerry Brown Papers.

27. At a meeting in his office to discuss the transfer of power shortly after Brown was elected governor, Reagan served Brown two hamburgers and a Coke for lunch.

CHAPTER THREE

1. John F. Kennedy once said that life is not fair, a statement to which fellow politician Waldie could relate. He was an important player in pursuing the truth about Watergate, introducing a House resolution to impeach Richard Nixon, and he was a member of the House Judiciary Committee, which was preparing a committee vote to impeach Nixon. The vote came in July 1974, a month after the June California primary. Waldie gave up a safe seat in Congress to run for governor against Jerry Brown. Then, for all practical purposes, he gave up his race for governor to fulfill what he believed was his duty to the congressional Watergate investigation of President Nixon. Whether Waldie could have won the Democratic nomination against up-and-coming crusader Brown will, of course, never be known for certain. But if he had devoted all of his time and energy to the campaign instead of his formal duties in the Watergate probe, Waldie would have significantly cut into Brown's image as the leading political reformer in the Democratic primary, and he could thereby have seriously eroded Brown's subsequent success. Yet even at a time when the nation was caught up in the Watergate affair and the impending impeachment of Nixon, Waldie was unable in California to take full political-media advantage of his role. Waldie's loss involved more than his sacrifice of campaign time to perform what he regarded as his duty in Washington. Unfortunately for Waldie, unless the news involves a scandal, preferably one involving sex, individual members of the House of Representatives, like individual members of the state Legislature, seldom make statewide headlines outside their home districts, no matter how meritorious their service. In addition, most members of legislative bodies, with the possible exception of Waldie and Jesse Unruh, are unable to make the intellectual leap from legislating to broad-brush, emotion-based statewide campaigning. Ironically, while Waldie was in the center of the nation's greatest political scandal, Jerry Brown, on the outer fringes of Watergate but a statewide elected official

headquartered in Sacramento with a poised-to-jump Capitol Press Corps, created advantageous headlines for himself by revoking a notary public license. Jerry Waldie died in June 2009. He was eighty-four.

2. The board has occasionally served as an effective platform to attract media attention to causes advocated by individual members. Regent Ward Connerly, for instance, campaigned against affirmative action programs both in California and eventually nationwide. The Board of Regents has been described as "the closest thing California has to the House of Lords."

3. Ironically, in 1971, only three years before the 1974 primary, the Citizens' Conference on State Legislatures named the California Legislature the best in the United States. It was regarded as a model by many other lawmakers and political scientists across the nation.

4. Associated Press article in the *San Bernardino Sun-Telegram,* May 24, 1974.

5. In one of the most wrongheaded analyses of California politics ever published, nationally syndicated Washington-based columnists Rowland Evans and Robert Novak, a few days before the balloting, declared, "The reason for the largely unspoken Democratic self-doubt is that young Brown scarcely seems the ideal candidate to cash in on those Republican weaknesses. What's more, this self-styled 'reformist's' campaign may be a basic misreading of the public mood" (Jerry Brown Papers, Regional History Collection, Doheny Memorial Library, University of Southern California). As it happened, Brown made an almost perfect basic reading of the public mood. The largely unspoken Democratic self-doubt was largely unspoken because it didn't exist.

6. Secretary of state's official summary of election results, 1974.

7. Dymally, a native of Trinidad, had a lilting Caribbean accent, and when he talked, "it sounded as if you should be hearing steel drums in the background," said one anonymous Capitol wag (pers. comm.).

8. Jerry Brown, first inaugural address, January 6, 1975, www.governors. library.ca.gov./addresses/34-jbrown01.html.

9. More than three decades later, collective bargaining for state employees became a hot national issue in 2011, as governors in Wisconsin and Ohio have attempted to reduce the power of state employee unions.

10. Robert Pack, *Jerry Brown: The Philosopher Prince* (New York: Stein and Day, 1978), 234.

11. Ibid.

12. Late in 1974, as Reagan was preparing to leave office, Democrat Riles, accompanied by me, walked the two blocks from the Department of Education building to Republican Reagan's Capitol office to bid him a

cordial and unpublicized farewell. The two stood amid packing boxes and exchanged smiling good wishes. At the time I was Riles's special assistant (press secretary).

13. Jerry Brown, internal memo to department heads, June 1975, Jerry Brown Papers.

14. As part of Willie Brown's role as Jerry's nemesis, later in their political careers Willie became fond of calling himself "the good Brown." In 1988, years after the negotiation of the Agricultural Labor Relations Bill, Willie Brown himself played a key role as speaker of the Assembly in secret negotiations at Frank Fat's restaurant that led to a "peace agreement" among the California Medical Association, the tobacco industry, and medical malpractice lawyers. The agreement was sketched out on a restaurant napkin and then quickly rammed through the Legislature. An enlarged replica of the napkin was displayed near the entrance to the restaurant as late as 2011. Fat's, famous for its banana cream pies, has been a legislative-lobbyist hangout for decades.

15. Signing statement, Jerry Brown Papers.

16. John C. Bollens and G. Robert Williams, *Jerry Brown in a Plain Brown Wrapper* (Pacific Palisades, CA: Palisades Publishers, 1978), 214.

17. Evelle Younger, prepared statement, February 1977.

18. Rose Bird, prepared statement, February 1977.

19. Lorenz wrote a book in 1978 accusing Brown of using "buzz words" in his 1974 campaign aimed at creating a favorable voter response while avoiding any specifics (James D. Lorenz, *Jerry Brown: The Man on the White Horse* [Boston: Houghton & Mifflin Co., 1978]). Lorenz's charge was akin to an observation that water flows downhill. Brown was guilty of doing what every candidate since the founding of the Republic did. Brown just did it better than most.

20. From material in the Jerry Brown Papers.

21. www.brainyquote.com/quotes/authors/j/jerry_brown.html.

CHAPTER FOUR

1. Doug Willis, e-mail interview with the author, May 23, 2011. Willis, who covered California politics for more than thirty years in Sacramento, is responsible for the most famous (some would say disgraceful) pun in the history of Capitol reporting. He was in a group of reporters being taken on a tour of the state Capitol renovation, a major project that lasted nearly seven years, 1975–82. A member of the group noted the large number of fireplaces in the old

building but a lack of chimneys. The guide informed the group that the smoke from the numerous fireplaces was channeled to a central chimney on the roof. Willis then remarked, "Oh—only one flue over the cuckoo's nest."

2. Jarvis also did a commercial for Brown's Republican opponent, Attorney General Evelle Younger. Both campaigns ran Jarvis's ads. Jarvis said he did both commercials because he wanted Proposition 13 effectively implemented no matter who won.

3. George Skelton, interview with the author, April 26, 2012.

4. Interview by Carole Hicke, Regional History Office, University of California, 1995 and 1996, part of the California State Government Oral History Program, California State Archives, Sacramento, page 126; quoted in Joe Matthews and Mark Paul, *California Crackup: How Reform Broke the Golden State and How We Can Fix It* (Berkeley: University of California Press, 2010), 40.

5. John Burton, who was the chairman of the California Democratic Party in 2011, also served in the state Legislature, in the U.S. Congress, and then again in the Legislature.

6. Doug Willis, e-mail to author, May 23, 2011.

7. Willie Brown quoted in *Newsweek*, April 23, 1979.

8. Jerry Brown Papers, Regional History Collection, Doheny Memorial Library, University of Southern California.

9. Editorial, March 25, 1980.

10. Editorial, August 3, 1979.

11. Indicative of Davis's attention to detail, the Jerry Brown Papers contain a letter from an indignant motorist who claimed to have been passed by Davis's car doing ninety miles per hour en route to the Sacramento airport. The letter to Davis asked in conclusion, "What's your rejoinder?" The letter writer received a handwritten note from Davis: "Rejoinder—made the plane. And I wasn't driving."

12. Associated Press story, *Orange County Register,* December 25, 1982.

13. Vidal was probably too acerbically witty to be successful as a candidate, once declaring, "Half of the American people never read a newspaper. Half never voted for President. One hopes it is the same half" (www.brainyquote. com/quotes/quotes/g/gorevidal100434.html).

CHAPTER FIVE

1. Fred Branfman, "The SALON Interview: Jerry Brown: Moving toward the Abyss," June 3, 1996, www.salon.com/1996/06/03/interview960603/.

2. In a splendid turn of phrase, Jerry Roberts and Phil Trounstein, editors of the political Web site *Calbuzz*, declared that Brown had "bigfooted" his way into the chairmanship.

3. Tsongas suffered from cancer—non-Hodgkin's lymphoma—but died of pneumonia and liver failure on January 18, 1997.

4. Candidacy announcement, October 21, 1991, Jerry Brown Papers, Regional History Collection, Doheny Memorial Library, University of Southern California.

5. Ibid.

6. Quotation taken from the debate video at Media Burn (www.MediaBurn .org).

7. *New York Times,* April 8, 1992.

8. See www.wethepeoplefoundation.org.

9. *New Yorker,* June 8, 1998.

10. *San Francisco Chronicle,* March 26, 1998.

11. *New York Times,* April 2, 1992.

12. Robert Pack, *Jerry Brown: The Philosopher Prince* (New York: Stein and Day, 1978), 170–75.

13. Ivan Illich, "To Hell with Good Intentions," speech delivered at the Conference on InterAmerican Student Projects (CIASP), in Cuernavaca, Mexico, April 20, 1968.

14. Published in *Whole Earth* (Spring 2003).

15. Jerry Brown Papers.

16. One wonders what Illich would have had to say in the spring of 2011, when, under the auspices of do-gooder organizations originating in Western industrialized nations, airplanes designed and manufactured in Western industrialized nations, flown by do-gooder pilots trained in Western industrialized nations, brought Western industrialized foodstuffs into Africa to aid Somalis starving in their undeveloped country.

17. *Newsday* interview, March 2, 1994, carried in the *Los Angeles Times.*

18. Zazen is a meditative discipline that Zen Buddhist practitioners perform to calm the body and mind, thereby gaining insight into the nature and meaning of existence. Quoted in Branfman, "The SALON Interview."

19. Quoted in Orville Schell, *Brown* (New York: Random House, 1978), 230.

20. Ibid., 71.

21. Jesse Walker, "Five Faces of Jerry Brown," *American Conservative,* November 1, 2009, www.theamericanconservative.com/articles/five-faces-of -jerry-brown/.

22. Steve Glazer, interview with author, August 4, 2011.
23. Doug Fagin, interview with author, August 9, 2011.

CHAPTER SIX

1. Harris was so confident he would win his Assembly race that he traveled to Sacramento to discuss committee assignments. He lost to the Green Party's Audie Bock, becoming the first major party politician to lose a state legislative race to a Green Party candidate. He later became chancellor of the Peralta Community College District. The district trustees decided not to renew his contract, and Harris left the chancellorship in June 2010.

2. Editorial, *San Francisco Bay Guardian*, May 1998.

3. Bobby Seale ran for mayor of Oakland in 1973, losing in a runoff to incumbent John H. Reading by a margin of 77,634 to 43,749.

4. Author conversations with American Medical Response paramedics, 1995–98.

5. Ignacio de la Fuente, an Oakland City Council member, said, "While a lot of us worked on it, Jerry basically branded the 10K program. He was a great salesman." Interview with the author, July 21, 2011.

6. Chip Johnson, interview with the author, March 13, 2012.

7. *Wall Street Journal*, August 10, 1999.

8. Johnson, interview with the author, March 13, 2012.

9. De la Fuente, interview with the author, July 21, 2011. De la Fuente also said that he and Brown nearly lost their lives in 2001, when the two had been invited to be observers of an election in the state of Tabasco, Mexico. De la Fuente said the van they and a number of other people were riding in blew a tire at sixty miles per hour and rolled four times. No one was wearing seat belts. Brown and de la Fuente escaped with minor injuries. De la Fuente said that after ascertaining that the other injured passengers were receiving medical attention, he and Brown repaired to a bar.

10. *East Bay Express*, March 19–25, 2003, 15.

11. De la Fuente, interview with the author, July 21, 2011.

12. Observation made during a panel discussion at the UC Berkeley Institute of Governmental Studies, January 22, 2011.

13. Faigin, interview with the author, August 9, 2011.

14. Johnson, interview with the author, September 14, 2011.

15. The elected city attorney in Los Angeles, rather than the district attorney, is responsible for prosecuting misdemeanors.

16. *Los Angeles Times,* June 21, 2007.

17. *Los Angeles Times,* September 1, 2005.

18. Governor Arnold Schwarzenegger nominated Poochigian to the California Court of Appeal, Fifth Appellate District. Poochigian was confirmed and was serving on the court as of 2011.

19. Brown news release, November 13, 2007, available at oag.ca.gov.

20. Brown news release, April 30, 2007, oag.ca.gov.

21. Brown news release, June 25, 2008, oag.ca.gov.

22. The headline coverage began when San Francisco mayor Gavin Newsom committed an act of civil disobedience two days before Valentine's Day in 2004, while Jerry Brown was struggling to improve Oakland schools and revitalize its downtown. Newsom ordered the San Francisco city clerk to begin issuing marriage licenses to homosexual couples, ignoring state law against same-sex marriages. Newsom himself presided over the marriage of two lesbians who had been together for fifty years. Newspapers across the country featured photographs of men in tuxedos kissing each other, thereby inflaming evangelicals and adding to San Francisco's, and California's, reputation among social conservatives as wanton twenty-first-century versions of Sodom and Gomorrah. For nearly a month, before the state high court issued its first ruling, the clerk's office continued to issue marriage licenses to gay and lesbian couples, stoking continuous outrage among religious fundamentalists.

23. Brown news release, August 4, 2010, oag.ca.gov.

24. The four winners are Warren himself, Edmund G. "Pat" Brown, George Deukmejian, and Jerry Brown.

CHAPTER SEVEN

1. California Secretary of State Report of Registration as of October 19, 2010.

2. Keynote speech, January 21, 2011; see Ethan Rarick, *California Votes: The 2010 Governor's Race* (Berkeley, CA: Institute of Governmental Studies Press, University of California, 2012).

3. Part of Agen's analysis as a panel member at the Institute of Governmental Studies' postmortem on the 2010 campaigns, January 21, 2011; see ibid.

4. Ibid.

5. Ibid.

6. Steve Glazer, interview with the author, August 4, 2011.

7. The Center for the Continuing Study of the California Economy reported that, in 2009, California had the fourth-lowest number of full-time equivalent state government employees relative to population among all states and that California's ratio of state government employees to population was 25 percent lower than the national average. The State Department of Finance reported that in fiscal 2010–11, California would have approximately 345,000 full-time equivalent state employees in the proposed budget for that year. That would be a drop of nearly 20,000 from the fiscal 2008–9 budget.

8. Public Policy Institute of California, "Just the Facts" report, September 2010.

9. Note that it took a much higher turnout percentage by Republicans to even come close to the number of Democratic voters—an indication of the much larger number of Democrats in California.

10. The Federal Election Commission reported that Barack Obama spent $7.39 per vote in winning the presidency in 2008.

11. "Breaking the Bank: Primary Campaign Spending for Governor since 1978," report by the California Fair Political Practices Commission, September 2010. www.fppc.ca.gov/reports/Breaking_the_Bank.pdf.

12. Gavin Newsom, news release, posted November 2, 2009, on www.calbuzz.com/2009/11/inside-story-why-newsoms-governor-bid-collapsed/.

13. Office of the California secretary of state.

14. Public Policy Institute of California, September 2010 survey report, www.ppic.org/content/pubs/survey/s_910mbs.pdf.

15. David McCuan, e-mail to author, July 6, 2011.

16. Jerry Brown, news release, October 28, 2010, www.jerrybrown.org/desperate-and-flailing-whitman-throws-kitchen-sink-oven-and-blender-brown.

17. *San Jose Mercury-News,* October 9, 2010.

18. *La Opinion,* October 20, 2010.

19. KTTV interview, July 4, 2010.

20. Part of a panel discussion at the Institute of Governmental Affairs postelection conference, January 21–22, 2011; see Rarick, *California Votes.*

21. Glazer, interview with the author, August 4, 2011.

22. Ibid.

23. *New Republic,* April 4, 1985.

24. Debate transcript, www.livedash.com/transcript/ten_o'clock_news/204/KTVU/Tuesday_September_28_2010/463948/.

25. Debate transcript, available at www.youtube.com/watchTV=odyrv_xgia.

26. Allred statement made at news conference, September 29, 2010.

27. California secretary of state's office, statement of vote revision, January 6, 2011.

28. Campaign spending reports filed with the secretary of state's office, January 31, 2011.

29. Debra J. Saunders column, *San Francisco Chronicle*, available at www. creators.com/opinion/debra-saunders/loose-change-and-propositions.html, accessed September 25, 2012.

30. Reagan had, however, served seven elected terms as president of the Screen Actors Guild.

31. Robert Naylor, remarks made as a panel member at the University of California at Berkeley's Institute for Governmental Studies' postelection conference, January 21–22, 2011.

32. Author observation during panel discussion at the Institute of Governmental Studies' 2010 election postmortem held January 20–21, 2011 (transcription available in "California Votes: The 2010 Governor's Race," UC Berkeley Institute of Governmental Studies, 2012).

33. Ibid.

34. Glazer, interview with the author, August 4, 2011.

CHAPTER EIGHT

1. Results from a joint UC Berkeley–Field telephone survey of 898 registered voters in February 2011, news release no. 2370, March 18, 2011, http://field. com/fieldpollonline/subscribers/Rls2370.pdf.

2. U.S. Bureau of Labor Statistics, compiled as of August 5, 2011.

3. Kousser made his remark at a conference on redistricting sponsored by UC Berkeley's Institute of Governmental Studies on September 30, 2011.

4. As of August 19, 2011, at least a dozen members of the California Legislature were eyeing potential runs for the U.S. Congress.

5. The California Citizens Redistricting Commission. Republican leaders filed a lawsuit on September 15, 2011, in the state Supreme Court, seeking to repeal new legislative district boundaries for the state Senate. The suit was prepared by attorneys for the group Fairness and Accountability in Redistricting (FAIR), backed by the California Republican Party and Senate Republican Caucus. The court rejected the suit in January 2012.

6. Doug Willis, interview with the author, August 17, 2011.

7. Dan Walters, interview with the author, August 24, 2011.

8. Ibid.

9. Sherry Bebitch Jeffe, interview with the author, September 15, 2011.

10. Doug Faigin, interview with the author, May 6, 2011.

11. Jeffe, interview with the author, September 15, 2011.

12. *Los Angeles Times,* August 17, 2011.

13. Walters, interview with the author, August 24, 2011.

14. Barbara O'Connor, interview with the author, August 23, 2011.

15. Steve Glazer, interview with the author, July 20, 2011.

16. Darrell Steinberg, interview with the author, September 27, 2011.

17. Jerry Roberts, interview with the author, August 28, 2011. Phil Trounstine is the former political editor of the *San Jose Mercury News* and communications director for Gray Davis; he and Roberts are coproprietors of *Calbuzz,* a prominent California political Web site.

18. *Fresno Bee,* August 17, 2011.

19. Statement at a *Fresno Bee* editorial board meeting, August 16, 2011. The California Delta is an inland estuary formed by the confluence of the Sacramento and San Joaquin Rivers, covering approximately eleven hundred square miles on the western edge of the great Central Valley. An elaborate system of levees in the 1850s has reclaimed much of the area for farming. A proposal being debated in late 2012 would divert fresh river water entering the delta to giant tunnels that would in turn deliver water to aqueducts carrying water south to farmers in the San Joaquin Valley and to Southern California. The project was originally envisioned as a "peripheral canal," but a more accurate current description would be "peripheral tunnels."

20. See State of the State Address, January 31, 2011, www.gov.ca.gov/news.php?id=16897.

21. O'Connor, interview with the author, August 23, 2011.

22. Speech before the Sacramento Press Club, August 16, 2011.

23. A "deliberative poll" of more than four hundred participants sponsored by "What's Next California?" on June 24–26 in Torrance showed a rise from 52 percent to 72 percent in approval for "reassessing non-residential property more frequently than now." A deliberative poll measures respondents' opinions before and then after two days of briefings and discussions of state issues.

24. Walters, interview with the author, August 24, 2011.

25. *Los Angeles Times,* August 17, 2011.

26. George Skelton, interview with the author, April 26, 2012.

27. Peter Schrag, interview with the author, August 11, 2011.

28. Quoted in the *Los Angeles Times,* August 17, 2011.

29. Quoted in the *Sacramento Bee,* August 14, 2011.

30. Kevin Starr, interview with the author, September 24, 2011.

31. Skelton, interview with the author, April 26, 2012.

32. See "State of the State 2012: California on the Mend," www.gov.ca.gov /news.php?id=17386.

33. *California Progress Report,* Monday, January 23, 2012.

34. Quoted in the *New York Times,* January 19, 2012.

35. Field Poll released June 27, 2011.

36. O'Connor, interview with the author, August 23, 2011.

37. In August 2011, Whitman became CEO of Hewlett-Packard.

APPENDIX ONE

1. Constance Brown Carlson died on August 27, 2011, at age ninety-nine.

APPENDIX TWO

1. Peter Schrag, "A Century of Initiatives: Anybody Want to Celebrate?" *California Progress Report,* September 19, 2011, www.californiaprogressreport. com/site/century-initiatives-anybody-want-celebrate.

BIBLIOGRAPHY

Bailey, Thomas A. *The American Pageant.* 2nd ed. Boston: D.C. Heath and Company, 1961.

Bean, Walton E. *California: An Interpretive History.* New York: McGraw-Hill, 1973.

Bollens, John C., and C. Robert Williams. *Jerry Brown in a Plain Brown Wrapper.* Pacific Palisades, CA: Palisades Publishers, 1978.

Boyarsky, Bill. *Big Daddy: Jesse Unruh and the Art of Power Politics.* Berkeley: University of California Press, 2008.

———. *The Rise of Ronald Reagan.* New York: Random House, 1968.

Branfman, Fred. "The SALON Interview: Jerry Brown: Moving toward the Abyss." June 3, 1996. www.salon.com/1996/06/03/interview960603/.

Brown, Jerry. *Dialogues.* Berkeley: Berkeley Hills Books, 1998.

———. Gubernatorial inaugural addresses, 1975, 1979, 2011. www.governors. library.ca.gov./addresses/34-jbrown01.html; www.governors.library.ca.gov ./addresses/34-jbrown02.html; www.governors.library.ca.gov./addresses /34-jbrown03.html.

———. Papers. Regional History Collection. Doheny Memorial Library, University of Southern California.

"Brown Says Top Solons Trying to Cripple Him." *Long Beach Independent, Press-Telegram.* June 17, 1972.

California State Government Oral History Program. California State Archives, Sacramento.

Cannon, Lou. *Ronnie and Jesse: A Political Odyssey.* New York: Doubleday & Company, 1969.

Cleland, Henry. "California." In *The Encyclopedia Americana*, 205. New York: Americana Corporation, 1952.

DeWitt, Howard A. *California Civilization: An Interpretation.* Dubuque, IA: Kendall/Hunt Publishing Company, 1979.

Illich, Ivan. "To Hell with Good Intentions." Speech delivered at the Conference on InterAmerican Student Projects (CIASP). Cuernavaca, Mexico, April 20, 1968.

Lorenz, James D. *Jerry Brown: The Man on the White Horse.* Boston: Houghton & Mifflin Co., 1978.

Lustig, R. Jeffrey, Dan Walters, Lenny Goldberg, John Syer, Ronald Schmidt Sr., and Mark Paul. *Remaking California: Reclaiming the Public Good.* Berkeley: Heyday Books, 2010.

Mathews, Joe, and Mark Paul. *California Crack-Up: How Reform Broke the Golden State and How We Can Fix It.* Berkeley: University of California Press, 2010.

McWilliams, Carey. *California: The Great Exception.* Berkeley: University of California Press, 1949.

Mills, James R. *A Disorderly House: The Brown-Unruh Years in Sacramento.* Berkeley: Heyday Books, 1987.

Montgomery, Gayle B., and James W. Johnson. *One Step from the White House: The Rise and Fall of Senator William F. Knowland.* Berkeley: University of California Press, 1998.

Pack, Robert. *Jerry Brown: The Philosopher Prince.* New York: Stein and Day, 1978.

Rapoport, Roger. *California Dreaming: The Political Odyssey of Pat and Jerry Brown.* Berkeley: Nolo Press, 1982.

Rarick, Ethan. *California Rising: The Life and Times of Pat Brown.* Berkeley: University of California Press, 2005.

———. *California Votes: The 2010 Governor's Race.* Berkeley, CA: Institute of Governmental Studies Press, University of California, 2012.

Richardson, James. *Willie Brown: A Biography.* Berkeley: University of California Press, 1996.

Schell, Orville. *Brown.* New York: Random House, 1978.

Schrag, Peter. *California: America's High-Stakes Experiment.* Berkeley: University of California Press, 2006.

———. "A Century of Initiatives: Anybody Want to Celebrate?" *California Progress Report*, September 19, 2011. www.californiaprogressreport.com/site/century-initiatives-anybody-want-celebrate.

Schwartz, Stephen. *From West to East: California and the Making of the American Mind.* New York: Free Press, 1998.

Starr, Kevin. *California: A History.* New York: Modern Library, 2005.

———. *Golden Dreams: California in an Age of Abundance, 1950–1963.* New York: Oxford University Press USA, 2009.

Walker, Jesse. "Five Faces of Jerry Brown." *American Conservative,* November 1, 2009. www.theamericanconservative.com/articles/five-faces-of-jerry-brown.

INDEX

"JB" refers to Jerry Brown.